# Baptized Into Hope

EMMANUEL SULLIVAN

LONDON
SPCK

First published 1980
SPCK
Holy Trinity Church
Marylebone Road
London NW1 4DU

Printed in Great Britain
at the University Press, Cambridge

ISBN 0 281 03759 0

*To*
*the many Christians*
*with whom I have worked*
*during a decade of ecumenical growth*
*and Christian renewal*

Weeping may tarry for the night,
but joy comes with the morning.

*Psalm 30.5*

# Contents

# Acknowledgements

Thanks are due to the following for permission to quote copyright sources:

Burns & Oates/Search Press: *The Theology of the World* by Johannes Metz, translated by W. Glen-Doepel (US publisher: The Seabury Press)

Fontana Paperbacks: *A New Hope for Christian Unity* by John Huxtable

*Third Way*: Article by John Stott

The Scripture quotations in this publication are from the Revised Standard Version of the Bible, copyrighted 1971 and 1952 by the Division of Christian Education of the National Council of the Churches of Christ in the USA.

# Preface

Baptized into hope! The phrase came to me, stuck with me on first reading the common declaration of Pope Paul VI and Archbishop Coggan signed at the Vatican on 29 April 1977. It was used to express their common will to bring their communions into one communion of life, worship, and mission: 'To this we are bound to look forward and to spare no effort to bring it closer: to be baptized into Christ is to be baptized into hope. . . .' Neither had in mind a facile union or a pragmatic merger, a submergence of conviction and differences. But I wonder to what extent either Pope or Archbishop grasped the breadth and depth of the words they used? We are often reminded that baptism initiates us into the Church as a community faith. Baptism is the real reception of God's very life, a life that is marked with a quality of love that moves us progressively beyond ourselves for living for others. But hope is all too often based upon the feeling of security that comes from human resources and aspirations rather than upon the promises of God and the inspiration of the gospel. Hope is both a dimension and a dynamic of Christian life. It links and enfleshes faith and love. It is the Christian commitment to become a fellow worker with God within the mystery of creation and redemption at a given time and place. Hope gives rise to a new consciousness that the Holy Spirit has been poured out on all flesh and is present and active in the whole world. Hope creates a sense of responsibility for discerning the action of the Spirit and its direction.

This book is not about a particular theology of hope. Nor is it written to counteract the voices of despair, strident or quiet, which the ferment, friction, and fragility of our times evoke, not least in the Christian community itself. I have no wish to promote a shallow optimism. Such an effort could be as counterproductive and naive as is much of our contemporary pessimism with its apocalyptic mentality that waits for the world to come crashing down or be blown sky-high. I hope it will not be judged a harmless exercise in futurology, a kind of parlour game in which you guess what the future might turn out to be. It is not within my scope or ability to muster impressive statistics, to indulge a kind of educated guessing about the future that often bolsters hope or confirms despair. Such futurology can lead to private fantasies, projected on the public, often a splashover from a thinktank, much more effective as science fiction than established fact. I certainly have no wish to indulge in any gratuitous form of prophecy, prophecy without discernment.

I am trying to indicate and illustrate a substantive content for contemporary Christian hope. Faith and love are expressed in the context of events and movements, the particular situations of history. So is Christian hope. What I have done is to focus attention on the base for Christian hope in a spirit of discernment. It is the discernment of the activity of the Holy Spirit in the Church and the World that is the essence of hope. Believing that the personal love of God has been poured into our hearts by this Spirit of the living God (Rom. 5.5), we are called to make the presence of this love real for our world. This puts a responsibility on us for the quality of our lives. But it demands equally a sense of awareness and commitment to the deepest human needs. The gift of hope is a real power to commit our lives to the Kingdom of God by active enlightened involvement in the problems and aspirations and movement of the world.

All I have tried to do is present a scenario, a sketch or outline with some main points for a script yet to be written. I have selected five areas of church life for this purpose. This is not a random selection. These are areas which separately and by promise of future convergence give some faint outline for the shape of the Church to come in its renewal and its mission. These movements are at a very early stage but they hold in themselves the essential ingredients for a Christian community that is once more challenged by the radical newness of life. These substantives of hope are: the Ecumenical Movement, the Catholic–Evangelical convergence, the liberation movement, the neo-Pentecostal movement, and the community movement.

This book is concerned with each of these movements as they are presently developed, in terms of what can be explicitly said of them right now. But it is always encouraging the reader to discern what is implicit in each of them and in their mutual interaction. In this respect I have put the burden on the reader, though giving him the utmost freedom for his own discernment. The real work of demonstrating their substance and interaction for renewal and mission will have to be done when they take more shape than they have at present. This will be the work of experts in the several areas. I want to impress on church leaders and active articulate church members the importance of recognizing the main areas of church life where the action of the Spirit can be discerned already and to which we are called to share, on which we are invited to build a renewed community of faith for our witness and mission among men.

My observations and convictions have been conditioned by the intimate association of my Christian ministry with the various activities of ecumenism and renewal within the British church scene for the past ten years. The brief given by my religious superiors has allowed me an unusual measure of freedom to explore new areas of church life. I am grateful to the Franciscan Friars of the Atonement for this freedom; for the support and encouragement that have accompanied it. But this is not surprising. For eighty years this small community has lived in a frontier situation, dedicated to Christian unity and mission.

I hope that this book will encourage fellow Christians. I hope it will be a genuine contribution to the encouragement presently needed to continue to build on what the Lord has already done in our midst. The Lord of history has called us to build a civilization of love that will manifest the central meaning of the Christian gospel. As always he has gone before us and asks us to follow. The fidelity of our response will have to be sustained by hope. In the years ahead all of us will be forced to re-examine the roots of our Christian life. Perhaps it was expressed by Pope Paul VI when he welcomed the visit of Archbishop Coggan with these words: 'The civilization of love is our shared hope – something which is utopia for the worldly-wise, but prophecy for those who live in the truth.'

# 1

# Baptized Into Hope

. . . God works through us . . . let us not lose sight of
his action in us and on us, and, above all, not allow
our sensitivity to his promptings and guidance to be
dulled. The signs of the times are encouraging.

*Cardinal Hume to the Church of England Synod*
*1 February 1978*

To say that a Christian has been baptized into hope is not an
exercise in rhetoric. It is supported by the very nature of the
Christian life flowing as it does from the meaning of Christian
baptism. We are in a period of Christian renewal. If this is to
mean anything, it must mean a renewal of our appreciation of
what 'baptism into Christ' calls and commits us to be and to do
in God's world. That there is an elaborate development in how
Christians have understood and applied the significance of baptism
need not deter us from looking for a fundamental meaning in this
sacrament. The sacrament itself represents a basic character of
the overall mystery which St Paul refers to as 'the mystery hidden
for ages and generations but now made manifest to his saints'
(Col. 1.26). In Christian understanding this is just what a sacrament means. It is a sign by word and action that God is revealing
and sharing his life among men. The revealing and the sharing are
not for the sake of a chosen few, an élite or an elect. It is to make
known among the nations how great 'are the riches of the glory
of this mystery, which is Christ in you, the hope of glory' (Col.
1.27). Baptism is not initiation into a secret sect. The secret, i.e.,
the mystery, is for the whole world. One who is baptized is already
an affirmation that the universal claim and power of Jesus is at
work within his own life. The very quality and direction of his
light ought to proclaim the unique meaning of Jesus in human
life. For Jesus is the sign of God's love and presence in the world.
It is not an ideal world. It is filled with grief and anxiety, joy and
hope, poverty and oppression, affluence and power.

However, to explore the fundamental meaning of Christian

1

baptism we quite naturally turn to the New Testament. Two texts
come to mind: Romans 6.3–4 and 1 Peter 1.3–5. In the first text
Paul states the essential Christian mystery expressed in baptism,
namely that out of death comes life. 'Do you not know that all of
us who have been baptized into Christ Jesus were baptized into
his death? We were buried therefore with him by baptism into
death, so that as Christ was raised from the dead by the glory of
the Father, we too might walk in newness of life.' Paul gave this
principle content and context.[1] Confident that Christ reigns
supreme we identify our lives with his life issuing in death and
resurrection for total healing and transformation. This transformation is not focused on self or individual ethical behaviour only.
Our entire outlook, our social awareness, all our relationships are
marked by their real identification with the whole meaning of the
life, death, and resurrection of Jesus Christ. Christians are called
to consider themselves 'dead to sin and alive to God in Christ
Jesus' (Rom. 6.11).

The second text which expresses the fundamental meaning of
our Christian baptism has been more intimately associated with
the liturgical rite of baptism.[2] 'Blessed be the God and Father of
our Lord Jesus Christ! By his great mercy we have been born
anew to *a living hope* through the resurrection of Jesus Christ
from the dead, and to an inheritance which is imperishable,
undefiled, and unfading, kept in heaven for you, who by God's
power are guarded through faith for a salvation ready to be
revealed *in the last time.*' Far from being a statement of 'merit
theology', it is a reminder to Christians that the serious oppression
they are experiencing, whatever the precise nature of it might
have been, is part of their mysterious involvement with Jesus. It
is not an exhortation to 'hang in' or 'hang on' because it will soon
be over. It is much more a statement of fact, the fact being that
new life comes to the Christian through the risen life of Jesus
received in baptism. This new life which is indestructible is the
very content of Christian hope. These Christians were being
exhorted to interpret their situation in the perspective of hope.
God gives us a share in his life and safeguards it. The life he gives
and shares is not an endurance contest. It cannot have arbitrary
limits put on it. It is life that demands basic freedom for development. It is life that has to renew itself, be reinterpreted at any
time in any new situation, a life that remains open to new possi-

2

bilities of thinking and acting. It is *life*. And the meaning of life is growth, something more than movement and activity. It has a future that cannot be pre-planned or pre-packaged. It is God's life and very much part of God's freedom and future.

Perhaps we get an uneasy feeling when we speak about God's future. We have all been shaped in our thinking about God as the changeless one who protects the purity of his perfect being at a safe distance from our world and its sordid little affairs. God is timeless and perfectly fulfilled. He has no need of a future. Yet he is the God of Abraham and the Father of Jesus. His relationship with us in creation and redemption is real. The gift of freedom he gives us is real in order to make our response to his graciousness a real response. Grace and freedom constitute one economy. God has a plan, something in mind for the world, 'a salvation ready to be revealed in the last time'. In this sense God has a future. Jürgen Moltmann says that 'although it is clear that faith in God and expectation of the future are indissoluble in the Old and New Testaments, Christian theology has paid far too little attention to the future as a mode of God's being.'[3] We cannot speak of God breaking into time without taking on the conditions of time, and time has a future condition. If we were to take God's future seriously, we would take the condition of the world seriously. Moltmann says: 'A Christianity which has for so long believed in God without his future in the world, now will seek, in recognizing the practical responsibility of hope for the future of man and the earth, to shape the possibilities and forces of the contemporary world which arise in an almost unmanageable intensity.'[4] Nor does this mean that we have to latch on to one or more humanistic or even Christian ideologies. Hans Küng has presented us with a litany of these and their limitations in his apologia *On Being a Christian*.[5] Our hope for the future is not Christian because of a particular ideology that seems to defend a gospel principle or conform to ecclesiastical polity at a given time. It is Christian because Jesus tells us that the future belongs to God and 'in the light of this future of God we must shape the present, both of the individual and of society'.[6] Christian hope, rooted in Christian baptism, the sacrament of our association with the death and resurrection of Jesus, cuts across the difficulties for Christian theology created by Greek philosophy with its tensions of how God acts both in the world and above and beyond the world. We have to learn that the transcendence of God is temporal as well, that he is before us, ahead of us always. This is the forgotten dimension of divine transcendence.[7] It allows God a future in his world and enables us to cope with the Christian message.

## The relationship of hope to faith and love

Because baptism obliges the Christian to explore the extent and intensity of his spirit of hope, it also induces him to reflect on the requirements of faith and love. It would be unreal to view these in too scholastic a fashion, i.e., as theological virtues relating us to God as their immediate object, as though they governed our internal relationship to God on a one-to-one basis, with only a peripheral reference to God's relationship in the affairs of the world around us. The passage from 1 Peter 1.3–5 calls us to a living hope and promises us salvation through faith. But it is a salvation that is part of God's plan yet to be realized. That plan gives all of God's world a future and therefore the potential of hope. Baptism creates hope in us as a virtue, i.e., a real power, as real as the powers of faith and love. These powers must be tested, exercised, matured in the future of God which is being realized in our world. Faith and love and hope do have God as their object – but a God very much involved in his world. Hope is not a weak sister. And the development of a theology of hope is a genuine theological development. For as Moltmann says: 'Hope leads us into life, into the whole of life. It encourages faith so that it does not degenerate into faintheartedness. It strengthens love so that it does not remain enclosed within itself . . .'[8] The power of Christian hope is our part in God's future. This future rests on the power of grace to transform and transfigure man and his environment. Out of past conditions and present situations and developments comes a new creation. It is our faith in the meaning of the death and resurrection of Jesus, a new energy of love God releases in us (Rom. 5.3–5). This release brings us a new understanding of the world. The world is neither heaven nor hell. It is not yet finished. It is engaged in its history. It is a world of possibilities, some of which transcend the world as we experience it right now. The form of the world is changing (1 Pet. 4.7). It moves from Sinai by way of Calvary to Tabor to share in the glory of the transfigured Christ. It is a world in which there is room for Moses and Elijah, for Peter, James, and John, for all sorts. It is a world in which mountains can be moved, a world in which the possibilities of God's love cannot be exhausted, a world teeming with opportunities for creative redeeming love, a world where faith demands that we remain open to all that God's love makes possible now.

While there are areas of Christian theology in which one might speak of the primacy of either faith or hope or charity, it is important to grasp their intimate correlation as essential powers of that new life conferred in Christian baptism. For this reason Moltmann says, 'the theme of *hope and the future* is therefore not a momentary theme or passing fashion. It is the essential theme of Christian faith and of that love which in the modern context and today more than ever has to be worked out.'[9]

## *Hope and spirituality*

Spirituality flows in our baptism. There is a Christian spirituality. To say this is not to deny pluralism in our understanding and exercise of Christian life, a manifold expression of the mystery of being in Christ. Just as there are theologies to express Christian thinking, a variety of ways to articulate and interpret the Christian mystery, a faith that seeks understanding, so there are a variety of approaches to Christian living. Corresponding lifestyles and ways of seeking communion with God in Christ hold different attractions for different people. This is certainly one way of expressing our unity in diversity to build up the Body of Christ (Eph. 4. 1–16). A call to live and witness to a dimension of the Christian mystery is a gift of the Spirit and not simply a matter of pious choice or inclination. So there have been Benedictine, Franciscan, Ignatian spiritualities; there have developed Catholic, Orthodox, Protestant spiritualities; contemplative and active spiritualities. These are related to our experience of faith. They can become a brand of piety that often obscures genuine faith or limits seriously our growth in faith. At the present time these spiritualities that have grown out of spiritual experience of the past seem less important than they once seemed. A growing number of Christians are searching for a renewed understanding of what is common and essential for healthy Christian life. At a time when Christians are working towards the reintegration of the Church's unity for its mission in the world, priority is given to this search for a unifying pattern of spirituality, a basic way of living as

Christians in the world and for the world.[10] This is not to devalue the manifold riches of Christ which pluralism in spirituality manifests nor to limit the action of the Spirit. But we have to link diversity to unity, churches to Church, theologies to theology. It would be dangerous to play off pluralism against unity, to try to manifest unity by denying pluralism, or fail to seek an underlying unity in the name of 'healthy pluralism'.

The inner dynamism of Christian spirituality is a joyful trust that the reconciling power of God is at work at the heart of the world. The Church as a community of faith is a prophetic community announcing the good news that 'we have now received our reconciliation' (Rom. 5.11). For the Christian the greatest sin is despair, because his existence is built on hope. Ecumenical spirituality must more and more mirror that hope to the human community. The purpose of ecumenism is to place the unity of the Church on the vast horizon of human unity. It is a tremendous task that demands a corresponding spirituality, a spirituality of hope. Christians can face the tensions of the present and the uncertainties of the future precisely because they have a future already begun in Jesus Christ. Christians take their courage from Jesus and his message, a message that anticipates the fullness of life in the Kingdom of God. Christian hope affirms that new life is always beginning, always reaching out to what can be. Man can always be more truly human. We can always seek to be the kind of community of persons that truly represents and manifests a fullness and richness of life. The philosophers and theologians refer to this as 'hominization', the making of man, the ascent of man. We are free to be ourselves right now and participate fully in the human community without any fear of ultimate meaninglessness. This is not true for all men everywhere, because of tyranny and poverty. But it remains their most basic right and our most basic responsibility to join the struggle to secure this right for the last underprivileged person. So Christian hope is active and creative. It is a creative trust that the future is with God who is utterly trustworthy, but who here and now entrusts us with the gift of freedom and responsibility for our brothers and sisters. 'For great is his steadfast love toward us; and the faithfulness of the Lord endures for ever' (Ps. 117.2). A spirit of hope flows from the grace of baptism. Authentic spirituality makes this evident. This hope is not an indifference to the shape of this world which is passing away. The second coming of Jesus is a real presence in our lives. It is so real that Christians ought to be searching and seeking in every situation that fullness of time in which his coming is anticipated and things must be as the Lord of history would have them be – a world liberated from sin and oppression, healed in its poverty and pain, given courage and joy for anxiety and despair. Christian hope brings together this anticipation of that end time (eschatology) and the assurance that God has already come to us in Jesus (incarnation). His message and his promise fuse in the practical plans and events of life. This is neither optimism nor ideology. It is the substance of God's word in Christ, fully and definitively expressed in Jesus.[11] The Christian knows that the condition of the world must be changed for the better. He is also aware that the human condition makes backsliding, retrogression, all sorts of 'diminishment' possible. He accepts the final sentence of Teilhard de Chardin's *Phenomenon of Man* as part of the Christian mystery at work in the world: 'Nothing so resembles the human epoch as the way of the Cross.'[12] Christian spirituality in no small part is a matter of responsible hope for the world. It would be a false spirituality that would remain apathetic to what is happening in God's world or would throw God's cause to the ideological lions. Johannes Metz warns us that the 'responsibility of faith becomes boundless' and that 'the hominization of the world must not be left to the ideologies'. Rather, 'it must be taken hold of in hope as a burden and a task'.[13] No one is exempt either in cloister, commune, or rose garden.

In the last analysis perhaps spirituality could be described as a sensitivity we bring to all our relationships, the relationship to God in and through the world, a relationship of openness and integrity, an integrity that looks for wholeness in every sphere of life. In the Bible spirituality is a matter of obedience, a listening to what God is saying through his word and in contemporary happenings. Today events are thrust upon us by new avenues of communication. As members of a prophetic community Christians have to interpret these events in the spirit of the gospel. Christian asceticism may dictate the need to protect the interior life from the onslaught of mass media. But it is equally important to get our asceticism right, to make sure we do not abandon a sense of responsibility for the hope of the world. Metz speaks of the true nature of Christian asceticism in *The Theology of the World*:

7

Ascetic flight from the world should never be simply a flight out of the world, for man cannot in fact exist without a world. Such a 'flight' would only be a deceptive entry into some artificial world beside this one (generally only the more convenient religious world situation of yesterday). Not flight from the world, but flight 'forward' with the world is the basic movement of ascetic flight from the world: flight from the world that is established only in the present and in what is controllable, whose 'time is always here' (John 7.6). St Paul's call to renounce the world, above all his warning 'Do not be conformed to this world' (Rom. 12.2) must be correctly understood. Paul is not critical of solidarity with the world, but of conformism with it. He is critical of men who in their self-prestigiousness seek to fashion the world's future entirely by themselves and to turn everything into a function of the present. He is calling not simply for some undialectical denial of the world, but for the acceptance of painful conflict and self-sacrificing disagreement with the world, for readiness to challenge the present in the name of the promised future of God. What drives the Christian to the flight of asceticism and denial of the world is not, therefore, contempt for the world, but responsibility for it in hope – in hope for that world future as it is announced and sealed in the promises of God, against which we constantly harden our hearts in pride or despair.[14]

## Accountability for hope

We hear a good deal today about 'accountability'. To render an account is no new thing and has become part of ordinary language. Perhaps we need a term like 'accountability' to reflect a new way of thinking and speaking about authority, entailing, as it does, an emphasis on collegiality, conciliarity, consultation, and dialogue. There is a special instance of accountability in the first Letter of Peter. In chapter 3, verse 15 the writer exhorts the Christians who were under some kind of oppression: 'Always be prepared to make a defense to any one who calls you to account for the hope that is in you. . . .' They are to justify, as the Jerome Biblical Commentary says, 'not just a conviction about future expectations, but the very essence of the motivation of the new people of God'.[15] What makes Christians stand up for counting? For the baptized to whom this letter is addressed the ground of hope seems clear. Living in a situation of oppression they seem sure of this ground and of who they are. In a time of renewal the theme of accounting for hope is not an easy assignment. In the opening report to the meeting of the World Faith and Order Commission at Accra in July 1974, Dr Lukas Vischer addressed the theme of the meeting and asked why there was such spontaneous interest in the study: 'Giving Account of the Hope'. Under the theme of the meeting 'Uniting in Hope'[16] he said:

> Unless I am mistaken, it was due mainly to the desire of the churches and possibly even more so to the desire of so many individual Christians, to understand more clearly the significance of their Christian faith. In face of the tremendous changes taking place in our world and in ourselves, what can we say about the gospel? How can we connect up the faith in Christ and the demands which all these changes make on us? In the long run, the faith cannot simply be taken for granted; if it is to be a living force, it must be explained and unfolded, not just for others but perhaps first and foremost to ourselves. Most of the groups had their origin in this approach. Only a few chose to concern themselves with the differences and agreements between the confessions. The great majority of them were prompted by the question how to understand and proclaim the gospel, each in its own situation.

Christians and the churches to which they belong may be tempted to underestimate the depth and extent of the changes under way already. If so, they will underestimate God's summons to render an account. We will look at this question of change. Thus far we have tried to review the significance of the dimension of hope arising from Christian initiation. What follows in this book is one Christian's effort to indicate certain factors and some basic movements which he thinks are significant if Christians are to understand what it means to be born anew to a living hope. Before that, however, I want to look at a whole new climate of hope that has developed in Christian thinking.

## The development of the theology of hope

We cannot pretend that the development of a theology of hope is incidental, optional, or peripheral to growth in faith. Theology

9

is not the *queen* of the sciences as it was in the medieval synthesis of knowledge, with the various disciplines of human knowledge hierarchically arranged around her. In such a structure of human knowledge philosophy was the humble handmaiden, ancillary to theology. Today it is necessary to regard theology in the service of Christian faith itself, with a vital role to play in the expression, the piety, the discernment of faith. To detach theology from the service of faith would be as wrong as to confuse it with the substance of faith. It keeps piety attached to faith. It enables Christians to find a way forward to a contemporary mode of expressing their faith, renewing forgotten dimensions of their faith, exploring new frontiers for Christian living and believing in new unprecedented situations. I feel it necessary to make these remarks. All too often we find an anti-intellectual bias or disdain for theology among Evangelical Christians, pious Catholics, and neo-Pentecostals. Of course there are times when theological discourse and speculation seem beyond the ken of ordinary mortals, when the distance between podium and pulpit seems unbridgeable, when conflict between official orthodox teaching, theological opinion, and blackboard speculation divides the Church and leaves the people of God, to say nothing of non-Christians, thoroughly bewildered.[17] Perhaps it would be easier for all concerned were we to regard the ministry of the theologians as teaching and prophecy. Both teaching and prophecy are gifts of the Spirit for building up the life of the Church. Such teaching and prophecy are expected to be exercised in the context of a believing community with a sense of responsibility for the gospel's proclamation in spirit and truth. They are also to be exercised to some extent in all churches subject to an official teaching authority which has a pastoral charge and care. Teachers and prophets, pastors, and the community of faith itself must be reconciled in the unity of faith.[18] As there is development in our common understanding of the content of faith, so is there a development in theological understanding. Christians ought to remain open to such a development and the fruit of such a development. For these too are graces and gifts of the one Spirit. These too are nutrients of hope. Living in a time of renewal in Christian life and mission we ought to be encouraged by a theology of hope; living at a time of expanding social consciousness we ought to welcome a theology of liberation; living in a time of 'new Pentecost' we ought to welcome a theology of the Holy Spirit.

There are two theologians whose names are particularly significant in this development of a theology of hope. They are Johannes Metz, a Roman Catholic theologian, and Jürgen Moltmann, a Lutheran theologian.[19] The approach of Metz is to create a new way of thinking about the world and the relationship of the Church and the world. Specifically his purpose is to establish a new way of thinking about the political sphere of life. This sphere must be given its proper autonomy and freedom in order to avoid mixing politics and religion as the Church did in its reaction to the Enlightenment and to Marxism. At the same time it makes clear that there is a social dimension to the Christian gospel that is neither secondary or derivative nor accidental, private, abstracted from the social sciences. The Church cannot be limited to God-talk. It is an institution of social criticism. This is not a negative notion, because the Church exists to preach hope in the coming Kingdom of God. Metz is quite aware that the Church is not practising what it ought to be preaching to the extent that it itself is not liberated and is not a liberating institution. But he argues that if the Church makes a real beginning in its critical function within society as a prophetic institution, it will find a new awareness of itself and a new effectiveness within society. For Metz there can be no peaceful coexistence between a private faith and a fully secularized society that will reduce the function of theology to providing an ideology for an advanced industrial society. A Latin American theologian, while criticizing him, acknowledges that Metz has recast the question of the Church in the modern world and has described his work as 'a breath of fresh air for European theology'.[20] Moltmann, deeply influenced by Ernst Bloch, a Marxist humanist philosopher,[21] develops the important biblical themes of God's coming to establish his Kingdom with the associated themes of promise and hope. God reveals himself as the one who is on his way to meet us. We wait for him both in the shadow of the cross and in the light of the resurrection, in the power of the mystery that begets an active hope.[22] God's promise is a profound challenge to the existing order of things. Because of faith in the risen Christ, man is free of the limitations of the present to think and act completely in terms of what is to come. This emphasis on the resurrection was felt by the liberation theo-

11

logians to be deficient because the challenge to the existing order of things seemed to be without content. The promise of God had no relation to human, concrete, historical experience. It would be more of a lure to keep going and enduring without really attempting to change the present order. As Rubem Alves says, God would resemble the prime mover of Aristotle 'pulling history to its future, but without being involved in history'.[23] While Moltman insists in his *Theology of Hope* that resurrection theology is not an easy acceptance of the *status quo*, that it does not sacralize the present, it would seem that earlier on he left himself open to the charge of naive optimism about a victorious march into the future without a genuine struggle for liberation here and now. As I have indicated, he has developed and corrected his theology by complementing his theology of resurrection with that of the cross. The cross is the place where the Christian discovers his identity and makes his commitment to his brothers and sisters of the world. Like Metz, Moltmann has his critics, especially from Latin America. Yet José Miguez Bonino, a protestant liberation theologian, does not hesitate to cite Moltmann as 'the theologian to whom the theology of liberation is most indebted and with whom it shows the clearest affinity'.[24] And Guttierez is generous in his acknowledgement:

> Despite these critical observations, Moltmann's work is undoubtedly one of the most important in contemporary theology. It offers a new approach to the theology of hope and has injected new life into the reflection on various aspects of Christian existence. Among other things, it helps us overcome the association between faith and fear of the future which Moltmann rightly considers characteristic of many Christians.[25]

Moltmann has no doubt about the timeliness for a development of a theology of hope. He finds that today 'those very hopes with which the technocratic society were built up are disintegrating'.[26] It is precisely this point in time 'that gives man an unambiguous certainty of hope . . . when he can no longer see any future ahead of him' and 'simultaneously places him in the open question of how he wants to fulfil, personally and together with society, that hope which God has placed in him and this world'.[27] This makes hope come alive and gives it its particular religious quality whereby 'we do not have the feeling that we must plan the future but rather that we must be responsible for the present in the face of the future'.[28]

As I understand the significance of these theologians of hope, it is their creation of a new Christian apologia of hope. It is indebted to Bloch's dictum: Where there is hope, there is also religion. This is an apologia of practice, not of intellectual appeal alone. As such it is not another ideology. It rests on the need to make certain that 'Christianity will no longer bear the train behind society; instead it will bear the torch ahead'.[29]

## Christian hope and utopia

If there is to arise in the Church a genuine spirituality of hope and an adequate apologia of hope, it is vital that the Christian is clear about the distinction and relationship of hope and utopia; of ideology and wishful thinking. Eschatological thinking is part of Christian theology and piety. There is nothing new in this respect for it is a way of thinking about the Kingdom of God. With regard to modern biblical scholarship we can cite Albert Schweitzer's *The Quest of the Historical Jesus*, published in 1906 as a pioneer work which stressed a futuristic (eschatological) interpretation of the New Testament. What is true for biblical theology is true for systematic theology as well.[30] However, there has been a change in focus of the utmost importance. The theologians of hope work within this change. The old focus was on the free decision of the individual person to respond to God right now in a moment of free personal decision in the light of God's promised advent and judgement. It was based on a very private salvation theology. A lot of preaching and evangelizing has been done on this basis. 'Paradoxical as it may now seem, it was an eschatology of the present rather than of the future.'[31] The new focus is on the future, and as a theology of the future 'readily combines with a political eschatology'.[32] The point in noting the difference is to stress the need for a theology that does not opt for present or future as a total explanation of New Testament perspective. The old focus had many limitations; the newer focus holds as many. We can turn it into a mania or enthusiasm for futuristic theological novelty to bolster the most recent ideological passion. Alfredo Fierro notes:

The gaze of some theologians is so bent on what lies ahead that they can easily fall into the trap of mythologizing the future. Thus genesis myths give way to eschatological myths. Nor can one be sure that those theologians have freed themselves from an ingenuous conception of historical progress, because their image of the future is so abstract and optimistic. The 'God ahead of us' seems to function as the culminating symbol of a gilt-edged future.[33]

These two perspectives need not be mutually exclusive to the point of dividing Christians further. What is needed is the recognition of a basic content of Christian life and participation that leads to a sense of community action that is both moral and political. These perspectives can be united in the renewed emphasis on the Kingdom of God in the New Testament. This affects vitally attitudes towards the Church as a Spirit-based institution in the world. As such it will have a direct bearing on subsequent chapters of this book.

When one enters the realm of utopia he enters a jungle of definitions and presuppositions. When he explores the relationship of utopia to Christian hope, he may find himself tossed by wild bulls on the horns of more than one theological dilemma.[34] Regarding dilemmas, however, Fierro says 'it is not theology that decides but rather faith and hope'.[35] Utopia in the first instance must be liberated from common language where it has served as a synonym for illusion, lack of realism, the irrational. Guttierez speaks of its revival as an 'historical plan for a qualitatively different society . . . to express the aspiration to establish new social relations among men'. And he characterizes the notion by three elements, namely 'its relationship to historical reality, its verification in praxis, and its rational nature'.[36] Fierro describes it as 'an image that stimulates and incites people to action, that is based on a high valuation of the person and collective human happiness, and that suggests historical alternatives very different from those embodied in the present'.[37] Far from being associated with what is understood as irrational, utopia is what is rationally possible, a critique of reality, the hinge on which any historical change in ideas moves. It actually highlights authentic reason by going beyond an already obsolete stage of reason in an effort to amplify reality.[38] Guttierez differentiates utopia from ideology on the basis that the latter masks reality and preserves the established

14

order, whereas utopia leads to authentic and scientific knowledge of reality and to the practical transformation of what presently exists.[39] Despite its varied meanings ideology signifies a set of ideas related to established principles. It possesses a measure of coherence based on the adoption of a worldview. Utopia, on the other hand, provides a human focus for economic, social, and political action, involving the use of the creative imagination.

Related to Christian hope there arises the question of how the gospel either is or contains a utopian message. Theologians like Moltmann and Rahner maintain that hope relativizes and makes provisional all historical utopias because of its basis in the absolute future of God. And Metz says that 'Christian eschatology is not an ideology of the future' for 'it cherishes the poverty of its knowledge about the future'. He describes it as 'primarily a "negative theology" of the future'.[40] Another way of putting the question is: How are we to envisage the coming Kingdom of God – in earthly terms of praxis or in heavenly terms of absolute hope? This is not an academic question. It affects the whole question of the nature of religion, the relationship of the sacred and secular, of historical detachment and historical engagement or commitment. How do theory and praxis meet? How do justice and peace kiss? My own conviction leads me towards the solution offered by Helmut Gollwitzer, cited by Alfredo Fierro in *The Militant Gospel*. He distinguishes between the *absolute utopia* that is the object of Christian hope and the *relative utopia* that is the object for a theology of social action. Between these two orders of utopia there is a strict logical relationship – not an option for one or other. He says:

> From the absolute utopia of the new society in God's kingdom *there follows* a relative earthly utopia as a guiding image for the alteration of existing relations and the dismantling of all injustice, servitude, and abusive power.[41]

The main advantage of adopting this position is its function of safeguarding Christians from confusing the Kingdom of God with a specific stage of history. The Christian commitment to work for justice and liberation and healing in the historical situation is in view of the coming Kingdom of God.[42] It is important to note that what is truly the basis of human hope functions as *a real part* of the Christian hope in the coming of the Kingdom. Whether a

15

particular movement belongs more to the spiritual or temporal realm, if it is truly discerned as a sign of hope, as the activity of the Holy Spirit in the Church and in the world, then it commands our attention and solicits our respectful interest, some measure of commitment. Such attention, interest, and commitment are qualitatively different from that of either Gamaliel (Acts 5.34–40) or the Athenian philosophers (Acts 17.16–32). In this book five basic movements have been selected as significant for the future, as signals of Christian hope here and now. Three of these involve the life of the Church immediately, while bearing a definite relationship to the Church's mission in the world. I am referring to the Ecumenical Movement, the Catholic–Evangelical convergence, the neo-Pentecostal movement. The liberation movement touches not only the life of the Church and its mission, but the intimate immediate concerns of society at large, with special reference to the 'third world' where religious and secular issues meet more directly. The community movement is a secular-Christian phenomenon of our times, holding much hope for the renewal of our understanding of the Christian Church as a community of faith ready to make its particular contribution to the human search for essential human values in a period of profound social and historical change. In these movements it is possible to detect the beginning of a subtle, immanent process of convergence and unity. A significant shift in human consciousness that realizes a progression towards unity of the profane and sacred spheres of life is the present function of Christian hope. I would not want to argue the case for a particular interpretation of human history. Christian hope does not rest on a particular philosophy of history. Nor does it rest on giving our age an identity tag. But in modern terms Christian faith, the substance of things hoped for, is about bridging the gap between the sacred and the secular.[43] Christian spirituality rests on an imperative to subdue the earth. I am not thinking simply of some primitive agricultural cultivation of the earth, nor of technological mastery and manipulation of the resources of the cosmos. Much more is involved. We are committed to bring every element and dimension of our world under the victorious grace of Christ. In christological terms this is a matter of death and resurrection. We have no promise that this struggle is without pain and loss, that tensions between the sacred and secular realms will be entirely eliminated (Rom. 7.21–3; 8.

19–22). Christian hope is a matter of willing, not simply wishing that things could be other than they are. Wishing is the imagination playing about as it were with random possibilities. Willing is our capacity, informed by God's Spirit, to move in the direction to which one feels drawn and committed. Beneath all this we live with a deeper tension, one that seems built into the very heart of the world, indeed into religion itself. Paul Tillich expresses this tension of 'original sin':

> Asked what the proof is for the fall of the world, I like to answer: religion itself, namely a religious culture beside a secular culture, a temple beside a town hall, a Lord's Supper beside a daily supper, prayer beside work, meditation beside research, *caritas* beside *eros*. But although this duality can never be overcome in time, space, and history, it makes a difference whether this duality is deepened into a bridgeless gap . . . or whether the duality is recognized as something which should not be and which is overcome fragmentarily by anticipation. . . .[44]

This is an expression of hope based on faith in God. The authenticity of a Christian spirituality of hope rests on a conviction that there ought to be some measure of progress, some evidence of organic union in the sacred and profane elements of human existence, without confusion or separation. Unless church work reflects this commitment to a stage where God is everything to everyone (1 Cor. 15.28), where the creative and redeeming activity of God can be seen at the secular as well as the religious level of life, Christian life becomes narrow and churchy and petty, deserving to be caricatured as all gas and gaiters. The Christian spirituality of hope makes us sensitive to what God is doing in human history. Christians may often feel up to their necks in the swirling waters of contradiction and ambiguity. They may be caught in the cross-currents of creation and redemption. They may well ask: Is it a moment to take risks, to explore new frontiers of the human spirit, to avail themselves of new techniques that promise a better life? Or is it a moment to hold fast to tested truths, to stem the tide of corruption, exploitation, and permissiveness; to heal the wounds of the human spirit, avoiding the subtleties of an expanded or deepened consciousness; to leave the world to disentangle the threads of its own increasing complexity? This latter option would assume that Christians are exempt both from the complexity of the world and from their own confusion and division. It would be opting out. And it would be a serious misjudgement about the relationship of the Church and the world. Only sensitivity to the Holy Spirit can bring us through these problems. Prayer is the way we develop this sensitivity. In prayer God gives us the courage and love we need to tolerate and integrate a diversity of Christian life and witness. The ongoing mystery of creation and redemption is a meeting of waters, of life and values, of thought and emphasis. At times it is a gentle flowing together; at others the meeting takes place in a mighty roar. The creating and redeeming love of God is what Christians are called to witness to and make present among men. However we choose to respond, it will be less for the cause of Christ if we ignore that spirituality of hope that looks to the progressive integration of God's world. There is nothing radical in this – except our hope. It is time to make radical our Christian hope. For there is only one reality hope has as its object – the Kingdom of God. The contemporary approach to spirituality is very much based on this subject. The validity of religion itself in the modern world is at stake.

## The Church and the world

What we have said about the relationship of Christian hope and utopia with its primary application to the general realms of the sacred and secular has a more defined application when we come to speak of the Church and the world. In every discussion along these lines there must be three terms: Church, world, Kingdom of God. How explicit the third term is will vary. But it is necessary to be clear that neither Church nor world is coextensive with the Kingdom. In his *Theology of the World* Johannes Metz notes that 'despite the many discussions about the Church and the world there is nothing more unclear than the nature of their relationship to one another'.[45] Working from the biblical notion of the Church as an *eschatological* and *exodus* community, the Church exists as an institution that is provisional and meant to pass away. The Church lives for the Lord to come. Metz quotes Rahner: 'The Church always lives in a certain sense from the proclamation of her provisional character and from her historically progressive surrender to the coming Kingdom of God.'[46] Metz concludes: 'The Church has a hope and witnesses to a hope, but its hope is not in itself. It is rather a hope in the Kingdom of God as the future of the world.'[47] To stress the provisional character of the Church is to argue for a more intimate relationship with the world, indeed for a mutual inclusiveness of the Church and the world for 'the end of all things is at hand' (1 Pet. 4.7). Christian hope is hope for the world based on the promise of God made good in Jesus Christ. Both Church and world are in time and space. The Kingdom means God's reign or rule. Quoting M. Dibelius, Hans Küng notes that 'God's Kingdom thus becomes the designation for God's cause'.[48] Later he defines the Church as 'the community of those who have become involved in the cause of Jesus Christ and who witness to it as hope for all men'.[49] Such an understanding implies a relationship of the Church to the world as an institution of hope that is in the world for the world. Yet this definition, while leaving the world as principal beneficiary of the Church, fails to take into account that the world is not only the place where the action is, where the agenda is prepared, but where the new heaven and the new earth have been inaugurated. 'Our hope presupposes faith in the world as God's creation.'[50] Karl Rahner provides a very helpful theological lead here, taking into account his mutual inclusiveness and intimate relationship between Church and world. In an essay entitled 'Redemption within creation' he claims that the question of the Christian apostolate in the world can be stated thus:

> . . . if, instead of placing the orders of redemption and creation alongside each other, we speak of the order of redemption *within* the order of creation; this states the thesis that divine grace, the fruit of redemption, actually penetrates the created order itself, healing and sanctifying it; that it incorporates the world, in all its abiding naturality, into the *mysterium Christi*; and that this process of taking the world by grace into the life of God is to be carried out by the activity of men. . . .[51]

If we are patient with the heavy style of this great theologian, he brings us to the intimacy and inclusiveness of the Church and the world because he shows that the primordial unity of nature and grace which have been brought to a final stage in Christ enables us to think and speak of the redemptive order within the created order, without fear of confusion or separation. In this way we are able to avoid giving social, political, family values second-class status, assigning religious and personal ethical values as primary, i.e., as God-given with no reference to their total human context, their flesh-and-blood condition. The Church as part of the world is not so much a *new religion* as it is the *new creation*, a community under the Spirit and in Christ, made anew in the image and likeness of God.

The Pentecost event described in Acts 2 necessarily completes and expresses what we have been saying. Following this event Peter explains what has happened. He quotes the prophet Joel: 'And in the last days it shall be, God declares, that I will pour out my Spirit *upon all flesh*. . . .' (Acts 2.17). Whatever problems of redaction and exegesis attend the expression 'upon all flesh', it indicates a final epoch of redemptive history and a universal out-pouring of God's Spirit. A few years ago it was often said that the doctrine of the Holy Spirit was one of the most neglected areas of Christian theology. This is probably more true of the Western Church than of the Eastern Church where a great theological and spiritual tradition have been united. Eastern theology can hardly be said to have neglected the role of the Holy Spirit in the life of the Church. But in both East and West such an opinion might be verified if we are thinking about the development of a doctrine of the Holy Spirit that more effectively speaks to the experience of contemporary Christians.[52] In practical terms a sound doctrine of the Holy Spirit is vital for an understanding of the relationship between the Church and the world. In a lecture given some years ago, Professor John Macquarrie said:

> The Church is the 'community of the Spirit' not in the sense that it has some kind of monopoly of the Spirit but rather in the sense that in the Church there is going on that work of the Spirit which, in a more diffused way, is also going on through the whole of creation. . . . We could also say that the work of the Spirit is the spiritualizing of all creation. This does not mean in the slightest that the creation becomes rarefied or that creatures are withdrawn from their material environment. . . . It means rather that the creatures too are enabled to 'proceed' forth from themselves; in the case of man, his 'existence' . . . is more and more established or, in other words, he becomes more and more truly human . . . and is less and less just a thing or an organism, a mere item in the world's furniture.[53]

In such a perspective, within the very structures of both Church and world there are clues to the activity of the Holy Spirit. This activity has an intimate link with human experience. The Spirit is experienced by a quality of life that differentiates men from their physical and material environment. In the order of creation when we say that man is made in the image of God we are not simply speaking about his faculties of intellect and will. We are speaking about his use of them in openness, freedom, creativity, and the capacity to move beyond his present situation. We are speaking of his thoughts and his prayers, of his hands and his actions. In the New Testament the 'image of God', i.e., the quality of the life man expresses, is judged by the fruit of God's Spirit – love, joy, peace, patience, kindness, goodness, fidelity, gentleness, self-control (Gal. 5.22–3). These are more than personal qualities of individual ethical behaviour. They move the one with them beyond himself to a new life marked by the very possibility of a new kind of life marked by openness to establish the basis for a new human community. If you will, the natural life of man is opened to the creation of a 'spiritual' man who lives for others.

We cannot understand the activity of the Holy Spirit in the Church if we do not think of it as an activity which gives shape and builds a new heaven and a new earth out of the chaos of the present world. The Church is in that world, not as a perfect society within an imperfect one. The Church needs the ongoing reformation and renewal of its own life. It can only claim to live in society as a community that strives to anticipate imperfectly and proclaim God's Kingdom. The Church is the 'community of the Spirit' in which the work of the Spirit in the whole world is focused, concentrated, sacramentalized, i.e., becomes a sign-bearing institution. The Church is a growth point, a place and space where the upbuilding and unifying work of the Spirit is demonstrated, where the final community of love is anticipated, where the Kingdom of God is already in the world's midst, where the entire world is called to become the people of God, the Body of Christ, the temple of the Holy Spirit.[54] As part of the world and of mankind created anew by God's Spirit, life in the Church demands an ever maturing sensitivity and obedience to the Holy Spirit who works both in the religious and the profane sphere. Religion as such is not the special concern of the Christian Church. Obedience to the word, attention to the work of the Spirit in bringing creation and redemption to completion and fullness is the proper concern of the Church. So, to speak of the Church is to speak of a community concerned with the relationship and correlation of the sacred and secular in human life. Christians belong in the marketplace among men and ideas. Their activity, as a friend of mine once described it, is not limited to looking at the world through the sacristy keyhole. *How* to relate and bring together these two spheres of life often finds Christians in disagreement within and beyond denominational borders. Such division became marked in the 1960s. It seems we can be more hopeful of a more balanced and integrated approach as we come to the beginning of the 1980s. However we articulate this theologically it is a fact that the Church is associating increasingly closely with the quest of society as a whole for further liberation and development in the human community. For it believes that this quest is linked *causally* with the fullness of life in the Kingdom of God which Jesus proclaimed (John 10.10).

## The norms for discernment

We are now at a stage of this initial reflection on the meaning of 'baptism into hope' where we have to ask how the Holy Spirit is working in our time in the Church and in the world. What are the norms for a genuine discernment of this divine activity? In speaking of norms for discernment we have to take it for granted that the biblical record of a God who reveals himself and its authentic interpretation through the Church's tradition is the fundamental norm.[55] Peculiar to this norm is the concept of the Kingdom of God established in Christ, of whose kingdom there will be no end, as the Nicene Creed expresses it. Neither a particular history nor the whole of history is the history of the Kingdom of God. But where the Kingdom receives its specific history in the world, there the Holy Spirit is present and active. The Church witnesses to the inauguration of the Kingdom in Jesus and has the assurance that the basic norm for an activity of the Spirit either in the Church or in the world is love. This is not a sentiment. It has been manifested and given its full value in Christ. We cannot go about putting 'love' as a convenient label with a transcendent advertising sound on what conforms to our comfort and meets our expectations. For love is about an unselfish and self-giving attention and involvement with others whose needs are not met or whose rights and dignity have been violated. The economy of the Spirit has a very specific historical dimension. Pentecost happens at specific places, in and among specific persons. Not all places or times, not all of mankind manifest the Spirit, not all Christians manifest the Spirit and those who do manifest the Spirit do so very imperfectly. But if a specific *praxis* can be related to the Kingdom proclaimed by Jesus and to his acts of loving kindness and mercy that eradicate evil, then the Spirit is present and active. Salvation takes place where there is exercised the power of Jesus' ministry of preaching and healing, of liberating and exorcizing. There is no fixed content by which the Kingdom is discerned or brought into existence. There are only the words and deeds which overcome evil and destruction. There ought to be only responsive hope and joy among Christians whenever and however this is happening, be it in social liberation movements, in the neo-Pentecostal movement, in the Ecumenical Movement, between Catholic and Evangelical Christians, in the movement towards building community. Such is the most generalized norm for Christian discernment.

But how does the Christian discern in particular instances? How does he or the Christian community discern what is really in the interests of the Kingdom of God? Are we dealing with liberation, licence, or anarchy? Is it raw violence or a struggle for liberation? Is this the release of the Holy Spirit or mass hysteria, or sheer emotional release? Is it an opportunity for Christian unity or pragmatic ecclesiastical joinery? Are we running from the responsible adaptation to a science-based culture to a more traditional culture appropriate to the nineteenth century with its communal romanticism? Is it development, deviation, or revolution that is occurring? What has a Christian to say about the conflict in Northern Ireland, the European Economic Community, Amnesty International, immigration and integration in a multi-racial society, women's liberation, transcendental meditation and eastern mysticism, or sexual freedom? How do we discern with the rest of society in the political-social milieu what is good and bad, what is right and wrong? This brings us into the moral dimension of human experience and Christian hope, the latter grounded on the gracious acts and promises of God that are for our ultimate wholeness, justice, and peace. Human secular experience has its element of hope too. We may not be able to put this under a theological microscope to discover its precise significance and its source of energy for human endeavour. But it is there! An Irish theologian,

Dr Enda McDonagh, dealing with the theme 'On Discerning God's Action in the World' says that 'hope is the key to continuing moral efforts. . . . It is not easy to explain it as a human phenomenon, much less to justify it. It occurs. It keeps one going.'[56] Nonetheless such hope reflects both a moral dimension and the need for norms when we look at all that is going on around us and beyond our national limits. Are we not in danger of so much pluralism that we will get swamped in the wake of relativism and scepticism? We live in a supermarket of ideas, panaceas, plans and projects, and movements. Everything must be tested as worthy of this human hope. In some sense what is happening must become the ground of human hope.

What then is the underlying moral basis of the movements I am suggesting Christians regard as significant for the renewal and mission of the Church? It consists in a profound respect for persons *as persons*, i.e., not atomized, but living in society. Persons are ends in themselves, never to be treated as means to ends or idealistic goals. In a speech on the occasion of his reception of the peace prize of the German Book Trade in 1953, Martin Büber said: 'From my youth on I have taken the real existence of peoples most seriously. . . .'[57] Without this respect morality loses its distinctive human features behind a stolid mask. It is powerless to transform human nature. The basis of this respect lies in the unique 'otherness' of man. Unlike anything else in the world people cannot and may not be absorbed, possessed, or eliminated as a distinct centre of knowledge, freedom, creativity, or as a distinct centre of decision-making and loving relationships. McDonagh says: 'Attempts to assimilate through posesssion or destruction refuse to recognize this final otherness and their frequent frustration can be found in the records of family and political history.'[58] To talk about the other *as other* is not existentialist jargon. To enter as intimately as possible into another's subjective world, to get inside the skin of another as it were, is a supreme effort of unselfish, self-transcending love. It lies at the heart of all human efforts at counselling, dialogue, community, liberation, and reconciliation. It is not a sentiment or superficial sympathy, or even sincere compassion. In practical terms it is a process which makes man more truly and fully human. It is the recognition that the development of individual human potential and of man in society is a process of continuing discernment. This discerning process is concerned with finding the true direction of movement and growth for the person in community. In Christian terms, finding the true direction for an authentic expression of hominization, man becoming fully alive, is a norm for judging whether or not the Holy Spirit is present and active in a personal situation or social movement. This is not to set aside a basic common morality in favour of an individualistic or situational ethic. Self-identity is achieved in a community, in society. Recognizing others involves a discernment of the world in which they live with its cultural, moral, religious, political character. The upbuilding of the human personality and the human community are two sides of one coin.[59]

If the world is the place where the Church discerns the action of God, it is no less true that the Church is the place where the world ought to find evidence that God is really interested in and truly active among men. In other words there ought to be some evidence of the signs of the coming Kingdom of God. Pauline Webb, Secretary of the Overseas Division of the Methodist Church in Britain, sees five principal signs of the Kingdom which the Church ought to manifest in a pluralistic secular society.[60] Miss Webb, an ecumenist with both national and international experience, speaks to the British situation in a world context. The signs are:

(*a*) The Church as a sign of celebration;

(*b*) the Church as a sign of discernment and dialogue among men;

(*c*) the Church as a sign of a new kind of community;

(*d*) the Church as a sign of peacemaker and reconciler;

(*e*) the Church as a sign of a community of hope.

She concludes: 'So in joyful anticipation as well as present struggle we are called to live as a community which celebrates, which discerns the signs of the Kingdom, which creates a new kind of community, which actively pursues peace, which lives for the future.'[61] This is the right combination for the Church to discharge its responsibility to the world, show its true face, and function as a norm by which the world can undertake its own discernment. Bishop Barry once noted that 'the secular substitute for Christian hope – the belief in an imminent, self-redeeming Progress . . . has been killed by catastrophic disappointments and has no secure foundation on which to build'.[62] This is an echo nearly forty years later of the prophet and philosopher Nicholas Berdyaev. In a work which first alerted me to the depth and extent of the changes occurring in the world and which were soon to be felt in the Church, he said: 'The rhythm of history is changing: it is becoming catastrophic.'[63] Berdyaev believed that the West was witnessing the end of the Renaissance and approaching 'the dark beginnings of a middle age, and that we have got to pass through a new civilized barbarism, undergo a new discipline, accept a new religious asceticism before we can see the light of a new and unimaginable renaissance'.[64] It is the significance and magnitude of such a change that provides both Church and world with a norm for ongoing discernment. In suggesting this as a norm I am aware that a particular philosophical or religious interpretation of such change can be challenged. Certainly historians and social scientists are right to bring their critical apparatus on facile assumptions. But between such an assumption and the arbitrary denial of any deep significance in present social change, there is, as Alvin Toffler says in *Future Shock*, 'a growing body of reputable opinion' which 'asserts that the present moment represents nothing less than a second great divide in human history, comparable in magnitude only with that first great break in historic continuity, the shift from barbarism to civilization'.[65] Hans Küng in his *summula* of Christian faith, *On Being a Christian*, sees contemporary change in the last quarter of this century as a 'turning point in the history of ideas' and 'the upheaval of our lifetime . . . the second great break in the history of mankind . . . the transition from barbarism to civilization'.[66] Between the first writing of Berdyaev's *The End of Our Time* and Toffler's *Future Shock*, a period from 1919 to 1970, the eruptions predicted by Berdyaev have been part of our world.[67] And with these eruptions there has come that 'mass bewilderment in the face of accelerating change' that forms Toffler's thesis. Another version of this could be expressed as the human dilemma. How is man to cope with the disproportion between low human complexity and high technological complexity? Our sophistication hardly matches our sophisticated weapons and machines. When David Brown speaks of the birthpangs of a new age, he enumerates four characteristics of the age 'which makes some people think that it heralds some new and dramatic

leap forward in the Ascent of Man'.[68] Along with scientific technological development, increased control over natural resources,
and the necessity of interdependence between nations, he adds
the exposure of people to pressures of all kinds. Bewildering,
depressing, and frightening! It was more than hyperbole when
Berdyaev said that we 'are entering into the realm of the unknown
and the unlived, and we are entering it joylessly and without much
hope'.[69] The point in saying all this is not to give comfort to the
doomwatchers, the Cassandras on the city walls, nor to encourage
false apocalyptical expectations.[70] I want to stress both the magnitude and the seriousness of the change in order to discern the
activity of the Holy Spirit and the corresponding demands on us,
especially in our response of Christian hope. In *The Times* article
referred to above, Bishop Barry spoke to this: 'Christian hope
depends on trust in God, by whom alone it can be substantiated.
It rests not on illusion but on reality. It never pretends that the
worst does not happen. It shines through the very heart of the
human tragedy by the act of God in the cross and resurrection.'
The changes in our world and the shift in consciousness create at
very least a new and serious situation.[71] It is more than culture
shock, the sudden immersion in a new culture, e.g., post-indus-
trial, post-Christian. Such culture shock does not seem to account
sufficiently for the newness of our situation, new to a point of
losing continuity with the past. Dr Immanuel Jakobovitz has said
that 'the world is now faced by an acute crisis of more universal
dimensions than any since the Flood'.[72] The role of religion is
vital because the great religions of the world are concerned with
the origin and destiny of man, his roots, his memory of divine
encounters and human events, expressed in the richness and depth
of his myths and symbols. Both Judaism and Christianity affirm
that man is made in the image and likeness of God; that he is
called to live under the promise of God's final advent. The Christian Church is a point of continuity with the mighty act of God in
Jesus. Implicit in this is the vocation to serve the human community. 'All this is from God, who through Christ reconciled us
to himself and gave us the ministry of reconciliation; that is, God
was in Christ reconciling the world to himself . . .' (2 Cor. 5.18–
19). Christians share the world with other men, with other religious people in this time of radical change. With them our sharing
must be mutual and our dialogue an honest exercise. Our dis-

27

cernment is a joint one. If the Christian attitude is such that we give the impression we have everything to give and nothing to receive, the possibility of real discernment of the Spirit's activity is diminished. However, our first responsibility is to look to the inner life of our Churches, our communities of faith, to discern what the Spirit is saying to the Churches (Rev. 3.6). In the next five chapters of this book, five major areas of church life are proposed to help church leaders and responsible members in such discernment. Neither the choice nor the method is random or arbitrary. These are five paths that will meet ultimately in a Church renewed for mission. This is not a sociological analysis, though such an analysis needs to be carried out in the near future. In discerning the activity of the Spirit we ought not to neglect the competence proper to human disciplines. In particular we cannot dismiss the methods of discovery and analysis proper to sociology.

In assigning significance to these five principal areas of renewal in Christian life, there has to be a defined context. The sociologist would say there has to be a particular meaning system. It supposes that there is some measure of acceptance of the premises and assumptions of the Christian life. This would have special application to the areas of renewal, ecumenism, and mission. Sociologist John Hughes says that 'this does not mean that there are no criteria by which to evaluate the ultimate postulates, only that there are no *absolute* criteria'. And he continues: 'There are plenty of criteria, rules of evidence, of procedure, and so on within the system of meaning itself, but our confidence in them comes from the attachments and human commitments we make to them.'[73] So, in some sense a commitment to the work of renewal, ecumenism and mission is presupposed and a basic content of understanding is assumed. There will be little interest or openness to what follows if there is not some measure of understanding and commitment to these movements and their mutual interaction. They involve growing numbers of participants. There is no evidence that they are going to go away. There is evidence of growth and development notwithstanding the need for further development and maturity in themselves and in their interrelatedness with one another. Some may think that these five paths are running parallel or indeed away from each other, that any one of them or all of them could take the Church off course and put it in a wrong direction. Feelings are facts, but we have to get our facts right.

We have to try to see each movement as it is in itself, let each movement disclose itself and reveal its inner meaning. Secondly, at the present time we can only let the implications, legitimate relationships, and interacton of these movements find their own level. This cannot be forced. Most of the movements are in a very early stage of development. This does not mean we are unable to interpret these movements in the *context of renewal*. Renewal has to be defined in such a way that there is some common understanding, though exhaustive definition is impossible. As a definition I suggest the following: Renewal is the manifestation of the new age that has already broken upon the world in Jesus Christ who forms a community of faith dedicated to live in his Spirit, to extend his liberating mission by the power of his Spirit, and to live ever more perfectly in obedience to the Spirit of Jesus. This definition implies two other factors, namely ecumenism and mission. By ecumenism I refer to 'the movement among the Christian Churches for the recovery of their visible institutional unity'.[74] And by mission I understand the authentication, articulation, and communication of the gospel in a particular place and at a particular time.[75] While these definitions provide a defined context, a meaning system for what is under discussion, they do not preclude a measure of pluralism in the way Christians react to and interpret these five movements I am suggesting as signs of ongoing renewal in the Church, as signals of hope for a new age of the Church in renewing its inner life for its mission to the world. Renewal, then, is the principal factor in this analysis; ecumenism is its major signpost; mission is its destination.

The five movements are as many paths indicating that there is a renewal movement of historic proportions in progress. It is no time to get landlocked or bogged down in traditional attitudes and reactions; no time for internecine strife, no time for party politics. It is the fullness of time, a unique opportunity to begin speaking the truth in love in order to grow up as Christians (Eph. 4. 14–16). We are in the early stages of this development. How early is difficult to say. Perhaps these movements are birthpangs, inarticulate groanings. The Church is in travail, sorrowing because her hour has come. One day she will no longer remember the pain and anxiety for joy that a child is born into the world (John 16.21). Or it could be dawn and time for rejoicing (Ps. 30). At very least these movements are opportunities for living in hope.

Towards the end of his *Mystery and Imagination* R. P. C. Hanson reminds us that 'Christian hope is founded on the freedom and resourcefulness of God'. He continues on this note by saying that Christians need not surrender to any form of determinism for 'we cannot dogmatically exclude any possibilities which are consistent with the known character of God as long as we are in his hands'.[76] This is what the challenge of Christian hope is all about. This is where the Christian is asked once again to account for the hope that is in himself and his church community.

We have been speaking of these paths of renewal as movements. A movement has to be judged by more than a body count. It has to have and hold some discernible direction. It has to exhibit a quality of life. It must participate already in that which it anticipates. Participation in some way is an essential principle for judging a movement. John Hughes says:

> To try and catch the interpretative process by remaining aloof as a so-called 'objective' observer and refusing to take the role of the acting unit is to risk the worst kind of subjectivism – the objective observer is likely to fill in the process of interpretation with his own surmises in place of catching the process as it occurs in the experience of the acting unit which uses it.[77]

In non-sociological language this means that if a Christian does not bring some sympathy, interest, openness, and willingness to be taught by the Spirit, he is in no position to judge the value of the movements described and evaluated in the next five chapters. But there must be some levels of interest and participation that will allow involvement and experience without demanding final commitment. There are at least two levels of participation possible:

(*a*) A *participant observer*, i.e., one who questions, watches, listens, and acts; who tries to share as intimately as possible in the life and activities of the movement, in its world of meaning;

(*b*) an *observer as participant*, i.e., one who initiates contacts and develops these as enduring relationships with individuals within the movement, sincerely trying to discover meaning through friendship, respect, and dialogue.

These possible levels of participation reflect two attitudes with which one can approach the material of this book in the chapters which follow. I dare suggest they are basic Christian attitudes. I have been a participant observer in the ecumenical, neo-Pentecostal, and community movements. While I have come to these movements from a critical and analytical direction my participation has been wholehearted and my experience direct. These have been a source of joy and hope for my own life and the basis of that hope which I hold for the Church. The Catholic–Evangelical convergence and the liberation movement have engaged me principally as an observer participant who has come to treasure contacts with Evangelical Christians, the spiritual friendships formed, the opportunities for spiritual sharing and doctrinal dialogue. These Christians have struck deep responsive chords in my own Christian life. The liberation movement is more in the nature of a vicarious experience for me. I say this because of its wide and diffuse social applications. But both the content and the method of the theology behind these various struggles for liberation and justice seem to me in the main to be valid, and moving Christians in the right direction. But the struggle itself speaks fully to my mind and my heart. The aim of securing genuine human freedom on an unprecedented scale is in itself the greatest opportunity offered to the evolving human community. For Christianity it is an unprecedented opportunity to bring together the meaning of its own word and action, its *theoria* and *praxis*. God's word is never unfruitful because it reaches into the real world of human concern (Isa. 55.10–11). The presence and action of the Holy Spirit are assured to the extent that we are prepared to make the word of God alive and active in our world both by our convictions and our lives. We need not be afraid that our Christianity will be tainted by politics or secularized by humanistic goals if we are really pledged to discover the meaning of freedom anew. 'Where the Spirit of the Lord is, there is freedom' (2 Cor. 3.17). Just as renewal with its factors of ecumenism and mission happen simultaneously, so do these movements that give renewal, ecumenism, and mission their inner meaning and content. At this stage of renewal it is important not to be too eager to predict how the convergence of these movements may happen. It is enough for now to look at these movements in themselves, to examine whatever relationships can be discerned already among them, to explore how tenuous or deeply mutual these may be. I am convinced that an honest look at these movements in openness to the Holy Spirit will lend substance to our hope for the future of man and the future of God in his world.

# 2

# The Ecumenical Movement

. . . our quest for Christian unity is not just a matter of group-interest. It is part and parcel of our calling to serve God's plan 'to unite all things in Christ.

*Cardinal Hume to the Church of England Synod*

The Ecumenical Movement is a movement of parts, of many faces, but with one name. William Temple referred to it as the 'great new fact of our era'.[1] As usual the Greeks had a name for it, rooted in their word for 'house' or 'dwelling' and by extension for 'family' or 'household'. By further extension it came to mean 'all the world' or 'the whole inhabited earth' or 'the civilized world'.[2] As the Christian Church developed historically and doctrinally the word *ecumenical* shifted its secular usage to designate the Church in its catholicity, i.c., the Church of the whole world. When a general council was held, it was called an *ecumenical council* if it was thought to involve the whole Church. Otherwise it did not merit such a title. Later, with the schism between East and West (1054) and with the Reformation in the sixteenth century, a difference in the reckoning of the number of ecumenical councils arose between Roman Catholics and other Christians. When the movement towards reunion began in the early part of the century, it was referred to as the 'Ecumenical Movement' to indicate that no Church could claim to be *the* orthodox or *the* catholic Church as long as there were denominational divisions. It was thought that when the Church rediscovered and made visible the unity willed by Christ for the Church, then and only then would it be truly ecumenical and catholic. This theological position was reflected in the remark of William Temple: 'I believe in the Holy Catholic Church and sincerely regret that it does not at present exist.' Both the Orthodox and Roman Catholic Churches were unable to accept this position.[3] In this period also there was an effort to secure some sort of peaceful coexistence among Christians and this had to be distinguished from the proper goal of the Ecumenical Movement. Ecumenism can easily get

33

confused with eirenicism. The goal of visible unity in Christ is more than peaceful coexistence among Churches. The Ecumenical Movement has laboured under the suspicion that it is a false eirenicism which attempts peace at any prize.[4] At any rate, by 1910, when we usually date the beginning of the modern Ecumenical Movement, the word 'ecumenical' entered into Christian theological vocabulary with new meaning, the Churches' search for visible unity.

The concept behind the word can be expressed with different emphasis on various dimensions of the movement. Thus a real definition of the movement sees it as an effort to foster unity among Christians in order to extend the Christian mission to the world. Or it could be defined as the movement of Christians *towards* unity *for* mission *by* renewal. An American ecumenist suggests the following: 'The personal and communal celebration of an already existing unity amid sinful division with the ultimate goal of celebrating healthy diversity in full unity.'[5] More could be suggested. However, simply taking these three definitions, we note that the first stresses the relationship between Christian unity and mission; the second stresses the same relationship while introducing *renewal* as the principal factor; the third stresses the imperfect unity already existing between Christians and their Churches and introduces the notion of a future full communion that will respect unity in diversity and pluralism. Unity and mission, renewal of the Christian Churches, imperfect and full communion, unity in pluralism and diversity – all are essential factors in the Ecumenical Movement and the convergence to which it leads. More and more Christians see the wisdom and the will of God in their increasing acknowledgement that Christian unity has to be visible, organic, and full if the mission of the Church is to be effective. This does not mean that they agree on how this happens. Nor does it mean that they agree on what is essential to achieve and express it. This was expressed at the third world conference on Faith and Order held at Lund in 1952:

> We differ in our understanding of the relation of our unity in Christ to the visible, holy, Catholic and Apostolic Church. We are agreed that there are not two Churches, one visible and the other invisible, but one Church which must find visible expression on earth, but we differ in our belief as to whether certain

doctrinal, sacramental, and ministerial forms are of the essence of the Church itself. In consequence, we differ in our understanding of the character of the unity of the Church on earth for which we hope. (Lund Report)

Here the theological dialogue tries to get back beyond the disputes that have divided Christians. When the Faith and Order Conference of the World Council of Churches (WCC) was convened at Montreal in 1963, it was felt that more progress could be made in dialogue if the Churches discussed theological issues prior to their historic divisions. This was not advocated to avoid necessary and difficult points of theology or doctrine. Rather it was intended to avoid a purely polemical comparative approach that would only tend to harden dialogical positions, rendering them immobile and sterile. Hopefully such an approach will continue to produce evidence of growing agreement in such areas as Eucharist, ministry, authority. Today it is sometimes called 'consensus theology'.[6]

Today Christians are less satisfied with and enthusiastic about halfway measures in solving the problem of Christian disunity. They are less satisfied with solutions based on federation schemes which really paper over cracks. Again, feelings are facts, but we have to get our facts straight. It is important that ordinary Christian people have some feeling and sympathy for what professional ecumenists are trying to do. But it is equally essential for the professionals not to forget their responsibility to all the Christians in all the Churches. While I am not writing or even outlining a history of the Ecumenical Movement, it is important to indicate the fundamental dynamics behind the movement. Otherwise the real purpose behind theological dialogue and union plans will continue to be misunderstood and misinterpreted by those in whose interests they are undertaken. It is often said that the Ecumenical Movement is a case of pragmatic ecclesiastical joinery. 'Let's all hang together or we will all hang separately.' Bryan Wilson, writing in *Religion in a Secular Society* in 1969, attributes the enthusiasm among church leaders for ecumenism as 'a growing recognition of the essential weakness of religious life in the increasingly secularized society' and a recognition by these same church leaders of 'their essential marginality in modern society'.[7] But the birth of the movement, with the exception of Methodism, coincided not with decline but with evangelistic success. And so we can say that the modern Ecumenical Movement was born more of 'optimism in prosperity' than of 'hope in adversity', despite the decline of a generation later and the deepening of the secularization process. With reference to the Methodist problem of inner divisions, Barry Till notes that their 'ecumenical plans were linked with missionary hopes, rather than with fears of decay'.[8] Historically speaking then, the real causes of the Ecumenical Movement were and are a sense of mission and the inherent theological difficulty of a divided Christian Church. To use any other pragmatic consideration as a basic motive is to betray the Ecumenical Movement. The problem was and still is one of understanding the nature of the Church in relation to its mission. In the Bampton Lectures of 1966 Stephen Neil suggested that 'the classical Reformation statements of the Christian faith . . . were drawn up to refute fellow Christians rather than with a sense of mission to non-Christians, with the result that the doctrine of the Church . . . is set forth in terms of *being* and not of *function*'.[9] The same could be said of much Reformation and counter-Reformation polemic. A simple statement of the difference between being and function can be expressed in two brief questions. What is the Church? What is the Church for? Since the General Assembly of the World Council of Churches at Uppsala in 1968 and Nairobi in 1975 it could be said that the effort to understand catholicity and ecumenicity as one and the same work has been intensified. However, some along with the Orthodox and Roman Catholic Christians would be reluctant to accept a simple identification of the two terms. It has caused serious difficulty for the Ecumenical Movement and inter-Christian dialogue. Older Protestant theology used the notion of a more or less imperfect 'manifestation' of unity in the essentially invisible Church. In this theology catholicity is the fullness of the Church which has not yet appeared; ecumenicity is the concrete appearance of the one true Church from time to time. Roman Catholics and Orthodox have maintained that the Church is as essentially visible as it is invisible. The term catholicity for them expresses an ever valid essence of the Church as the gift of Christ which is characterized by its oneness, its continuity with the discipleship of the Apostles, and particularly by the holiness of its members. Ecumenicity on the other hand expresses the mission of the Church to the whole world dividing believers from unbelievers. Thus ecumenicity was more of a dynamic element for Protestantism and more of a static element for Roman Catholicism and Orthodoxy. Neither theological camp intended to make catholicity and ecumenicity mutually exclusive terms. Going beyond this difficulty the contemporary search for Christian unity is expressed as a search for a genuine understanding and respect for one another's communities of faith. There is the common feeling that our Churches are somehow lacking and incomplete in the fullness of life they are meant to express as the one Body of Christ; that they are deficient in the witness they give to non-believers; that their prophetic role in human society is seriously diminished or obscured. Contemporary ecumenism seeks for the Church a renewed sense of its vocation. As Christians we are constantly summoned by the Holy Spirit to rediscover and express that essential unity which Jesus willed for his disciples and for which he prayed to his Father (John 17). The search is not for an old unity. It is for a more perfect, more profound, more full and rich unity than heretofore realized. This is the ongoing responsibility of the Church under the Holy Spirit. It must go on until its consummation in the final appearance of Christ the Lord. The Ecumenical Movement recognizes that there has been a serious and essential breakdown in mutual life within the Christian family. Some Churches feel that the essential *data* of Christian unity have not been lost because of God's fidelity to the Church. But it would be foolish to deny that the unity Christ willed for his Church has received a serious diminishment, that the measure of unity the Church was able to express through the Spirit of Jesus, the *datum* of unity, does not represent a real loss. All ecumenists believe that we owe Christ a fundamental obedience to rediscover the essential data of unity and share the riches of Christ.[10] The gift of unity becomes a Christian responsibility to turn to the world in the powerful witness of visible unity, offering the universal 'Shalom!' of the new creation that belongs to a new inhabited world, a new *oikoumene*.

I referred earlier to false eirenicism. There are Christians who understand ecumenism as an exercise in tolerance and good will. But there it stops. Their notion of unity pretty much defers visible unity until the Second Coming. We enjoy an invisible unity now, in Christ, they argue. We shall have visible unity in the coming great new Church of heaven. Right now on earth its membership is partially discernible. It may sound plausible, but the actual thinking is muddled. The Church is a reality transcending space and time. It is also a visible gathering of Christians on earth. The Church on earth is the beginning of the Church in heaven, lacking fullness of perfection in truth and love where God is 'everything to every one' (1 Cor. 15.28). As we noted in the introductory chapter the Church anticipates the coming Kingdom of God imperfectly and proclaims God's saving will towards all men by its life and mission. Precisely because of the imperfect life of the Church here and now we are constantly 'straining forward to what lies ahead' (Phil. 3.12–16). In saying this I am not saying that we are to be indifferent to the life and work of our own particular denomination. Far from it. It is the renewal of Christian life, having the mind of Christ Jesus (Phil. 2.4–8) within our own denominations, that offers the greatest hope for Christian unity. Tolerance and friendship are of the Spirit. They are grounded at the deepest level of life in Christ. Our unity is not something we have to build up from the very foundations (Eph. 2.19–22) for our divisions do not go all the way down. At a very basic level we are united already, incorporated into Christ, however imperfectly our Churches are united. Ecumenism is the effort to give adequate visible human expression to the unity already existing in the Church as a gift of God. Ecumenism challenges Christians progressively to increase both the reality of their inner unity and the fullness of its outward expression.

Ecumenists are sometimes suspect in their own denominations because of their willingness to work out the implications of theology. They try to work out the practical conclusions in the meaning of the Church as catholic, as provisional of the Kingdom of God, of the Church as historical. We also have to talk about the 'one Church of Christ'. This introduces an expression that takes into account both the reality of our Christian unity and our lack of it. John Coventry, a Roman Catholic ecumenist, in commenting on the Decree on Ecumenism of Vatican II, said:

> The greatest theological step taken by the Decree on Ecumenism can best be explained by saying that it introduces a third term between the Kingdom of Christ, which is a heavenly reality, and the visible and historical Church, which is an earthly reality. This third term is 'the one Church of Christ'. We may miss the significance of this step if we do not observe

that . . . the Decree first treats of 'the one Church of Christ', or 'the entire Church', or simply 'the Church', before going on to treat of the Catholic Church. No patterns of thought are going to be fully adequate to express the Church . . . But this way of thinking in three levels about what is one mysterious reality helps us to realize the inadequacy of other patterns; and it helps us to see further into the mystery of the union that precedes both the outward expressions and structures of union, and their partial breakdown in divisions.[11]

Looking for the third term is not to be regarded as a search for a lowest common denominator; it is a way of working with the highest common factor. Recognizing the reality behind the third term, as Coventry calls it, Christians are free to interact as 'loyal representatives of distinct traditions under the guidance of the Holy Spirit'.[12] To think of the Church as the Body of Christ, as the People of God, as Sacrament, already acknowledges the 'third term'.[13] It is the very legitimacy of a plurality of images in the New Testament to describe the Church that indicates the validity of the third term and allows us in the present ecumenical stage to speak of the Church and the Churches. The Church is not a finished product, an end in itself, a self-enclosed institution, an efficient organization to save souls. It would be bad theology, if not bad faith, to deny the Church the practical needs it has for the organization of its institutional life. But the institutional model is inadequate to reflect the true being and function of the Church.[14] The Church is subject in its inner life to the will and activity of Jesus Christ reaching out through the Holy Spirit to men in every age and under every condition (Eph. 4. 7–10). Because men and human affairs change, it is the very nature of the Church to change, to adapt, to renew itself. Such change is for the sake of the world in order to meet its needs. The Church does not wait for disciples to come. By the command of Jesus his disciples go into the whole world to make disciples (Matt. 28.19–20; Mark 16.15; Luke 24.47). The Church is not free in this matter. It is under obedience to Christ. And so it must change. Sometimes it is a change of reform and sometimes a change of renewal. Always change is subject to the activity of the Holy Spirit. Consequently the Church has to allow for its charismatic element where the Spirit frees us for the contemporary work of

Christ and bestows appropriate gifts on the disciples of Jesus for this work (Mark 16.17; Luke 24.49). The activity of the Spirit prevents change from becoming a search for novelty, and an expression of faddishness, hitching a ride on bandwagons; it dispels what is illusory and superficial in the change; it provides the discernment to judge the character of the change and keep it within the spirit of the gospel; it provides the power and wisdom to manage the change. It is the activity of the Spirit which is at the heart and at the base of the institutional Church. His activity runs throughout its whole life, keeping Christianity orthodox in its concern for the truth of Jesus, Catholic in its concern for the mission of Jesus, Protestant in its concern to offer prophetic witness to the prior claims of the Kingdom of God on human society. The Church must bring together somehow this threefold life of orthodoxy, catholicity, and protest in one visibly united community of faith. These elements of concern are meant to be its ongoing witness, work, and character. I am not suggesting that this will be an easy thing to do, or that it will be a facile synthesis. It is urgent, but it is also subject to the laws of organic development and growth. We are not simply challenged as Christians to reconcile differences in theology or divergent views. We are challenged to be part of a growth and renewal under the Spirit that will bring together in visible organic unity elements of the Church's life, mission, and witness. Ecumenism is not an option. It is a dimension and spirit in the whole life of the whole Church.

Undoubtedly the spirit of ecumenism begins with self-examination and criticism, with genuine reformation and renewal. When a debate arose at the third session of Vatican II over a draft document on what was to become a pastoral constitution on 'The Church in the Modern World', Edward Schillebeeckx, a well-known theologian, is quoted as saying: 'It is precisely in this document that the proof will out: whether the institutional Church considers herself the be-all and end-all, or whether she deems herself an instrument in the hands of Christ, at the service of all mankind.'[15] These words reflect a desire to look at the whole meaning of the Church on the horizon of the world, on the horizon of time as well as eternity. This phenomenon of self-awareness in the Church goes beyond councils and synods. Christians instinctively feel that truth has to be a meaning for their lives and not simply a fixed grasp of facts. When the aura and excitement of

Vatican II were dissipated Roman Catholics might well stand back and exclaim, 'What happened?' If we are to believe the American Management Association, this Church was second only to General Motors in organizational efficiency prior to Pope John's Council. Pope Paul VI had the unenviable task of seeing through or at least continuing what had been begun. In his encyclical letter *Ecclesiam Suam*, issued in 1964, he said that 'the first thought is that this is the hour in which the Church should deepen its consciousness of itself . . .' (n. 10) and that the attitude of the Church in its renewal is that of one 'standing before a mirror . . . to examine interiorly the image of Christ which he has left us' (n. 11). 'We think that it is a duty today for the Church to deepen the awareness that she must have of herself . . . The Church in this moment must reflect on herself. She needs to feel the throb of her own life' (n. 27). When the Pope opened the third session of the Council on 14 September 1964 he said: 'The Church must give a definition of herself and bring out from her true consciousness the doctrine which the Holy Spirit teaches her . . .' What this Church has tried to do in recent years now involves many Churches. All Churches tend to let the force of their own rhetoric die away. Churches as well as individuals can look into the mirror, forget what was seen, and walk away. But the one 'who looks into the perfect law, the law of liberty, and perseveres, being no hearer that forgets but a doer that acts, he shall be blessed in his doing' (Jas. 1.23–5). It is this commitment to an honest examination of our inner lives and the inner life of our Church congregation that offers hope to the Ecumenical Movement. If we look at our Churches as they are, we may well wonder if there is any point in promoting the Ecumenical Movement as it has evolved in church relationships. They seem to be getting on quite well and the new pluralism in theology seems to ease old aches and pains and relieve tensions.[16] Here we have to recall that the unity we seek is a unity of faith, not a unity of theologies. Ecumenism operates not only at the level of competitive and comparative theologies. It operates within the actual experience of Christians. So, when we emphasize self-awareness we are asking Christian Churches to ask out of their collective experience what being a Christian today means. It is not a question of taking a fumbled ball from theological hands, nor setting aside order and discipline to take matters into their own hands. Informed by the honest research and discovery of the

41

theologians and guided by proper pastors Christians have to ask themselves this question. Two such Christians, one a theologian and the other an educationist, have done this. By way of example I want to cite them at some length:

> First, it is able to handle in practice the total reality of the present situation while respectfully leaving it to the theologians to persevere in their legitimate and necessary argument. For the conviction that life is more than its explanation is a basic law of the modern consciousness. This is an appeal to the instinctive sense of the modern mind for life, and for the wholeness of all horizons. It is 'common sense', not in the sense that this is a practical, compromising attitude to a question that is unresolved, but in a sense that the present community of mankind has the mysterious ability to trust its instinct for living resolution of its issues in this way.
>
> Secondly, the present experience knows how to find in the lived mystery of Christ a focus of faith in a radical sense that is sufficient dynamism for its pilgrimage. This amounts to a 'mystical' sense of Christ that comes from faith – 'mystical', not in an esoteric sense, but in the sense of the mysterious quality of a believing that forms its own mentality, unity, and life.[17]

Christians who have experienced shared life in the new ecumenical climate of our times know that a firm convergence is already under way, an idea whose time has come, and more than an idea, a mighty movement of the Holy Spirit. Those who have shared church premises and buildings know that much more than Christian generosity is involved. There is shared life. One cannot share a pastoral ministry and not experience a concern for all God's people. Instead of jealous pastoral oversight of one's 'own flock' there develops a sense of community in which all share. Shared retreats and pilgrimages serve to unite spirituality and piety, devotion to Christ combined with a veneration for the manifestation of his life and holiness in persons and places associated with his presence among men. Shared mission, when it is undertaken properly, creates an ecumenical consciousness that the gifts and grace of Christ are for everyone, believer and non-believer. This is a way of participating in the spirit of ecumenism that was understood in the ancient Church, the original and basic meaning of ecumenism that was developed early on. Unfortunately this sense of mission is too often lost amid the confusion of goals and methods, by a spirit of competition and proselytism, by nose-counting and head-hunting, by the numbers game.[18] There are two significant movements of the Spirit creating this ecumenical experience and consciousness. These are the neo-Pentecostal and community movements. But precisely because of their significance it is necessary to give them separate consideration in the last two chapters of this book.

Nor must we underestimate the more ordinary ways in which 'common-sense' ecumenism works. Teacup ecumenism is not to be despised and history may reveal that tea disposed Christians to receive the more heady distillations of ecumenical church councils and theological commissions. Every occasion of friendly conversation with fellow Christians enables us to share perceptions of truth. Friendship leads or flows from the intimacy of dialogue and casts out fear about sensitive issues arising, e.g., the papacy, devotion to Mary, the ordination of women, a disputed point of history, difficulties with certain devotional practices. Friendship does not make these topics an embarrassment. It is gracious and soon discovers ways of sharing in one another's church tradition with sympathy and increasing understanding. So groups of Christians meet as friends to listen to experts lecture and lead them in study, to keep as informed as possible.[19] They undertake common Bible study as a primary spiritual ecumenical activity, listening anew to God's Word, taking it as a rule of life for their new life together. New ways of sharing life and Christian ministry are always appearing. While we have to assign priorities among the ecumenical activities in which we engage, we cannot be selective in the sense that we arbitrarily select *how* we are going to be ecumenical. We have to remain open to all that is happening and to all that is consistent with our informed convictions and present disciplines. Openness to the diverse charisms of ecumenism for building up the new life of the Church in a new era is essential. When the first Life and Work Conference of 1925 was convened at Stockholm to provide impetus to the Ecumenical Movement by its insistence on 'practical Christianity', ecumenists learned that you cannot talk about service and worship together while excluding questions of faith and order. They learned that you cannot discuss practical Christian living without reference to theology.[20] But there is a practical way of doing ecumenism. You rejoice

43

when a way forward in ecumenical progress is discovered, even if one's own Church cannot be involved immediately. We have to keep the movement moving. At the time of the Anglican–Methodist scheme and presently in the case of the Ten Propositions for Unity, committed Roman Catholics have been involved in the work, discussion and planning inevitably associated with such schemes and propositions. Such joy and optimism and hope keep ecumenism a spontaneous living creation of the Spirit. They keep ecumenism as close to actual life as possible. In the past ecumenical consciousness has had its forerunners and its prophets. Today, however, we are in a higher stage of its development. There is the acknowledgement in our mainline Churches and at an official level that it is the work of the Spirit for which there can be no turning back. There will continue to be a need for a prophetic ecumenical ministry until the spirit of ecumenism has got into the mainstream of church life. The Church needs members with the charism of ecumenicity to build up a new sense of catholicity for the whole Church. Ecumenicity is a charism, a gift of the spirit to build up the Church until it becomes what Christ wants it to be in the service of his Kingdom. As such it is something to be desired and prayed for. All this needs to be said. Too often ordinary members of our Churches feel that ecumenism is the preserve of clerics and theologians. Only general good will, tolerance, patience, and social co-operation in the wider community are left to them. But in fact it is essential that Christians in ever greater numbers open their lives to the imperative of Christian unity and an awareness of the issues it involves. All too often the Ecumenical Movement is held back by those who do not know anything about it and those who think they do. The growing consciousness and 'common sense' we have talked about exceed uninformed enthusiasm. It is a movement to bring the Church into obedience to Christ. It cannot be supported for ever by the few. Barry Till says that 'the World Council of Churches is the institutional response of the institutional western Churches to their conscience about their disunity.'[21] Personally I do not think there is any doubt about this. Yet it would be a tremendous loss to the Ecumenical Movement if rank-and-file church members were to see no relationship between the WCC at Geneva and their own efforts in Muddlesthorpe. As R. M. C. Jeffery noted in his invaluable report on local Councils of Churches in Britain, it is a mistake 'to equate Councils of Churches with the ecumenical movement'.[22] What I am saying is that the WCC has played an indispensable role in the growth of the movement and is still indispensable to that growth. It is not simply a church forum or place for theological dialogue. It has helped create an ecumenical awareness. From Amsterdam to Nairobi the WCC has been plagued by unfair criticism and suspicion that it identifies Christianity with secular humanism and political socialism; that it adopts the role of a super-Church constituted by a federation of disunited Churches, when it ought to be preparing the way for a united catholic Church. If one traces the spirit of the WCC by a quick look at its various general assemblies that have been held since 1948, it seems clear enough how unfounded these criticisms and suspicions are. Moreover, it will be evident how faithful the WCC has been to its basic constitution as 'a *fellowship of Churches* which confess the Lord Jesus Christ as God and Saviour according to the Scriptures and therefore *seek to fulfil their common calling* to the glory of the One God, Father, Son, and Holy Spirit' (italics mine). These assemblies reflect and announce new growth in the search for unity, a growth from inward concern to outgoing, outreaching commitment. Each general assembly begins with a theme and ends with a slogan, a kind of dismissal in the spirit of what has emerged in the course of the assembly and which tells us something of where the worldwide Ecumenical Movement has got to:

| ASSEMBLY | THEME | COMMITMENT |
|---|---|---|
| Amsterdam 1948 | Man's Disorder and God's Design | 'We intend to stay together' |
| Evanston 1954 | Jesus Christ, the Hope of the World | 'Growing together' |
| New Delhi 1961 | Jesus Christ, the Light of the World | 'All in each place' |
| Uppsala 1968 | Behold, I Make All Things New | 'Move out together' |
| Nairobi 1975 | Jesus Christ Frees and Unites | 'Suffer and struggle together' |

Here we get the sense of the irreversibility of the Ecumenical Movement. The commitment is to go beyond a period of growth for more growth, turning it to the advantage of the cause of Christ. We have an opportunity to experience the fraternity and charity of the Christian family in an unprecedented way. Our world is smaller, a house we want to turn into a home. New Delhi reflected this pattern of growth by its insistence on unity as a local reality which can be seen by everyone everywhere. New Delhi envisaged unity not in terms of a grand-scale conference that would present the Church as the bearer of good news throughout the world. It wanted to stress the catholicity of the Church in the daily lives of Christians everywhere. Uppsala created a balance and healthy tension within the WCC, which again reflected a changing pattern in Christian life. Ecumenism was once more focused on mission. The issues of racism, exploitation, development, and the unity of mankind were the substance of Uppsala. The assembly was concerned with revolutionary ferment, questions of social and international responsibility, war and peace, ecology, the third world, social change. A new dimension, a new face of ecumenism was seen. It was referred to as *secular ecumenism*. This did not signify a lapse into the older 'life and work' syndrome to which I have referred. It recognized the real relationship of the Church and the world and the pattern of hope intrinsic to any healthy relationship of the two. The Uppsala Report reflected this pattern:

> The Churches, while wishing to affirm the reality of God in the world, often do so at the expense of the reality of man and the world, thus provoking a denial of the reality of God. Secularization can recall us to true worship which affirms the reality of God, of man, and of the world.[23]

The Report defined its understanding of secularization in the context of openness to the future and therefore of Christian hope. It said: 'In secularization', understood positively, 'man refuses to absolutize any authority or structure of the created order and insists on maintaining an open view of the future.'[24] At Nairobi 'the basic attitudes at Uppsala were not called in question, but the assembly had been forced to see them in a more total dimension – both spiritually and in terms of effective action'.[25] Dr Philip Potter spoke of the mood of Uppsala as one of Exodus, going out to change the structures of society and the perspective of races. But he noted that 'we find ourselves in the wilderness . . . a pilgrim people in conflict and penury. . . .' Then he had to confess further: 'We have had to understand the inability of our Churches and congregations to face together what it means to believe in Jesus Christ.'[26] Nairobi taught the Churches how impotent they were to implement their well-intentioned generous programmes apart from renewing themselves in the Holy Spirit on a truly catholic basis. Nairobi taught the Churches, not the WCC, that the concomitants of grace, i.e., community and liberation are costly (1 Pet. 1.18–19). It taught them to take up their cross, their responsibility for making ecumenism a priority in the life of the Church. They would have to suffer and struggle together in love for both truth and justice.[27] The WCC and other councils of Churches were meant to be instruments in making ecumenism a priority. They were not meant to become scapegoats. Bob Jeffery commented in his survey of local councils of Churches that 'the Churches have allowed their ecumenical commitment to be conducted, as it were, by proxy'.[28] In my opinion, Nairobi sent the ecclesiastical pigeons home to roost and was a success precisely for this reason. The issues of the world are too vital and imminent to be handled by servant-bureaucrats from any world-centre, be it Rome or Geneva. They can only be met by 'all in each place'. This demands the renewal of Christian life and mission. It is not the task of any council of Churches. Dr Lukas Vischer says that councils 'are in fact an ecclesiological anomaly which ought not to continue indefinitely in its present form'.[29] Nairobi renewed the instrumental and transitional function of the WCC and other councils of Churches, reminding the Churches of their anomalous character which was made in the image and likeness of that greater anomaly of Christian disunity. That such bodies were meant to lead the Churches into a renewed relationship was precisely expressed in the Report by the General Secretary of the WCC:

> The World Council exists to assist the Churches to move forward into the fullness of conciliar fellowship – that unity of a fully committed, charismatic fellowship of all the Churches in each place and in all places. Our task at this assembly will be to see how the World Council can be the privileged instrument of God to further this goal in the coming years.[30]

More and more the Churches will be asked to respect the instrumentality of the WCC and other councils of Churches. But the

Churches themselves have to reflect a new maturity and responsibility for leadership in the Ecumenical Movement. Faith in the Ecumenical Movement as a summons of the Spirit has been largely 'notional'. It will become progressively real as the Churches take up their ecumenical responsibility. The oft-quoted Lund principle is seldom seen in context. As a principle it has had supreme value. It is this: The Churches ought to do together all things except those which doctrine or conscience require to be done separately. Aside from not being applied very extensively since its formulation at Lund, on the occasion of the Faith and Order Conference of 1952, this principle is frequently put forward as a matter of counsel or suggestion rather than a demanding directive to the Churches. Put in fuller context it can be seen as such:

> We would, therefore, earnestly request our Churches to consider whether they are doing all they ought to do to manifest the oneness of the people of God. Should not our Churches ask themselves whether they are showing sufficient eagerness to enter into conversation with the other Churches and whether they should not act together in all matters except those in which deep differences of conviction compel them to act separately?[31]

If a Church commits itself officially to the Ecumenical Movement, it commits itself to this directive. Nairobi was a signal to the Churches that it is time for mere notional faith to be translated into real faith at the level of ecumenical life according to the Lund directive. Small groups of ecumenically minded Christians have tried to implement this, often with little encouragement from their Churches and church leaders. Nonetheless they have prepared the way for a more official and generous response from the Churches. The level of ecumenical awareness has been prepared for wider and deeper official involvement. The history of the WCC reflects this. Daily life in the Church and the world indicates that the time is ripe for such response and involvement.

The Christian community has come through the experience of schism, heresy, enmity, hot and cold wars of religion, right up to peaceful coexistence. Here we are speaking of relationships between Churches. There have been and are the moral heresies, the failure of the Church to respond to the demands of the gospels in society and within church life. And Christian still kills Christian. However, the Christian community cannot be concerned primarily with repairing and reconstructing history. Its task is to make all things new. A reading of the second chapter of Ephesians will demonstrate this. The Ecumenical Movement exists to bring Christians to a condition of reconciliation or at-one-ment, a condition whereby they learn to live for one another, a condition of proexistence, and beyond this a life lived and sacrificed if need be for all our brothers and sisters throughout the world. Paul knows that God unites Jew and Gentile in Christ, not for mere tolerance or even friendship but to create 'one new man', i.e., a new humanity (Eph. 2.14–16). The Ecumenical Movement is about evolution, spiritual evolution, human evolution.[32] Evolution is one of those words a good number of Christians still feel uneasy about, if not downright disturbed. It is all too easy yet to hear the old charge of *modernism* in this context.[33] I use the term 'evolution' to describe and define a view of man and his world that is based on a model that is an upward linear-spiral that will account for the freedom of God to act among men in history and time, and yet will account fully for the freedom of man to respond to God. This freedom of God is absolutely prior and unconditioned. It is the first article of the Nicene Creed. God not only calls, invites, draws men to a transcendent destiny and life, but also acts in human affairs. Creation, exodus (liberation), incarnation, pentecost are the mighty acts of God. Though they are related and in continuity, they are new and unprecedented. They are God's freedom and promise in time. God enters our history and our time, not to diminish or make nonsense of our freedom, but to do something new and summon his people to respond. This is the worldview, a biblical view. The Bible is more than a resource book written in and about the past. It has to be understood as 'the beginning of the ongoing tradition towards the fulfilment of Yaweh's promises'.[34] This is a matter that will come up again in the next chapter. Christian consciousness is formed by the definitive act of God in Jesus. It is *definitive* but it is not *closed* to the further activity of God through his Holy Spirit. Jesus never viewed his life, mission, or death apart from the Spirit – and this is not only to 'bring to your remembrance all that I have said to you', but to 'teach you all things' (John 14.26). It is this Spirit of Truth who 'will guide you into all the truth' (John 16.13). The life, death, and mission of Jesus is an ongoing mystery lived through an historical community of faith under God's Spirit (John 7.37–

49

9). This relationship to Jesus through the Spirit is part of a whole that is coextensive with human history in Christian consciousness. Pentecost is an observable and movable feast. It looks to the mystery of the cross and resurrection and the final advent of Jesus, Lord of the world. Christian consciousness is further influenced by the promise of an ongoing relationship with God in Christ. This relationship is expressed in the terminology of spiritual childhood, divine sonship by adoption, of fatherhood with its inherent notions of care and dependence. Jesus taught us to call God 'Father' in a very special way. John's first epistle reflects, not an esoteric mysticism, but an intimate relationship with God that is unfinished and undisclosed (1 John 3.2). Our relationship with God simply exceeds all our expectations and remains open to the future action of God bringing us into full communion with himself and into full participation in his divine life. 'Beloved, we are God's children now; it does not yet appear what we shall be, but we know that when he appears we shall be like him, for we shall see him as he is.' One day the language of childhood and fatherhood will yield to an experience of communion with God that we are unable to find adequate language to express now. Our language, culture, and meaning are simply inadequate. It is a matter of a new developed relationship, a new awareness. There is so much truth in the saying: Be patient! God hasn't finished with me yet. We can all say that singly and collectively. We can say it even now about our institutions and Churches. We can say it about the Church. When we talk of 'the one true Church' or about 'full communion', we are working within the limits of human language to express what is a matter not only of time but of eternity as well. It is why we rely on a careful understanding of myth as part of the modality of language itself, the intersection of the time and the timeless, the experience of transcendence. We are on the way to the Father and the way is Jesus and the power is the Holy Spirit. In this perspective there has always been an ecumenical movement, a movement towards the perfection, the fullness, the final manifestation of unity. The modern historical Ecumenical Movement is a thrust forward, an essential integral part of that ongoing evolution of man in his relationship with God in a communion, a fellowship of those living in the divine life. It represents the way to 'the active realization and manifestation of that incomparable concreteness of the historical existence of the

Spirit of Christ which will be made visible only in the total course of history'.[35] And that is why ecumenical dialogue has to go beyond an inter-Christian exchange to include Jews and non-Christians. All the great world religions are concerned with unity and communion, the movement of man towards God. As such they are a vital component of the evolutionary movement. The secular concern with technological and sociological development cannot be conceived by the Christian in total dissociation from the quest for ultimate human fulfilment where God is all in all (1 Cor. 15.28). Man is in history. Christian faith affirms the perfection of Jesus who is the Alpha and Omega of history. So it is the Christian who cannot affirm some form of evolutionary conviction who is the anomaly, not the one who does make such an affirmation. A reaction to Darwinian evolution in its more crude forms cannot justify the total rejection of evolutionary awareness. Walter Ong says that 'the discovery of cosmic and organic evolution is part of man's discovery of himself in history'.[36] Evolution can be conceived as history, i.e., developments within human culture. This is the basis and the importance of widening the dialogue beyond the Christian confessions. It is the foundation on which the modern Ecumenical Movement integrates its search for unity for mission. Ecumenical consciousness intends the *oikoumene*, the inhabited earth. As this earth becomes a global village, as it shrinks, man's awareness of man and his human condition and responsibility for the earth expands in consciousness, giving new efficacy to political and spiritual commitment. The significance of a human act at these levels can be symbolic and prophetic on a scale heretofore unimagined. Without yielding to either a utopian or a myopic vision Christians are asked to see the newness and freshness and the unique opportunity of the present age. Christian unity will have a truly prophetic witness to give because people still live within the memory of its disintegration over four centuries. Therefore, this new opportunity is a maximum opportunity. Walter Ong has expressed this in warning us against a nostalgia for the past in the name of authentic tradition and continuity:

> We have to be careful about imputing to past ages a Christian synthesis. . . . You cannot have a valid Christian synthesis based on a false cosmology or even on a notably defective one. We must face the fact that earlier cosmologies were both defen-

sive and, in many crucial points, false. Nature was never until recent times effectively conjoined with history. The problem today is not to restore an old union but to implement a new one.[37]

Hence a new cosmological vision of unity and smallness, qualities reflected in that earth photograph taken by lunar astronauts in July 1969, corresponds to a new consciousness of one human community in one small world.[38] The witness of a Gandhi, a Dag Hammarskjöld, a Martin Luther King, a Mother Teresa, a Helder Camara, and so many others in our lifetime has a new quality of catholicity and immediate relevance for great sections of the human community, the civilized world, the *oikoumene*. We are in a better position to give a truly renewed Catholic–Evangelical witness than our fathers, than ever before. We are faced with the opportunity to achieve a Christian synthesis surpassing any yet achieved. Speaking out of a confrontation between evangelical and orthodox Christians within the WCC and of Roman Catholic ecumenical participation from outside that body, Professor Thomas Torrance speaks of a 'kind of ecumenical osmosis' that leads to 'a unity of the whole Church at a higher level transcending traditional differences in such a way as to reveal the basic validity within the differences on both sides, which can then be treated as necessary but mutually complementary contributions to the comprehensive unity on that higher level'.[39] Precisely because the Ecumenical Movement seeks that higher unity it has to be concerned with continuity. But this does not mean an endless search for the right conditions under which to repeat or re-enact an imagined 'golden age' of faith. Any significant movement into the future will be marked by transience, novelty, and diversity. Alvin Toffler, quoting John Gardiner, says that 'we must guard against the notion that continuity is a negligible – if not reprehensible – factor in human history'.[40] And then he says:

> In the light of theory of the adaptive range, it becomes clear that an insistence on continuity in our experience is not necessarily 'reactionary', just as the demand for abrupt or discontinuous change is not necessarily 'progressive'. In stagnant societies, there is a deep psychological need for novelty and stimulation. In an accelerative society, the need may well be for the preservation of certain continuities.[41]

For this reason ecumenism advances within a larger field force named *renewal*. This updating or *aggiornamento* as it has been called, is a shared journey not so much back as down to the roots of the Christian community. The vision is of a Church 'regarded as part of a universal movement within the creation in which all things visible and invisible are being reconciled and gathered into unity in Christ'.[42] Christians want this measure of continuity that will ensure a renewed understanding of how the world of God is living and active in their world through a valid tradition of faith. One of the dangers of the Ecumenical Movement, along with inertia and hostility, is impatience. It sometimes takes the form of a feeling of urgency lest renewal and mission overtake ecumenism and render it superfluous. It is an impatience with dialogue and discipline over doctrinal differences. These are little more than non-events, much too late, asking the wrong questions, expressing the wrong concerns. However sincere and well-intentioned, perhaps even prophetic and necessary, such proleptic prodding may be, it must not be allowed to turn the movement into a stampede. The Faith and Order Conference held at Montreal in 1963 was most helpful with its resolution to do ecumenical theology in such a way that it would get us back to common theological roots from which to attack our present theological and doctrinal sticking points. In this way continuity, consensus, and a comprehensive unity at the new level of which Torrance speaks becomes possible. But I must always insist that however important this theological work is, it is only part of the ecumenical process against the wider background of renewal. When we speak of doing ecumenical theology it is important to remember also that we are thinking of the traditional way of doing theology. This way is itself being challenged by a new generation of theologians speaking from a newly emerging third world, groaning under structures of oppression and the most profound injustice and inhumanity.[43] Theologians have a tremendous task to achieve consensus and bring such a consensus under the critical light of this newer approach to doing theology. This is not simply an intellectual task. It is something that presupposes the spiritual renewal of Christian life and calls for spiritual and theological giants on the earth. 'What is needed therefore is a renewed belief in the Holy Spirit and the creative power of Christ to transform mankind, and in that context a commitment to work out in close dialogue with the natural and social sciences constructive ways of realizing the coming world community in obedience to Jesus Christ the Head of the human race.'[44] To date, nothing has held out greater promise of meeting this need for renewed faith in the Holy Spirit and the transforming power of Christ to realize a new sense of community and theological responsibility than the neo-Pentecostal movement. This is a personal conviction and I have devoted a chapter to supporting the conviction. While spiritual ecumenism has been acknowledged as the 'soul' of the Ecumenical Movement, this has been all too nominal. Its intimate relationship to all areas of ecumenical endeavour has not been worked out effectively. With the maturation of the neo-Pentecostal movement this need will be met significantly. Moreover, there seems to be a greater interest in spirituality developing within renewal movements. In the general openness to finding God within the created and within the secular order of things, a renewed spirituality and liturgical life is attracting more people. In this climate the Ecumenical Movement is experiencing something positive and unitive beneath all faith and order questions, namely the oneness of Christian life and discipleship (Mark 9.38–40). It is this unity of discipleship that liberates us from our prejudices and presuppositions. It makes theological dialogue and consensus theology possible. For example, if I am to dialogue with a liberation theologian or a black theologian, I have to begin with his religious experience. This is prior to theological concepts and categories. Therefore I cannot enter the room in plumberlike fashion with my toolkit of Western European-North American presuppositions. It is the common discipleship and experience of the love of God in Christ that makes ecumenical experiences real and creates new possibilities for Christian life together. It is this growing spiritual experience that prepares ordinary Christians to receive in the right spirit, a spirit of understanding, what the theologians express through the findings of their consensus theology. Where there has been shared life at the ordinary level of church life, agreed statements on Eucharist, ministry, authority, and the like will be received with good will and even joy. Resistance to agreed statements and to ecumenism itself have a causal connection with the failure of Christians to develop a spiritual life, an understanding of Christian life rooted in the dominical signs of baptism and Eucharist.

Baptism for most Christians is the basis for their commitment to visible Christian unity. This is so, not because we have a ritual act to be performed or a particular ethical lifestyle to be adopted. The sacrament as such is focused upon the saving act of God embodied in Jesus Christ. Jesus is the content, reality, and power of the sacrament. Professor Torrance thinks it significant that the term *baptismos*, denoting a rite of religious cleansing, was set aside in favour of *baptisma* which the Church 'may well have coined, with the intention of expressing Christian baptism in this objective sense'.[45] Baptism into Christ is the reality. And so Torrance continues: 'Quite evidently the interest of the Church did not lie in the ritual act itself, indispensable as it is, but in the event that stands behind it and that impinges on us through it.'[46] We are baptized into the mission of Jesus, into his death and resurrection, into a new way of living in a new creation. Out of this event flows our response in faith and behaviour, a faith and an ethic in depth, ever initiating and incorporating *intensively* into our lives and our lives into it – the mystery of dying to live the life of God, a life profoundly interior yet stretching out to all (Rom. 6.11). It is the intensive appropriation of this mystery that characterizes and makes authentic Christian life and spirituality. If we can teach this fundamental mystery effectively, we have set ourselves already on the path to visible Christian unity.

This unity of experience and life, the life of the one baptism, is to be nourished and matured in the one Eucharist. Again this central sacramental act is neither a repetition of the one uniquely sufficient sacrifice of Jesus nor a sacred symbol with no real life-bearing value apart from that measure of faith and love which it evokes in the recipient. It is our celebration and entrance anew into the total mystery of God in Christ. It points to the unity of his person, his word, his mission as the one mediator of men with God. Also it expresses Christianity as a community, a communion or fellowship and it builds up this community into a people of shared faith and life. In the liturgical constitution of Vatican II liturgical worship is described as 'the summit towards which the activity of the Church is directed' and at the same time 'the fountain from which all her power flows' (no. 10, Abbot edn.). Here unity is brought to perfection and the community of faith, life, and mission expresses its visible unity. This is also the reason why the Eucharist continues to be not only a sign of unity for Christians, but a sign of contradiction as well. Some Christians feel that there is already a sufficient measure of unity and faith needed to express our life in Christ; others do not feel there is. Some will argue that we will only attain that maturity of faith and unity by eucharistic sharing; others feel that this is a vain attempt to express a unity of faith, life, and mission that is in fact lacking, unable to be made visible as yet. The hope of Christian unity does not rest on the immediate dissolution of this tension or difference. We are witnessing among Christians an 'emergence of eucharistic liturgies which manifest the same fundamental and traditional structure. . . . While our eucharistic liturgies still show rich variety in detail, this variety is seldom today so overstated as to obscure that common tradition.'[47] This might seem insignificant or even trivial for the future of Christian unity. But we have to remember that not so long ago as human affairs are reckoned there were suspicions, often deep suspicions 'that we were up to different things, and probably with different Lords'.[48]

Hope for the Ecumenical Movement through a renewal of Christian awareness rightly focuses on the sacraments of baptism and Eucharist. But if we regard them only *in the flat*, to use Torrance's expression, and not *in a dimension of depth*, we shall overlook the basic unity of faith and life that we share. Today it is common to speak of orthopraxy as well as orthodoxy. Our practical way of celebrating these sacraments ought to approximate much more closely our understanding of their significance and effectiveness in Christian life. Renewed pastoral practice in all Christian Churches at this stage could be more effective in the long run in the cause of Christian unity than putting on pressure for shared Eucharist. For example, baptism in the presence of a gathered parish community, often in the context of a eucharistic celebration, is renewed orthopraxy. Pastoral efforts to relate confirmation to baptism and Eucharist as one process of Christian initiation is another sign of growing orthopraxy. The effort to celebrate the Eucharist through a greater sharing on the part of the worshipping congregation by diversifying functions is another such sign. As orthopraxy develops, orthodoxy deepens and the possibilities of meeting in a deeper unity of faith become more realizable. There is still a lot of sacramental malpractice in the Churches in the form of indiscriminate baptism both regarding infants and young children and a superficial hurried catechumenate for adults.

Earlier on I stressed the Lund principle, indicating that it was time for a more officially generous response to its spirit. The principle is of particular application at local and regional levels of ecumenism. It was good to see a restatement of this principle in the Roman Catholic document *A Time for Building*.[49] It states:

> The Church must show that it believes in growing unity: by encouraging full co-operation at every level in those areas in which conscience does not force us to act apart; by looking honestly at the issues which still divide Christians and seeking together with others the truth of Christ which will bring unity and end divisions which hamper the Christian mission. (No. 65)

It seems to me that there are signs that Lund is beginning to be taken seriously by the Churches – only just beginning. More important will be the extent of its future application to church planning, especially in education and church buildings, shared social commitments. It would also find immediate application where liturgical renewal is in the pipeline. Definitive revisions of the liturgy ought to be avoided to prevent liturgical reform from running parallel rather than towards convergence. This is a way for all Churches to live provisionally and apply with rigorous practicality the Lund principle. Another significant statement in the document *A Time for Building* is the following:

> Catholics must plan not in terms of present disunity, but of the future unity which the Holy Spirit has in store for us; unity will grow through prayer, shared activity and reflection on what we do together. (No. 64)

This is significant because it is the recognition of the Church's orientation to a future built on a genuine hope and anticipation of future unity. It also holds together the life and work principle with the faith and order principle of the Ecumenical Movement. It introduces a dynamic relationship between spirituality and mission. A working principle of ecumenism is that unity is discovered in mission and is directed towards mission. This is a way of saying that unity characterizes Christian life. It is a quality that is basic to the integrity of the Christian Church. But without a sense of mission church life will become narrow and static and inward-looking, untrue to its nature as catholic and apostolic. I stress this to make a point. The holiness inherent in the Christian community has to be made relevant for the whole human community, the *oikoumene*. The effort to make this outreach sincere and effective is called mission. It is more than the oral proclamation of Christian beliefs, more than technological exportation, more than offering a moral philosophy of optimism, inner harmony and peace, creating spiritual euphoria. It is about sharing fully in the life of the human community, testifying by the open witness and quality of our lives that Jesus Christ is the unique centre of human life in its deepest meaning, life for and with others. This has to be said because of a growing feeling among many Christians that Christian community is more a myth than a tangible reality in a divided world.[50] Certainly the conviction that unity is the gift of God must be balanced with the conviction that it is an historical process of overcoming all that divides the human community, not setting limits to this process. Out of this concern, particularly in the third world, 'a new kind of ecumenism is being born'.[51] In conjunction with this new ecumenism a new dialogue is being fashioned by the Spirit. For a while the dialogue of East and West, Protestant, Orthodox, and Catholic will continue. But it will be changed in its nature and priorities as the new dialogue gains ascendancy. It will have to be far less pedestrian to satisfy the new generation of Christians, especially those from the Third World. This does not mean that we leave problems unresolved. It does mean that they will be solved in a larger perspective within a more complex hierarchy of truths. Christian problems are mysteries to be lived in ever greater depth and against a widening horizon. Dialogue is part of building community and a search for unity in faith is a search for community.

But we must ask if there is a genuine sign of hope given in the traditional dialogue within the modern Ecumenical Movement as we have known it. An extended illustration based on my more immediate experience may be helpful here. I would suggest that the Ecumenical Movement in Britain may well underline the movement as a sign of hope. I would suggest this for three reasons:

1 the interconnectedness and diversity of its national life, i.e., a small united kingdom by geography with historic and political significance in the world community; because of this a pattern of

ecumenical development can more easily be traced and its significance evaluated in the light of Britain's church history;

2 a renewed sense of mission against the background of nominal Christianity and the beginning of a new multi-racial society;

3 a developing future role as a cultural crossroad between North America and Europe of which it is a part and to which it is a gateway.

For these reasons the pattern and pace of the Ecumenical Movement will serve as a focus of ecumenism. However, before we take a closer look at British ecumenism it is important to have some idea of the *convergence* involved in ecumenism. Ecumenical convergence is a product of consciousness, a consciousness that inductively approaches theology, life, and mission. This is a way of saying that the ecumenist looks at the precise point of Christian presence or whereabouts in today's world and at this stage of history. Ecumenical consciousness wants to create real choices that will bring the Christian community closer to its fulfilment as a community prepared on behalf of mankind to reflect the unity and diversity of the divine life in which all men are called to share. Convergence is not based on broadmindedness nor on monolithic mergers between Churches. It is aware of the historical process which the Spirit keeps future-oriented, directed towards fulfilment. It is careful to remain loose in making judgements about how convergence is likely to take place. It is content to take the next practical step if such a step is discerned as the next step likely to get us to where we feel the Spirit bids us. Ecumenical consciousness if properly formed should be 'particularly conducive to the clarification of *contradictory* options'.[52] Far from creating contradictions it eliminates them. As such it is a work of the Spirit.

On 14 August 1960 there was a celebration of the World Missionary Conference which had been held at Edinburgh in 1910, at which the modern Ecumenical Movement had been born. For many British Christians it was an occasion for very sober reflection on the future of ecumenism in Britain. Britain had played a leading role in the initial impetus given to the Ecumenical Movement by the formation of the World Council of Churches. This is part of ecumenical history with the names of William Temple, J. H. Oldham, William Paton, and George Bell firmly and predominantly fixed in that history. However, historical consciousness lingers on long after the events in the souls of men. Church and chapel have been buried deep in the psyche and remain operative as sociological causes and factors in human behaviour. They are formative of human attitudes, underlie them, justifying them to an extent. At any rate church leaders in 1960 were increasingly concerned by the lack of ecumenical progress in Britain itself. Perhaps the malaise came from the expectations of a grand union movement. It was not entirely justified since a change in the ecumenical pattern was emerging through the growth of councils of churches in Scotland, Ireland and Wales. In a period from 1918 to 1945 local councils of churches grew from 3 to 126. In the next twenty-five years they increased to over 650. In this twenty-five-year period they became a normative part of church life in many areas.[53] Whatever attitude one has towards the overall effectiveness of such councils, they signal genuine growth in ecumenical consciousness, representing a firmer rooting of the movement in the local church with its historical and social particularities. At any rate it was against this background that the British Council of Churches (BCC) called its first Faith and Order Conference at the University of Nottingham in 1964. It was at this conference that the following resolution was passed:

> United in our urgent desire for One Church Renewed for Mission, this conference invites the member churches of the British Council of Churches, in appropriate groupings such as nations, to covenant together to work and pray for the inauguration of union by a date agreed among them.
>
> We dare to hope that this date should not be later than Easter Day, 1980. We believe that we should offer obedience to God in a commitment as decisive as this.
>
> We urge that negotiations between particular churches already in hand be seen as steps towards this goal.
>
> Should any church find itself unable to enter into such a covenant, we hope that it will state the conditions under which it might find it possible to do so.[54]

The resolution did not call for total union by 1980, but it did want to assure the sense of urgency and reality for the Churches already in dialogue and planning for unity. The choice of a date and a day was to indicate the serious intention behind the resolution.

Far from timetabling the Holy Spirit it was a call to responsible commitment and action, an attitude of responsible concern for the cause of Christian unity. As such it represented a big step in ecumenical awareness throughout Britain. While Anglican– Presbyterian plans came to naught, Anglican–Methodist plans came to the test, a test that failed. English and Welsh Congregationalists pressed forward with plans for uniting with English Presbyterians. They were to experience the Spirit's leading into a United Reformed Church. The rite of union took place on 5 October 1972, at Westminster Abbey. But I am getting ahead of my story. For around this event in the Abbey two other events were to have great significance for Christian unity in Britain.

The first event was the Church Leaders' Conference. A report of this has been provided by Canon David Edwards, presently Dean of Norwich, under the title *The British Churches Turn to the Future*.[55] The conference took place at Birmingham in September of 1972. It was not an assembly, synod, or council. Five hundred Christian leaders and expert ecumenists drawn from both clergy and laity met for nine days. All were equal participants. There were no consultant observers. Among the 500 were forty Roman Catholics. Already Roman Catholics were active in three-quarters of existing Councils of Churches. They seemed ready to join the Ecumenical Movement as full participants and fellow workers. It was an enthusiastic, remarkable conference that left its mark on ecumenical awareness in Britain. The spirit of the conference was one of vigour and charity. It was blessed with a sense of humour and stimulated by an element of criticism aimed at the oldguard leadership. It was as much about the real situation of the Church in the world as it was about church unity. It proved that truth could be as divisive as talk about unity. David Edwards was to speak of 'two Christianities' as traditional leadership met a more radical type in an open atmosphere. However, the divergence was tempered and the conference experienced unity as it shared common Bible study each morning and common prayer, and a measure of eucharistic sharing. Edwards observed that 'the real fight was to be seen against secularism'. The question of Christian unity was always at the forefront of the overall debate. It was expressed in the words of a Methodist leader: 'I came here believing church union to be right; I go away believing it to be inevitable.' And there was Cardinal Heenan's remark: 'This, at least, seems certain – Christians will never return to the old rivalries and enmities.' There was both disappointment and hope registered at this conference – disappointment over the Anglican–Methodist failure to achieve unity; hope that the Roman Catholic Church would join the British Council of Churches as a full member and partner. As things came to pass in the wake of that conference disappointment was changed into new hope and hope was disappointed by an unnecessary deferral to join the BCC on the part of the Roman Catholics.[56] But the new hope was such that it offered a new opportunity not only to Anglicans and Methodists, but to other British Churches to respond to a new move towards Christian unity. And this brings us to the second event.

At the Birmingham conference there was a feeling that the United Reformed Church which would shortly come into existence would be in a moral position for some sort of ecumenical leadership, that it could initiate a step that would help the Churches further along the road to Christian unity. The new sense of trust and friendship created at the Birmingham conference needed extension and concrete implementation. The expansion of the dialogue and a renewed will for unity had to be sustained in fidelity to what God had done at the Church Leaders' Conference. The burden fell on this small Church to be born the following month.[57] It was a burden the United Reformed Church gladly assumed in fulfilment of the law of Christ (Gal. 6.2). In the manual of the United Reformed Church devoted to the basis of the union we read:

> They see their union as a part of what God is doing to make his people one, and as a united Church will take, wherever possible and with all speed, further steps towards the unity of all God's people.[58]

On 5 October 1972, at the inauguration of the URC, the leaders of other Churches publicly pledged their Churches to continue the quest for Christian unity. It was the picture worth thousands of words as the Archbishop of Canterbury, the Cardinal Archbishop of Westminster, and the Moderator of the Free Church Federal Council came forward one by one to make the following declaration:

On behalf of the { Church of England
Roman Catholic Church
Free Churches in this country

I give thanks with you for this union and share your resolve to seek that wider unity which is Christ's will.

I do not want to give the impression that all initiative came from this official level. In the wake of the Anglican–Methodist union plan a number of people began to discern what new efforts God might be asking them to make on behalf of Christian unity. I shall refer to them as the Churches' Unity Group. The Group convened a conference at Christ Church, Oxford in January of 1973. It was meant to be fairly small and informal, but it turned out to be large and formal – though not official in any sense. The participants were from the mainline Churches. The nature of the exercise was the feasibility of initiating 'talks about talks' on a wider basis than Anglican-Methodist participation. Literally at the end of the day the plea for opening a multilateral theological dialogue that would include Baptists and Roman Catholics carried the day. It was understood that if, in the course of the dialogue, two or more Churches discovered a way forward into some kind of church union scheme, the theological dialogue would continue uninterrupted on the basis of continuing to build up ecumenical relationships and prepare the way for a wider and deeper unity to come. At the same time all the Churches in the dialogue would be as co-operative and encouraging as possible in the process of uniting the two or more Churches prepared to enter into a scheme of union or covenant. Once more British Christians are indebted to the United Reformed Church which, pressed by our sense of urgency, was encouraged to issue an invitation along these lines. The following invitation was sent out from the Spring Assembly of the URC:

> The Assembly, recalling the commitment in the Scheme of Union that the United Reformed Church will take, wherever possible and with all speed, further steps towards the unity of all God's people and welcoming the response given on behalf of other Churches in Westminster Abbey on 5th October 1972, now

(1) invites those Churches to share in discussions as to how that unity can be furthered in England.

(2) resolves to appoint eight people to be available to meet with similar groups from such other Churches as may be ready to accept this invitation.

(3) records its hope that these discussions will produce concrete proposals for conversations between those Churches able to commit themselves to seek the formation of a united Church.

The invitation was issued to the Baptist Union of Great Britain and Ireland, the Churches of Christ (United Kingdom), the Church of England, the Methodist Church, and the Roman Catholic Church. The Free Churches' Federal Council was asked to act as agent in securing representation from any smaller Churches wishing to participate. Since I am not writing a full account of these events, it is enough to say that the response to this invitation led to the formation of the Churches' Unity Commission in 1974. This Commission drew up ten propositions to be put to the membership of the participating Churches in order to determine what support there might be in the Churches for a further step towards visible unity. The propositions themselves concern issues about which the Churches must make up their minds. At this time of writing various responsible authorities in the Churches either have or are in the process of formulating definitive responses to the ten propositions. More important, under the influence of the Commission and with unofficial support, the Churches' Unity Group continues to muster support for the work begun by the Commission and seeks to help educate churchmen to the underlying issues involved in the ten propositions.[59] Whatever the future of the work initiated by the Churches' Unity Commission, the ecumenical ferment and relationships that preceded it and made it possible must not be allowed to diminish. This effort must be followed up by a new spirit of co-operation at all levels and by as many Churches at as many levels as conscientious conviction allows. The work of the Commission is a signal for British Christians to work for Christian unity with serious purpose and in a renewed spirit. Like all such commitments it looks not to the recovery of the old way back, but to the discovery of a new way forward. The words of Oscar Cullman commenting on the Decree on Ecumenism from Vatican II occur to me. 'This is more than the opening of a door; new ground has been broken.' In the events which I have been describing, the British Churches were encouraged through the propositions put to them by the Commission to take another step. A big step, an infant's faltering step, perhaps only an aged, feeble step; who knows? Out of the shambles of Anglican–Presbyterian, Anglican–Methodist union plans have come new hope and new Christian relationships, with greater denominational commitment and involvement than heretofore dreamed or even hoped for. Such is the power of the Spirit to work through human weakness. There is a new spirit behind the letter and the theological groping of the ten propositions. It is a spirit of proexistence, of trust, of friendship and life together. Something is possible that yesterday's ecumenist saw only in timeless vision. The success of the ten propositions does not depend on the number of propositions to which a Church can say 'yes' or 'no'. The propositional approach is not one of 'do you or don't you?', 'will you or won't you?' 'can you or can't you?' One Church may be able to go along with all ten propositions but in a spirit of benign indifference. Another may find them an acceptable basis for ongoing intramural debate, not wishing or ready for a definitive response. Another Church may find difficulties with a number of the propositions. The outcome may be less than unanimous but more than was previously hoped for. Another Church may not be able to enter into a covenant relationship at this time, while continuing to give sincere support to the Churches which can do so and opting for ongoing dialogue and co-operation at as many levels of life as possible. The triumph of the Spirit consists in changing our indifference, our lack of enthusiasm, our ambivalence, our present theological *obex* into a fervent, fresh, educated commitment to find a way forward to unity beyond the present in a foreseeable future. A change of attitude, a sincere conversion of church leaders and active members is badly needed. I feel it is happening. Our changed ecumenical climate in Britain, where history has struck such deep religious roots, is living witness to this hope for a united Church. Ecumenism is the invincible idea whose time has come. And Britain is the focus of that idea. It is not the change we must debate. It is now a matter of how we are to manage that change. For those who say that all this is unsubstantiated, that I am living in cloud cuckoo land, I would simply suggest they look around, indeed that they look back to see what has already happened. For those who say that this is an unfounded projection, I would offer the remark of G. C. Berkouwer that 'realism about ecumenicity is something different from a fatalistic view of the future'.[60] Far too many Christians do not think that visible Christian unity is possible. This is a position inimical to growth in Christian life and witness. This is not the same thing as questioning the precise means, the *how* of such Christian unity. We would have reason for a great deal of doubt and hesitation if we became too absorbed in predicting and planning the event itself. One step is enough. If ecumenists plan for union, it is in the spirit of openness to God to set aside such plans in favour of his own, willing to see our best plans never complete their predicted course. There is no reason for discouragement, faintheartedness, or fatalism because of this provisionality of all our planning within God's will. The answer lies in the unpredictability of the Holy Spirit. At the end of the Hoover Lectures of 1975 Raymond Brown said that 'the future of ecumenism is not fully predictable because it is not a question of human mergers or bargaining but a sign of God's action among his people'.[61] Christian faith has as its object the Holy Spirit, the Lord and Giver of life. Unity is God's gift and he alone bestows it, creating the best dispositions with which it is to be received. Berkouwer says:

> We must not rule out the possibility of surprises; the mystery of the Church forbids us to be fatalistic. Realism will keep us from misjudging the present situation, but it must not keep us from a believing consideration of the unity of all believers in Christ, of the reality of the One Shepherd and the one flock.[62]

In this chapter we have looked at certain events and attitudes that provide substance for our hope that the Christian community will be seen to be one once more, not for its own glory, but for God's and for the sake of his mission in the world. Hope for the Ecumenical Movement rests on something deeper in Christianity, namely its capacity to acknowledge its achievements and an uncertain future as the gift of God. In our relationship with God we live the provisional as a way of life, knowing that our future is God's future. Christian prayer is a conscious acknowledgement of this. We let 'things declare themselves to us in a new depth, so that we may become more truly the instruments of God'.[63]

Because our future is uncertain, prayer helps us overcome the obstacles in ourselves, in our Churches to becoming visibly one in Christ. Prayer creates a change in attitude, it creates repentance for the lack of love and care, of truth and justice among Christians and others. It begets an intention to work now according to the opportunities we have for furthering Christian unity. Prayer together renews our awareness of being one people of God. Little wonder ecumenists call it 'the soul' of the Ecumenical Movement. Abbé Couturier once said:

> The whole fabric of Christendom must be shaken to its very depths by the universal prayer of Christians; it must experience a supernatural shock which will break down its prejudices, rectify its superficial and false ideas, cause hearts to grow into one another, and finally unite minds in the eternal light of the one Christ.

All this happens in prayer. Prayer is not a cleverly devised psychological method to create enthusiasm or awareness. It is a spiritual condition for opening ourselves to be led by the Holy Spirit. It is an ecumenical activity. It is an activity integrated with a spiritual reality within ourselves. This reality is that the prayer of Christ for unity (John 17) is prayed in us and through us by the Holy Spirit. Couturier had grasped this essential mystery of prayer and could say that 'Christian unity will be attained when the praying Christ has found enough Christian souls in all confessions in whom he himself can freely pray to the Father for unity'.[64] Prayer is something that God does in us. It is not primarily our activity. We let it happen but God makes it happen. And because it happens, other things happen as well. Prayer is not a rarefied form of human-spiritual activity, not an exercise in mind control, or taken up as a psychosomatic discipline. It is man opening up his entire future to be realized by God as part of the free gift of God, the gift of eternal life, offered us in Jesus Christ (Rom. 6.23). Each dimension of prayer rests on this truth. Adoration, thanksgiving, intercession, repentance – all are the gift of God. The prayer for Christian unity according to the mind of Jesus is the most essential and effective, the most available and practical thing Christians can do to rediscover the beauty ever old and ever new which is also the witness of life together in the mystery of the

Church, the promise of our future, the power to renew the face of the earth.

# 3

# The Catholic–Evangelical Convergence

> May I suggest that we must not only listen to each other, but together listen to what the Spirit may be saying. . . .
>
> **Cardinal Hume to the Church of England Synod**

To speak of a Catholic–Evangelical convergence as an element of contemporary Christian hope could easily be judged to be without any real foundation, unless we are willing to go beneath the appearances of such a relationship. The terms themselves embrace a diversity of Christian life and doctrinal positions that would seem to render any general use of them quite meaningless. But if we remember that the Ecumenical Movement, while not setting aside what divides Christians at many levels, has taken renewal, the search for the essence of Christian life in the world today, as its wider context, it does not seem presumptuous to look for those things that seem to be drawing Christians closer from the extreme ends of the Christian spectrum of doctrine, life, and spirituality. When we set these extreme Christian positions side by side it may well seem like an exercise in mixing oil and water. Here older polemical attitudes and suspicions seem to linger on. Indeed, both sides seem firmly entrenched. It is true that for the most part the 'big guns' are silent. But they have not been dismantled. In the wake of the Anglican–Roman Catholic Agreed Statement completed at Venice in 1976 an open letter was issued in June of 1977 by an impressive number of Evangelical Anglicans throughout the communion. It was addressed to bishops and archbishops of that communion. It concerned relationships with Roman Catholics, Eastern Orthodox Christians, Old Catholics, and the ancient oriental Churches, namely Assyrian, Coptic, Ethiopian, Syrian, and Armenian. They insist that relationships with these Churches must 'have an adequate basis in the theology of the Bible'.[1] They also make clear that 'past apprehensions about Anglican rapprochement with non-reformed Christendom, and particularly with the Roman Catholic Church' have been well founded 'since previously there was no common quest for doctrinal agreement under the authority of Holy Scripture'.[2] As Anglicans of the reformed tradition, there were questions they wished to put to the non-reformed churches, Roman Catholic first and foremost. These questions concern doctrines of the Immaculate Conception and Assumption of the Virgin Mary, prayer to the Virgin and the saints, the universal primacy and ministry of the Pope, and the infallible teaching authority of popes and general councils with special references to sections 19 and 24 of the Agreed Venice Statement of ARCIC. The line of questioning continues: Does the Roman Catholic Church now agree that justification is essentially God's free gift of acceptance, bestowed on sinners by grace alone, in and through Christ, and received by God-given faith alone? If so, how does this affect traditional RC beliefs, namely, good works, merit, purgatory, indulgences, prayer to and for the departed, the necessity of sacraments and communion with Rome for salvation? The question put to the Orthodox Church is a variant of this: How do they see justification in relation to other aspects of Christ's salvation? Both Roman Catholics and the Orthodox are asked to state the grounds for their claim to be the Church exclusively. And Roman Catholics are asked specifically: How does the image of the Church as God's pilgrim people now adopted affect the conception of the Church as the extension of the incarnation? The Anglicans of the reformed tradition are forbidden to think of 'any particular historical form of the ministry being integral to the Church's identity, or of any Christian minister participating in the mediational work of Christ's high priesthood'.[3] Related to this question they note the lack of theological clarity in section 13 of the Canterbury Statement of ARCIC on ministry where the Christian ministry is described as 'not an extension of the common Christian priesthood but belonging to another realm of the gifts of the Spirit'. They question section 6 of ARCIC's Windsor Statement on the Eucharist on matters of 'true presence' with its footnote on transubstantiation. They declare their opposition to 'any views of eucharistic sacrifice which obscure the sufficiency, finality, and historical completeness of Christ's one sacrifice for sins on the cross'.[4] They counsel discipline in the matter of the ordination of women and regard the issue as an unfinished theological debate. The letter makes clear that intercommunion is not possible until there is fuller agreement on these issues. And it would seem that for them any notion of full communion or visible unity will have to interpret agreement in essentials and disagreement in secondary matters (a distinction to be explored) on the basis of a union such as Anglicans have with Old Catholics. A uniate basis or model of union implying complete identity of doctrine with Rome but with freedom in church order and discipline is less acceptable to them.

I mention all this in support of my opening remarks and to indicate an awareness of the problems that will have to be resolved as Catholics and Evangelicals grow together into a newness of life in Christ in a new era. The *Open Letter* is a grilling questionnaire to all of us in the Catholic tradition, including Anglicans of that tradition. It makes one wonder if the dialogue has even begun. There is the feeling that we have become locked in a period of history from which there is no exit, neither antecedent nor consequent history to liberate us from our deepest convictions. The Catholic does not like the feeling of being put against the wall or pushed into a corner, be the inquisitor ever so kind and well-meaning. He may well feel that the Evangelical expects simple answers to allay his deep suspicions when in fact a dialogue on the issues has been under way at many levels for some time now. On the other hand the Evangelical resents the feeling that he is being written off as a fundamentalist crank, one of an embarrassing minority, hardly worth taking seriously in the light of new developments and relationships. My own feeling is that it would be selective ecumenism to dismiss these questions either as impertinent or irrelevant. However, I think it equally important for Evangelical Christians to look at the whole theological history of the Christian Church. I think it is important to accept in good faith the stated intentions of any Christian Church when it undertakes a programme of reform and renewal. It is important to understand how certain practices have developed as well as being able to criticize where they have gone wrong and come loose from their doctrinal moorings. This is a mutual task we perform for one another in the Church and it is also the subject matter for internal examination of our own traditions. Even more important is it to understand that the Holy Spirit is creating a future for us in building up new relationships and preparing the Church to face new situations in new responses of faith to God's call. These factors do not justify striking the questions from the agenda of

formal theological dialogue. They do change the context and presuppositions in the dialogue. The dialogue must be conditioned
as much by the future as by the past, more so in fact. The dialogue
is not the only way forward. It is not the whole process of convergence and unity. There is a life and mission to be shared to
some extent even now. Convergence has to be judged by what is
happening within the life of each community involved. It is also
to be judged by those external factors forcing on Christians a new
awareness, fresh priorities, a renewed sense of urgency for God's
Kingdom. There is no area that I can think of where authentic
renewal will be registered more clearly than in a Catholic–Evangelical convergence. Attitudes are changing. Both traditions have
to repent of self-righteousness which is so often practised in the
name of being toughminded in the cause of truth. Misguided zeal
for God's cause has done more harm to that very cause than any
other single factor in history. By all means let the dialogue be
toughminded, but let our relationships be tenderhearted. Dialogue is as much an exercise in listening to God as to one another.
God is trying to do much more than work out an intellectual
consensus. He is trying to make us one again. 'Oh that today you
would hearken to his voice! Harden not your hearts. . . .' (Ps. 95.
7–8) Both Catholic and Evangelical Christians ought to write the
words of the prophet on their hearts: 'He has showed you, O
man, what is good; and what does the Lord require of you but to
do justice, and to love kindness, and to walk humbly with your
God?' (Micah 6.8). Abraham Heschel refers to this passage as the
reply to 'the most urgent question of religious existence: What is
the way of true worship?'[5] Surely the Christian believes that Jesus
Christ is the great sign of God's goodness, justice, loving kindness,
and humility; that he is our way to worship God in spirit and truth
(John 4.23–4); that he is the foundation of our dialogue, the alpha
and omega of our convergence.

The Roman Catholic biblical scholar Raymond Brown, noting
that theological reflection is involved in all formulas of faith and
theology, warns against separating faith and theology. He says:

> . . . it is too simple to say: Teach the faith and forget about
> theology. This is especially true today since modern theological
> discussion is not focused on marginal questions but on a con-

72

temporary reunderstanding of the *fundamental* teachings of Christianity.[6]

We cannot bypass theological dialogue. It is necessary to upbuild the Church, not simply to clear the ground of past misunderstanding and doctrinal difficulties. Christian theologians have to do theology together for the future of the Church. Here in England we have had our 'honest-to-God' debate and our 'myth of God Incarnate' debate.[7] There is a real danger at such times that language will simply fail to get ideas across, resulting in or even creating an intellectual and spiritual vacuum. The danger is not in trying to improve the medium for the message. It lies in adopting a too facile discontinuity with the history of Christian thought and doctrinal development. Contemporaneity is not enough for it is often subject to the creation of its own myths and a superficiality that simply fails to do justice to the Christian mystery. The myth and the language of myth must establish firm guidelines for reflection and life that are truly rooted in Christian truth. The new myth and its language have to take into account our present need. Also it must provide some promise of development in the self-understanding of Christians. It must be consistent with the basis of Christian hope. Now both Catholics and Evangelicals share a mutual concern in this area. It is unfortunate that the concern often takes the shape of a negative reaction to renewed critical reflection on the central truths of the Christian faith. However, Catholics are renewing their faith through a more intense and intelligent use of Holy Scripture, acknowledging the tools of modern critical scholarship. And it is equally heartening to find among the twelve Declarations of Intent formulated at the second National Evangelical Anglican Congress, held at Nottingham in April 1977, the following:

> We acknowledge that our handling of inspired and authoritative Scripture has often been clumsy and our interpretation of it shoddy, and we resolve to seek a more disciplined understanding of God's holy word.[8]

In the future Catholics and Evangelicals will have to question their own presuppositions – philosophical, cultural, spiritual – that condition the way they 'do' their theology. In their dialogue the difficult work of focusing properly 'on a contemporary reunderstanding of the *fundamental* teachings of Christianity', as Brown expresses it, will be a major task. And together we will have to carry out the resolution 'to seek a more disciplined understanding of God's holy word' as the Nottingham declaration states. We have to be sure that a 'return to basics' is not simply a fixed point of doctrinal understanding. If we return to basics, it is not to find a sticking point but to find a way ahead. This applies to church unity or to the mission of the Church. We have to be honest in our convictions, but our honesty has to be judged by our openness and prior commitment to be led into the fullness of truth promised by Jesus through the gift of the Holy Spirit. If Catholics and Evangelicals are wary of the 'thoroughgoing relativism' of which Michael Taylor speaks, it is not because we think that absolutistic thinking is any more supportive of faith.[9] It is because of faith in the absolute fidelity of God to man in Jesus Christ. Revelation is not simply information about God. It is a definite disclosure of God in Jesus demanding a response from the believer. Jesus is the fixed point of salvation history. Because of him there is content for our faith and implications for our living. Our differences arise from a difference about how best to discern our response to the divine disclosure in Jesus and what is normative for this discernment. Concern for doctrine, a return to basics is a search for norms of discernment as to the content and implications of our faith in Christ. This discernment is not limited to the past. It is about the present and the future. We are committed to the provisional approach because we believe the future belongs to God and we are offered his free gift of sharing it in Jesus Christ. Catholics and Evangelicals may lapse into absolutist forms of thought and speech. But they are committed to an openness to reformation and renewal by the Spirit. This is the spirit of Vatican II, of *The Nottingham Statement*, and of the Evangelicals at Chicago.[10] It is this power of the Spirit that brings us to repentance over wrong attitudes, acknowledging the transforming power of the same Spirit to keep us open to reformation and renewal. It lies behind a growing acceptance among Catholics and Evangelicals of some of the values for both ecumenism and renewal that are inherent in the neo-Pentecostal (or charismatic renewal) movement in the Churches.

Christians of both Evangelical and Catholic orientation will draw closer together as they are challenged more and more to articulate afresh the fundamentals of Christianity in a more disciplined understanding of God's word. It would be a questionable witness for them to close ranks when basic orthodoxy seems threatened as in the case of the 'myth of God Incarnate'.[11] There is need for a much more positive effort to come together on occasions where there can be some real sharing of life and resources. At Nottingham, speaking of his experience on the Anglican–Roman Catholic International Commission, Julian Charley confessed that his theological convictions had been enriched 'without changing them one whit' and that he had had prejudices towards Roman Catholics removed, many of whom he had come 'to love in the Lord'.[12] It is not unimportant or banal to say that many Roman Catholics could echo these sentiments towards Evangelicals. What is of God's Spirit in any theological conviction cannot be lost if we are open to the Spirit who is also a Spirit of Love (Rom. 5.5). Christians tend to emphasize denominational labels and churchmanship in such a way that getting to the truth about each other is difficult and makes it even more difficult to initiate new relationships. We have opposed the terms 'Catholic' and 'Evangelical', often equating fundamentalism with conservative Evangelicalism. One can detect the beginning of a new spirit, an honest effort to drop name-calling and labelling (a form of libel). There seems to be a genuine effort to clarify terms and provide a positive content for them. If we are to talk about 'fundamentals' this will not mean 'fundamentalism' nor assume that it means the same thing as the Evangelical slogan 'back to the Bible'. It does mean a concern for the central truths of the Christian faith and a common concern for discerning the will of God in Jesus Christ in the power of the Holy Spirit. It assumes a basic recognition of one another as authentic Christians.

One of the problems between Catholics and Evangelicals is this question of fundamentalism. James Barr has undertaken a sizeable attempt to explore this question.[13] Without attempting too succinct a definition of it, Barr says that it reflects 'a certain basic personal religious and existential attitude . . . I consider to be a pathological condition of Christianity . . .' (p. 5). He gives three norms for judging that 'there is something which many or most Christians perceive or classify as fundamentalism' (p. 1):

(1) There is a strong emphasis on the inerrancy of the Bible, i.e., the absence of any kind of error;

(2) a strong hostility to modern theology and to modern critical study of the Bible;

(3) an assurance that those who do not share their religious viewpoint are not 'true Christians' at all.

He goes on to say that 'I do not say . . . that all conservative Evangelicals are also fundamentalists; but the overlap is very great' (p. 5). What is of importance for our purpose is to note how careful we must be in the use of that label 'conservative' and even more careful not to assume that Evangelical Christians are fundamentalistic. Most Churches, if not all, have some streak of fundamentalism in their membership – a fundamentalism that forbids any interpretation of an imagined obvious sense which is contained in such simple patent propositions of faith as to make them valid for all time. An attitude which grants second-class citizenship, if that, to other Christians, is not confined to Evangelical Churches. The only response to fundamentalism is the exercise of Christian charity in all its depth and breadth.

More Christians of both Evangelical and Catholic traditions of church life recognize that there has to be a conservative element in Christian life expressing the basic commitment to be faithful in our response to the unique revelation of God in Christ. We may differ in how this revelation is best conserved or safeguarded. Likewise, many Christians in both traditions would want to think of themselves as 'radical'. To be a radical Christian is to get to the roots of Christian faith, life, and mission. It does not mean necessarily a critical attitude to the Church *as an institution*. In this respect there is a lot of false radicalism, a lot of cheap radicalism. To be conservative, radical, and evangelical is the ideal of every Christian. This combination rests on devotion to the gospel. It is devotion to the gospel that makes a Christian all three. There are many Christians, proud to be called 'Evangelical', who would not agree with John Stott when he said 'the first hallmark of the Evangelical is biblical supremacy'. Nor would they agree when he says that the second hallmark is the centrality of the gospel.[14] The centrality of the gospel is in no sense secondary. It is the primary hallmark of the Christian, the true Evangelical. It seems to me that it will be in this area that the greatest hope of growing together exists for both Catholic and Evangelical. The centrality of the gospel is a norm both of us can adopt as the basis of dialogue and shared life. The Bible is a faithful record of the gospel, the good news anticipated in the Old Testament and proclaimed in the New Testament. As such it is a vital constituent in the life of the Church and in the life of the individual Christian. It is a gift of the Spirit. Its vitality as gospel has been communicated in liturgy, art, in the sermon, the story, the stained-glass. But the vitality comes from the gospel, the message and meaning of Jesus. It is the gospel that can be devitalized, drained, diminished, even distorted. And to reduce God's word to a printed page is another form of devitalization of the gospel. The Catholic tradition loves the Bible, protects (at times has overprotected) it, teaches from it, illustrates it particularly by holding up the lives of the saints, enshrines it, and canonizes it, seeing it as a unique declaration of the good news of God proclaimed in Jesus Christ. The Bible shares in the inspiration of the Church by the Holy Spirit as a faithful record of the prophetic inauguration of the new creation and the coming Kingdom of God. When the Church grows in openness to the Spirit, it grows in its devotion and love for God's word in the Bible. It is this growth and devotion that makes a Christian and a Christian Church Evangelical. Questions concerning the Bible as normative and authoritative will continue as part of contemporary Christian dialogue. But as R. Marle says: 'Thus Scripture is invested with authority, the authority of God, only by becoming the gospel. The question then is to know how Scripture effectively becomes the gospel.'[15] This is the question Catholics and Evangelicals try to answer as they explore together their theological presuppositions and doctrinal positions. And this is a question to which I shall want to return. Right now it is important that each Church manifest its devotion to the gospel by its profound reverence for the Bible. An Orthodox theologian, Demetrios Constantelos, speaks of 'the evangelical character of the Orthodox Church'.[16] His thesis is that Orthodox theology 'in nearly every one of its ramifications is evangelical or biblical rather than patristic, philosophical, or liturgical'.[17] Here we have evangelical being equated with biblical. Constantelos views the Bible as both a divine and a human record of God's involvement in history, in time and space. As a record of God's disclosure it is for the experience and existential life of man. It is 'a theanthropic document, infallible and fallible, an eternal and temporal record at the same time'.[18] This is not a case of having it both ways or of 'double think'. It is an attempt to show a mutual relationship between the Church and the Bible. He can say that 'because of the central position accorded to the *Evangelion*, the Orthodox Church is an Evangelical Church *par excellence*'.[19]

> The recorded revelation was the work of 'churchmen', people of God, living within the community of believers, and speaking primarily to other believers for their edification . . . Thus Church and Bible are inseparably united into a harmonious and mutually supportive entity. As the repository of revelation, as the recorder of God's . . . involvement in history, the Church is by nature biblical, for she includes the Bible and is the official interpreter of the Bible.[20]

I have cited this theologian at some length to illustrate the relationship that obtains in some way between the gospel, the Bible, and the Church. The gospel is from God. The Bible is the inspired record. The Church is the community of faith where the gospel is heard and experienced and its primitive record in biblical form functions in the life of that community living still under the promises of the mighty acts of God to sustain, lead, and fulfil its prophetic mission in the world. Catholics and Evangelicals will continue to reflect on how these three elements are best related for the life of the Church in its mission to the world. This too is an area to which we shall want to return.

Since we have been trying to refine our understanding of the various labels Christians assign to one another, it is time to look at the term 'Catholic' in a bit more depth. In the historic creeds it is a mark characteristic of the Church. From the second century onward the Church has been called Catholic. Western Latin Christianity substituted Catholic for Christian to such an extent that Christians came to be called Catholics. Since the Reformation the term has been used polemically, or at least defensively, and as a mode of differentiation. The modern Ecumenical Movement has appealed to its more ancient use, at the same time appealing for a reinterpretation of its meaning for the Church of today. At Uppsala catholicity was defined as 'the quality by which the Church expresses the fullness, the integrity, and the totality of life in Christ'.[21] If we take a giant step backward to the *Catecheses* of

Cyril of Jerusalem, a work used to make ready those preparing for baptism in the fourth century, we can detect a way of speaking that is not unlike that of Uppsala, albeit in another theological dialect. Cyril says:

> It [the Church] is called Catholic because it extends through the whole world from one end to the other; and because it teaches *with wholeness and without defect all the truths that men need to know*, of things seen and unseen, of things heavenly and earthly; and because it disciplines unto *holiness* every sort of man, rulers and subjects, educated and ignorant, and because it provides *wholeness of healing* and remedy for every sort of sin, committed in the mind and in the body, and has within it every form of known virtue, in deed and word, and *all sorts of spiritual gifts.*[22]

It would seem that an emphasis on *fullness, integrity, totality* provides a general descriptive framework of any Church or church party to rethink its doctrinal development and examine its ethos. The adoption and adaptation of these basic concepts give the Churches room to manoeuvre in a genuine spirit of *aggiornamento* or process of updating, reaching for the deepest roots of our common Christian heritage, often well beneath the historic differences and separation that have turned us into Catholics and Evangelicals. There can be no updating or renewal of Christian theology and life without a return to the common sources of Christian thought and life. The French have a lovely word that expresses such a process and goes beyond *aggiornamento*. They refer to the process as *resourcement*. Without the latter process the former easily becomes superficial and trendy, creating even greater stumbling blocks within the communities of faith and for the mission of the Church. So it is with this notion of catholicity. It must indicate not only a unity within itself, but manifestly indicate a power of *wholeness* inherent in the Christian message and mission. Let us look at some signs of such catholicity.

## 1. *The avoidance of an autonomous spirit*

We need each other and the gifts with which God has enriched separate Christian Churches. Our new unity will be the richer because of the diversity that will have to accompany the historical process of reintegrating Christian unity. Four hundred years of going separate ways have created denominationalism and a sectarian spirit wrongly thought to support Christian freedom. However, the Holy Spirit has continued to bestow his gifts on the Christian communities of faith. These gifts are meant to nourish the whole life of the whole Church and their future unity. This unity will have to set aside such a sectarian autonomous spirit. This will be done, as is so often said these days, not by an act or practice of uniformity, but by mutual respect for the diversity that has been created and with equal commitment to be one visible community of faith with an essential visible unity.[23]

## 2. *Fidelity to the continuation of the mission of Jesus*

The Church is the Body of Christ. This is not accidental to God's work of salvation and sanctification among men. This image of the Church and its corresponding concept has to complement the image and concept of the Church as the people of God. It has to do this in such a way that its ministerial and prophetic function always points and is referred to the unique ministry, witness, and mediation of Jesus as Lord. The catholicity of the Church is more or less visible according to its fidelity to the ministry and witness of Jesus, in the way it receives and uses the gifts Christ has bestowed through the Spirit on the Church for its sacramental role in effectively making his presence and mission felt in the world. The Church needs repentance and renewal as preconditions for manifesting the reality and holiness of Jesus in his mission of bringing wholeness and healing to men, that ultimate sign of salvation and perfection to which God is leading all men. It is a long quest and the Church has an indispensable role to play in it.

## 3. *A sense of being a community*

Christianity is not about an institution that maintains a system of ethics for individual behaviour. 'It has pleased God . . . to make men holy and save them not merely as individuals without any mutual bonds, but by making them into a single people. . . .'[24] This sense of community, of Church, is of the very nature of Christian life because the gospel has social implications that are of its essence and because 'the Church is part of the gospel . . . as God's new community'.[25] The catholicity of the Church ought to be realized intensively on the local level, in each local community of faith. It is wrong to see catholicity solely in terms of territorial expansion. Obviously the local or regional church is obliged to extend its membership and service apart from considerations of race, nationality, or social class. It has to avoid the appearance of being another community club. Regarding smaller, spontaneous, unregulated, unattached groups of Christians meeting in houses, in voluntary task groups, in shared prayer or neo-Pentecostal gatherings, the Church must be neither contemptuous nor patronizing. Such groups must be allowed to grow into a sense of Church or Body of Christ under the Spirit in such a way that they will come to respect the catholicity of the Church. In the Spirit they are formed into communities of faith with a spirit of freshness and freedom that creates for the traditional Churches a ferment for reform and renewal. Such groups develop links with the Churches as part of their life and witness and are exposed to ours. This mutual upbuilding reduces the sectarian spirit and is itself a manifestation of sharing and catholicity. Together it is challenging the urban technological society in which it is dispersed as leaven and for which it provides an alternative in moral values and lifestyle.

In thinking about a future Catholic–Evangelical convergence, it will be necessary to think of Evangelism and Catholicity in more open ways. This new way of sharing will create a new rhythm of Christian life that will focus more directly on faith and discipleship of Jesus that makes real our shared life in the Church as a way of proclaiming the Kingdom of God. Evangelism will have to mean more than activism and pious propaganda; Catholicism will have to mean more than liturgy and contemplation. Both represent the presence and activity of the Holy Spirit in history and the human community. Both proclaim and witness that the future of man cannot be realized by human invention and social planning alone. Both are called by the Spirit to a maturity and awareness of the real needs of the world to which they proclaim Christ and witness to him. As long as we are unable to undertake the work of the Kingdom together, we remain infants and children in faith. The new hope rests on the faint stirrings and encounters in truth and love beginning to take place with greater frequency at theological and spiritual levels.

When we turn to look at the label 'Evangelical' in greater depth, as we have with the term 'Catholic', we have to keep the same exigencies of faith in Jesus and mission on behalf of his Kingdom before us. It would be fundamentalistic indeed to define the Evangelical position, as I heard it defined a few years ago, as 'the right and duty of private judgement in the matter of using the Scriptures for Christian living, i.e., a personal commitment to bring the gospel to men for acceptance of salvation through faith in Christ's vicarious death'. Likewise it would be fundamentalistic to describe Catholicism in terms of spatial extension, numerical quantity, cultural social variety, and temporal continuity. To get beyond such fundamentalism it is important to look at some basic issues that have created a type of churchmanship that we describe as Evangelical.

## 1. *Justification by faith alone*

This issue is central though not insuperable. It has been the centre of much post-Reformation controversy. This is not to say that the issue is a non-issue, a straw man. It is something that could arise at any time in the life of the Church because it is central to the life of the Church. But because of its special context at the time of the Reformation and its subsequent divisiveness as an issue it must be looked at anew if we are to be realistic in working towards a Catholic–Evangelical convergence. In the 1960s the English-speaking world had access to Hans Küng's *Justification*, which was subtitled *The Doctrine of Karl Barth and a Catholic Reflection*. Barth hoped, but remained unconvinced that his view of justification could be aligned with the Roman Catholic position.[26] If I refer to the letter he wrote to Küng, it is because its 'spirit' so marvellously demonstrates a spirit of love and openness to new reflection on this divisive issue. Barth reminds us that we are divided within the same faith because we believe in the same Lord; that we use the same mirror, namely the gospel, to look carefully at ourselves and to regard others in the best possible light. In discussing this issue it seems to me that we are talking about our relationship to Jesus as Lord. We are not talking about how to analyse an abstract act of faith that enables us to feel justified or which believes we believe because we are accepted as believers by others who share our sociological milieu. Nor is it a case of erasing technical theological difficulties such as someone of Barth's stature might discern in the documents of the Council of Trent. It is a matter of taking a more radical spiritual view of the issue. Thomas Merton refers to the 'religious genius of the

82

Protestant Reformation'.[27] He believes this genius to lie in its struggle with the 'problem of justification in all its depth'. Protestantism raised the question not only in its simplest form, namely the conversion of the wicked and sinful to Christ, but raised it in its most radical form, namely the conversion of the pious and virtuous to Christ. Conversion is a correspondence between the works and habits of a person and his new being in Christ (2 Cor. 5.16–21; Gal. 6.15–16). So we ought not to speak of conversion exclusively as a movement from bad habits to good ones, from being bad to being good, from being damned to being saved. Conversion is God's gracious invitation to be initiated as a new creature walking 'in newness of life' (Rom. 6.4). Nor is it a once-for-all decision. Conversion is a process related to the depths of being and living in Christ. To become a new man in Christ under the Spirit is an ongoing summons God issues again and again. And while we may speak of a flashpoint of grace or crisis in our life that moves us towards God or back to God in a significant way, we have to remain open to the Spirit on a daily, hourly basis to be drawn more intimately into this new life in Christ. This is the conversion that makes *the conversion of the virtuous to Christ* the central moral issue of the gospel. The fifth chapter of Luke's Gospel illustrates this. Sinful Simon Peter is called by Jesus along with James and John to become fishers of men; he cleanses a leper; he forgives the sins of a paralytic man to the scandal of the Scribes and Pharisees and heals the man's infirmity; he calls Levi and celebrates with him and his fellow tax collectors; when he is questioned about the company he keeps, he says simply: 'Those who are well have no need of a physician, but those who are sick; I have not come to call the righteous, but sinners to repentance' (Luke 5.31–2). He puts little emphasis on the works of fasting and prayers associated with the disciples of the Pharisees and of John the Baptist. Then he delivers the punch line: 'No one tears a piece from a new garment and puts it upon an old garment. . . . No one puts new wine into old wine skins. . . . And no one after drinking old wine desires new; for he says, "The old is good." ' (5.36–7, 39). Couched in irony and wit and offbeat gestures, the demand is radical. Jesus is inaugurating the Kingdom of God in a new, definitive dispensation. This Kingdom is so radically new that he puts forth a demand for radical conversion and transformation. He indicates that the demand is so radical that it can be met only by those who have nothing to lose but their sins. The good are unable to see how they could be radically better. Jesus cannot use them for the building of his Kingdom. He can use only the sinful, the tax collectors, the harlots as the nucleus of his Kingdom, his little flock. He can build his Kingdom only on the humble of the earth (1 Cor. 1.26–31). Only faith in Jesus qualifies one for discipleship in the work of the Kingdom. It matters little whether one speaks of good works or the pure graciousness of grace if one neglects the new life, the new being in Christ, new life in the Spirit. It is the need to convert 'the good', 'the just', to a life of obediential faith, to destroy complacency and self-justification that lie behind the issue of justification, by faith alone. It is as much a Protestant problem as it is a Catholic one in this perspective. For it is a spiritual problem. It has been the task of Evangelical witness in both Catholic and Protestant Churches to challenge worldliness and mediocrity and complacency, superficiality and laxity. All Churches need constant reformation and renewal on this basis of chapter five of Luke's Gospel. James Barr says:

> This sense that the man *within the church* may by his own religiosity and his own goodness, both actually encouraged and abetted by the church, become alienated from God and thus be ripe for a total conversion through the hearing of the gospel, is one of the deepest characteristic insights of evangelicalism.[28]

Even this insight can become a form of self-righteousness *vis-à-vis* others. Preachers experience this if they exclude themselves from hearing the word they preach. Here Merton is helpful:

> One cannot be justified by a faith that does not do all the works of love, for love is the witness and evidence of 'new being' in Christ. But precisely this love is primarily the work of Christ in me, not simply some thing that originates in my own will and is then approved and rewarded by God. It is faith that opens my heart to Christ and his Spirit, that he may work in me. . . . But 'the good' are solely tempted to believe in their own goodness and their own capacity to love, while one who realizes his own poverty and nothingness is much more ready to surrender himself entirely to the gift of love *he knows* cannot come from anything in himself.[29]

More and more Catholics and Evangelicals are working

together, sharing prayer, engaging in common Bible study, experiencing these deep truths of faith together in neo-Pentecostal renewal, increasingly aware that division and difference in theology does not necessarily imply division and difference within faith. As life together matures God's love in us, certain truths of faith are experienced and we become free to work through the doctrinal difficulties and theological positions fashioned in the past, inherited from our fathers in the faith. They may have eaten sour grapes. Why should our teeth be perpetually set on edge?

## 2. *Scripture alone*

Like the issue of justification by faith, the issue of what is normative and therefore authoritative in saying what is of Christian faith and what is not has become a sticking point between Roman Catholics and other Christians. But things are not as sticky as they once were. These two groups of Christians have come closer in a new appreciation and reverence for Scripture at the same time as cultural relativism, with a new radicalism and liberalism, have raised their heads and introduced as many problems and questions for Catholics as for Evangelicals.[30] Cultural relativism signifies two things: (1) biblical thought and assumptions are quite different from those of modern man and consequently our perception and interpretation of biblical events must be quite different; (2) such differences existed within the total biblical period, thus creating deep oppositions within the Bible, e.g., had the resurrection of Jesus occurred in the eighth century B.C. it would have been either meaningless or would have meant something different. All interpretations and theologies are conditioned. Radicalism and liberalism with reference to the Bible signify a fresh questioning about its centrality and decisive importance. James Barr indicates that both Protestants and Roman Catholics have been inhibited in their use of the notions of inspiration and inerrancy regarding the Bible. He thinks we will have to understand inspiration as God's way of communicating with men of the past and the present on the same terms and not assign an essentially different mode of divine communication to the Bible.[31] One thing seems certain. Both the Evangelical and Catholic Church traditions will be challenged in their basic commitment to the normative or authoritative character of the Bible. There is cause in all this, not for anxiety that wants to make common cause, but for hope – that together we will strive to understand anew the meaning of 'the word of God'.

This renewed understanding is already under way in the neo-Pentecostal or charismatic renewal movement. This spiritual movement is of such significance in my opinion that it will influence every other area of Christian hope expressed in this book. But for our immediate purpose it is important to note that it focuses attention on the centrality of the proclamation JESUS IS LORD! God reveals himself in the living Word which is Jesus. The Bible witnesses to this revelation which is Jesus Christ yesterday, today, the same for ever (Heb. 13.8). As people of God we take Jesus Christ as the authority and norm for our lives, individually and communally. Therefore, Evangelicals and Catholics must not leap from their traditional positions on Scripture and tradition to biblical hermeneutics, i.e., the science and methodology of biblical interpretation.[32] There are more basic questions to be asked: How does Scripture become gospel? Another way of saying this is to ask how Scripture becomes the good news of God in Jesus Christ. Secondly, since part of the good news is about the possibility of building a community of love through the following of Jesus, how do Gospel, Scripture, and Church relate? Catholic Christians take the Body of Christ image every bit as seriously as the people of God image of the Church. Jesus is Lord and he is Head of the Church. If the gospel is to function as the third term, as the term of mediation in our renewed understanding and dialogue with one another as Christians, Evangelicals will have to respect fully the Catholic emphasis on life in the Church as part of the mystery of life in Christ. John Stott's words at the end of the Nottingham Conference were most welcome: 'The Church is part of the gospel and the Church is God's new community.'[33] In any new united effort to make Christians truly a gospel people, we will have to take Scripture and tradition seriously, as integral parts of one gospel, as two sides of one precious coin. And if the use of Scripture and tradition evokes too many shades of past polemics and apologetics, it may be helpful to bear in mind that we are thinking in terms of a relationship between revelation and the ongoing life of the Church in faith, worship, and mission. In his profound and very readable *Visible Unity and Tradition* written in 1961, Max Thurian, noting the passing of the older apologetics from both Protestant and Roman Catholic circles, suggests a new look at the meaning of *tradition* from three complementary viewpoints:

(1) As the life of the gospel in the Church;
(2) as the act by which the Church transmits the gospel;
(3) as the product of this life and this act.[34]

Let us look a bit more at each of these three viewpoints:

(i) As Jesus lived and moved among men, especially his disciples and apostles, his message registered in individual and community consciousness as the word of God. The life of the gospel in the Church then constituted by those apostles and disciples sent out in the power and authority of Jesus was directed and controlled by the Holy Spirit poured out on them. Their word was transformed by the Spirit into his word. His gospel existed in them and was transmitted by them. The Holy Spirit would maintain the purity and truth of that gospel by holding them together in a shared and varied ministry.

(ii) It was this combination of personal testimony and the Spirit's direction that made this transmission or tradition of the gospel a living thing. Part of this transmission were written accounts of the words, deeds, and actions of Jesus. It was a practical, common-sense inspiration, a way to keep the word of God focused and fixed among the followers of Jesus, a handbook for proclaiming the central message of the gospel. 'Behold, I make all things new' (Rev. 1.17–18; 21.1–5). Gradually becoming aware that the old covenant was fulfilled in Jesus, these men were led to preserve the treasure of the gospel in written form. The writings making up the New Testament to this new covenant in Jesus are not an accident of history, though they were not intentionally added to the canonical books of the Old Testament. They are part of the divine-human reality of the word made flesh. So was the development of ministries in the Church. Those whose ministry was both a succession and a transmission of the apostolic experience understood their ministry as a responsibility to effect the accurate transmission of the gospel, not as a book to be published, but a living word to be explained and interpreted within the church community and proclaimed in its mission to the world. The Holy Spirit distributes many kinds of gifts for this living transmission of the gospel. He overshadows the Church, creating unity and diversity and life, raising up apostles, prophets, confessors, and martyrs.

(iii) The New Testament is what Thurian calls 'the preferential form of this treasury of faith' (p. 73). This canon or corpus of Scriptures became fundamental and normative in the life of the Church and in her mission of proclaiming the gospel. But they took shape in the context of liturgy. The rule of worship became the rule of faith, *lex orandi lex credendi*, especially in a baptismal and eucharistic celebration, in an ordained ministry, and in conciliar gatherings. But in some sense they were conjoined to creeds and dogmas as legitimate ways of safeguarding the deposit of faith and the transmission of the gospel. Such a reintroduction of a notion of tradition into evangelical thought and life would keep the Scriptures at the centre of church life and proclamation. It would keep the hermeneutical technicians in the service of the wider pastoral office and fellowship of believers. It is tradition that recognizes and acknowledges the authority of Scripture. It does not diminish the unique authority of it. In the fullness and richness of the Evangelical–Catholic life of a community under the Spirit we can welcome newly bestowed gifts for the ongoing understanding and interpretation of Scripture so that the written word of God may be also a living word.

## 3. *Salvation and mission*

One of the most promising points of convergence between Evangelical and Catholic Christians is that of evangelism. This is due in great part to the whole process of liberation under way in the Third World. The next chapter will be concerned entirely with this process. But it is also due to an upsurge of social consciousness and a corresponding sense of responsibility for global stewardship. This new awareness of emerging novelty and the magnitude of world events in a shrinking world has created a healthy dissatisfaction with the way we live and the way we do theology in Western Europe and North America. Prior to the Nairobi General Assembly of the WCC, Clifford Longley, religious correspondent for *The Times*, conjectured on the meeting as a 'watershed in the history of the Christian religion in the West'.[35] The reason he assigned lay in the western delegations' presence as learners rather than teachers 'for the predominant theological style of the assembly is likely to owe more to situations and events in the hungry and restless Third World than to the tradition of detached academic thinking in the West'. What Bruce Kaye notes in his introduction to the third volume of *Obeying Christ in a Changing World* is applicable *mutatis mutandis* to Catholics as well as Evangelicals.[36] He is referring to the deductive method of doing theology. This consists in working out basic principles from classical theological sources, e.g., the early Church Fathers or Councils. Then these principles are applied to contemporary questions and problematical events, attempting to discover the appropriate application of them to a situation. There is a major shift in progress to an inductive method of doing theology. This consists in facing an issue, analysing it in depth in order to see what is being asked of the Christian and/or his community of faith, finally discerning how Christian truth can be related to this particular issue or event. Many Catholics could agree with Bruce Kaye that the use of this more inductive method 'seemed to be an appropriate contribution to the developing theological awareness and activity of Evangelicals' apropos of themselves. There is no need to analyse this method here. It will be exemplified in the context of liberation theology.

What is important to note is the beginning of the formation of a common approach to evangelism. Not only is a sense of global stewardship emerging among Evangelicals, but a renewed sense of the Church is developing as well. The Lausanne Covenant says that 'the Church is at the very centre of God's cosmic purpose and in his appointed means of spreading the gospel'.[37] Trevor Lloyd speaks of 'the new realism Evangelicals have about the Church'.[38] In addition to this new realism the Lausanne Covenant expresses a desire for co-operation in evangelism which amounts to the affirmation 'that the Church's visible unity in truth is God's purpose'. And there is the pledge 'to seek a deeper unity in truth, worship, holiness, and mission'. Walter Hollenweger, Professor of Mission at the University of Birmingham, commenting on the Lausanne Congress, illustrates as factual that Evangelical Christians had to cope for the first time with a pluralistic approach to mission.[39] Hollenweger not only illustrates this pluralistic approach but indicates the potential for convergence in mission among Christians. In a chapter entitled 'Tracts or Tractors?' he indicates the banality of talking about evangelism and service (*diakonia*) belonging together. Evangelists and missionaries before undertaking development aid will have to ask: Who is being developed and with what goal in view? In this we are close to liberation theology. We are close to a theology of hope, for however we choose to talk about heaven or hell 'we have to sing our hymns of salvation in dialogue' and Evangelists 'have to express their hope against those who frighten us with their apocalyptic visions of hell'.[40] His final chapter forces Evangelicals and Catholics to face together the most difficult and essential question: 'Evangelism Today: Good News or Bone of Contention?' He concludes that even if we cannot articulate what is common to us as Christians, there is the conviction that we have something in common. If the good news divides Christians, it is because we have reduced it to a statement, whereas it is an event. This needs serious rethinking and reshaping. Our debates are within this event. Our debates about the truth are not real as such. They are debates 'towards the truth which was hidden in the event'.[41] 'A Christian's understanding of the good news is always in the making, fundamentally in the making.'[42] If Christians were aware of their mutual tendency to distort the good news, of the need for repentance and forgiveness, the willingness to have their convictions changed if these are in contradiction to the goodness and newness of the gospel, we would correct one another and move together with an unbounded trust in God. 'If people begin to pray and act like this they will have many a surprise. Insurmountable barriers disappear. They discover "so much in common".'[43]

The Roman Catholic approach to mission has been taking cognizance increasingly of both the inductive method of doing theology and the fact of pluralism in theology. In the document *A Time for Building* we hear that 'each generation has to discover for itself the spirit of the first Pentecost, and an understanding of the Church's mission to the world'.[44] In a joint statement of Roman Catholic–Presbyterian– Reformed theologians of the USA we read:

> Implicit in an ecclesiology modeled on the people of God of the new covenant is the principle of catholicity. This new people of God looks to all humanity, since the reason for this people's existence in Jesus Christ is to be a bearer of the good news to all humanity. Thus we cannot attempt to define the future

unless we also affirm that diversity and unity are not mutually exclusive. Pluralism is endemic to human beings and has richly positive dynamisms and creative possibilities. So also for God's people. Diversity of language, of culture, of religious and historical experience are not by nature divisive. Rather they are called to be part of a rich and manifold expression of that total reality of our reconciliation with God in Christ.[45]

This new feeling for induction and pluralism in theology is developed with greater particularity in liberation theology and what is entailed in that theology. What is significant is the new openness to discern the Church's mission in a more particular, situational setting and the willingness to associate the quality of catholicity with pluralism.

In December 1975, Pope Paul VI wrote his exhortation on *Evangelization in the Modern World* (*Evangelii Nuntiandi*).[46] It underlined three documents of Vatican II, namely *The Church in the Modern World* (*Gaudium et Spes*); *The Decree on the Missionary Activity of the Church* (*Ad Gentes*); and *The Declaration on the Relation of the Church to Non-Christian Religions* (*Nostra Aetate*). However, *Evangelii Nuntiandi* went beyond the more traditional understanding of mission to emphasize creative dialogue with non-Christians.

> The conditions of the society in which we live oblige all of us therefore to revise methods, to seek by every means to study how we can bring the Christian message to modern man. For it is only in the Christian message that modern man can find the answer to his questions and the energy for his commitment of human solidarity (n. 3).

Here we find the main concepts of mission – *proclamation, community, building the human*, and *dialogue*. Vatican II did not bring these together in a single doctrinal synthesis of mission. Gregory Baum wonders if such a synthesis is necessary in the light of the New Testament for 'it may well be that several concepts of the mission [of the Church] are in harmony with the teaching of the apostles . . . that it depends on the historical situation of the Church and on the guidance of the Spirit what particular understanding of the mission the Church acquires in a given age'.[47] But whatever dimension of the Christian mission is stressed, the heart of the good news is Jesus himself as the one who proclaims the Kingdom of God, liberating us from human oppression, sin, the Evil One, sharing with us the joy of knowing and belonging to God. In Catholic thinking there is a close link between Jesus, the Church, and the good news because 'those who sincerely accept the good news . . . gather together in Jesus' name in order to seek together the Kingdom, build it up and live it'. These words of the *Evangelii Nuntiandi* (n. 13) without dissociating the mission of the Church from the temporal–political order make it clear that 'evangelization will also always contain – as the foundation, centre and at the same time summit of its dynamism – a clear proclamation that, in Jesus Christ, the Son of God made man, who died and rose from the dead, salvation is offered to all men, as a gift of God's grace and mercy' (n. 27). While Catholics and Evangelicals want to stress the universality of this proclamation, they must see that the notion is qualitative and cannot be judged by numbers alone. The hope offered to men through the Christian proclamation is continuous and yet discontinuous with any situation arising in history which involves concrete human existence in its aspiration for liberation and human development, individually and socially. To say this is to reassert those qualities of which St Cyril spoke in the fourth century and of which the Christians at Uppsala spoke in the twentieth, namely, the wholeness of healing, the fullness, the integrity, the totality of life in Christ. Liberation is an essential element of the good news and is a catholic quality of life. As Pope Paul noted, 'the liberation which evangelization proclaims and prepares is the one which Christ himself announced and gave to man by his sacrifice' (n. 38). Liberation theology tries to work out the implications of this. Its task is vital in the renewal of the life and mission of the Church. James Cone says:

> If we take seriously the clue disclosed in God's Incarnation, namely the cross and resurrection of Jesus, then we know that we have a way of cutting through the maze of political and social confusions. Because the divine has entered the human situation in Jesus and has issued his judgement against poverty, sickness, and oppression, persons who fight against these inhumanities become instruments of God's Word.[48]

The healing, the wholeness, the fullness of life, the totality of life in Christ have to be related to the actual situation and needs of the men and women to whom the gospel is proclaimed. This is another way of saying that the proclamation must be both Evangelical and Catholic if it is to take into account the principles of continuity with the gospel and the particularity of the historical situation and the contemporary human context. As the Evangelical–Catholic missionary witness becomes a united witness, the proclamation will become an authentic proclamation not only because it is faithful to the central Christian message of Jesus but because it is faithful to the totality of human needs where it is proclaimed. The missionary experience and the reflection of this in Christian liberation theology is of course the basic sign of hope that the two streams of evangelism are converging. Closer to home and at the level of Evangelical leadership the ten affirmations on evangelism put forth by John Stott in the Evangelical magazine *Third Way* (December 1977), illustrate that the time is ripe for the beginning of a much more common witness because there is a real convergence under way. It is reflected in such documents as the Lausanne Covenant, the *Evangelii Nuntiandi*, and the statements of the WCC Nairobi Assembly. Mr Stott relates his affirmations to these documents. The *Church Times* (13 January 1978) called attention to these affirmations because they express a 'wish to find a consensus rather than a distinctly Evangelical position' that is explicit and impressive, as the *Church Times* put it. The editorial of the paper felt that these affirmations had been drawn up with great care and ought 'to be matched everywhere by an equal care in pondering them'. Perhaps I can do no better to end this section than refer the reader to the full context of the affirmations in *Third Way* and simply state them here:

(i) Christ sends his Church into the world as he was himself sent into the world. Whenever the Church withdraws from the world it denies an essential part of its nature and calling.

(ii) The Church's mission in the world comprises both evangelism and social action, while evangelism always remains a priority concern.

(iii) Evangelism is in essence the spread of the evangel, and this has been revealed to us in Holy Scripture.

(iv) The heart of the good news is Jesus Christ himself, who died for our sins on the cross and was then raised from the dead as the beginning of God's new creation.

(v) Through the death and resurrection of Jesus Christ, God offers us salvation, or liberation from sin and death. God also wills liberation from social injustice. But the two must not be confused.

(vi) The proclamation of Christ and the offer of salvation must lead to a summons to repent and believe, which is conversion.

(vii) Although God's salvation is a free gift of his grace, it issues inevitably in a costly discipleship which must not be concealed by the Evangelist.

(viii) Evangelism is a responsibility laid by Christ upon his whole Church and every member of it. So the people of God must be both mobilized and trained.

(ix) The Church can evangelize effectively only when it is renewed in its own life and unity, becomes an authentic embodiment of the gospel and penetrates deeply into non-Christian society.

(x) Evangelism is not just a human activity. Only the Holy Spirit can make the Church's witness powerful and draw people to faith in Christ.

## 4. *Hermeneutics or how to interpret the Bible*

I have deliberately dissociated this issue from the 'Scripture alone' issue. I have done this because I think the issue of biblical authority must not get confused with the modern technique of biblical historical criticism, form criticism, redaction history. And I think it important because the Bible is essential to the proclamation of Jesus as the bearer of the good news to the world as the proclamation has developed in the tradition of the Church. As *The Nottingham Statement* made clear, the Bible was 'written by particular men in particular historical situations'. Because of this 'we have to work responsibly at the task of understanding it'. We can use all the help we can get from the biblical scholars and the textual technicians. But if we are to use it as an effective instrument in the proclamation of the gospel, it is important to remember that 'understanding it involves being open to God in obedient dependence upon the Holy Spirit'.[49] Evangelicals and Catholics need this spirit of dependence if the written word is to become a living word. The Greek term *hermeneutics* meant an interpreter both in the sense of one who translates and one who explains. It was coined in the seventeenth century after the Renaissance and the Reformation had focused upon the classics of Greece and Rome and upon the Bible. It has become a science in modern times with its proper scientific rules. Applied to the New Testament it is a method used to help us discern in faith the original words and deeds of the historical Jesus (historical criticism), how the apostles and disciples proclaimed these words and deeds and expressed them in different literary forms, e.g., catechesis, narratives, testimonies, hymns, doxologies, prayers (form criticism), and finally with what dominant ideas were these accounts and letters edited (redaction history) to become the New Testament. It has opened up a whole range of questions which some Christians feel is an indispensable tool for the mature approach to faith. Others feel that an over-extension of the critical method undermines faith, emptying it of its precious content. Catholic and Evangelical Christians may differ on *how* they accept the Bible as normative and authoritative, but they do accept it as such. When a hurried reply was given to *The Myth of God Incarnate* under the title of *The Truth of God Incarnate*, Catholic and Evangelical contributors shared the responsibility.[50] Both believe in the historicity of salvation, that God touches our world and this event is felt and recorded. No ambiguity here. Both interpret the resurrection event as fact – not metaphor. The general tenet of the historicity of salvation is normative for our common sharing and understanding. If we are to bring together the historicity of salvation and biblical criticism as a way of bringing us to a more radical understanding of that historicity, we shall have to adopt a mutual commitment to truth as something that 'dawns' as well as 'explodes'. This is a way of saying that truth is the fruit of what is often, most often, a complex process of coming to fullness and fulfilment under the Holy Spirit, and in which we all more or less share. Theology is part of that charismatic process always involving a reflection on the Christian mystery which lies at the heart of the Christian myth and is expressed by the latter. But it is important to be clear in our understanding and use of myth in the service of the mystery of God in Christ. This brings us to a fifth and final basic issue after Evangelical and Catholic relationships and future convergence.

## 5. *Mystery and myth*

I believe that Catholics and Evangelicals are being invited together to reflect anew on the mystery of 'being in Christ'. Those responsible for pastoral and theological leadership have to face afresh the relevance of the contemporary awareness of the limitations of language in handing on the good news. Our language is both mysterious and mythical. The appeal to either mystery or myth will not do. As a term 'mystery' can become an escape-hatch, an inflated term that is synonymous with avoiding difficult theological questions or in-depth reflection on Christian truth. 'Myth' is too easily associated with unreality, even illusion, devoid of a genuine truth content, but capable of soliciting salutary emotions and religious sentiments that feed into practical moral life. To avoid such an either/or situation, they are to be thought of together. Their meaning has to be restricted and revalued if our common task of interpreting the Bible and teaching Christian faith is to bear fruit in the ministry of God's Word.

Mystery (*mysterion*) as it is used in the New Testament has often been considered an import from the Greek world of mystery cults via St Paul. That this is too facile has been revealed by modern scholarship.[51] At the conclusion of his study of the semitic background of this term Raymond Brown says that 'Paul and the NT writers could have written everything they did about *mysterion* whether or not they ever encountered the pagan mystery religions' for mystery 'was part of the native theological equipment of the Jews who came to Christ'.[52] That God has come into our world, expressing himself uniquely and fully in Jesus; that God has brought life from death goes beyond the 'mysterious' and paradoxical. Christianity openly and universally declares both promise and fulfilment. That it clings to an essential record of this revelation as a basis for its message and as a font of its proclamation, is not a secret. The Bible is an important source of Christian worship and teaching, an inerrant record of the faith of the Church. Here as nowhere else the medium is the message. It is proclaimed from the housetops (Matt. 5. 14–16; 10.27). It is a living message delivered by living men who say openly that it is meant for everyman in every age. As such it is cast and recast in human language at different times in different places. There is nothing mysterious, secretive, or gnostic about it. Yet it is a mystery – the presence of God among men, eternity in time, life in death. For this reason Christians are subject to the mythical dimension of life, to expressing the ineffable, the divine, that which cannot be expressed adequately, where time and eternity, death and life, the human and divine intersect. Christians have their symbols, their rituals, their stories and statements which collectively mediate the divine presence in our world. By means of myth they represent, orient, communicate, and identify their existence as a community. The myth gives them a certain coherence as the people of God and the Body of Christ. So mystery and myth are related and mutually interactive. Indeed, theology itself can be understood as 'an invitation to reflection upon the Christian myth'.[53] Simply looking at religion as a phenomenon in need of interpretation, myth can be considered 'as the representation of and response to the manifestation of the sacred in the midst of the profane'.[54] The Christian religion in this respect cannot be an exception. At the same time, while Catholic and Evangelical Christians may admit this, they are rightly concerned with what seems to them theological irresponsibility which attempts to question or challenge the Christian myth in such a way that the effectiveness of its truth content and value in the service of the Christian gospel is diminished. Whatever element is removed or changed or expressed in a new way must be replaced by a new mythical element in such a way that the new element becomes a truth-bearer of God's revelation in Christ. It is not enough to demythologize or criticize Chalcedon or post-Chalcedonian formulas of faith concerning the humanity and divinity of Jesus. Is there anything better to express the reality of Jesus as truly man and truly God? Theodore Jennings says:

> The irreplaceable function of the symbol is that of truly mediating, thereby making it possible for us actually to participate in the reality to which it points. This is precisely why it is ludicrous to think of creating new symbols and myths. For the power of mediating reality cannot be arbitrarily conjured or attached. It is a power which a symbol has because it resonates with the experience and history which it has also in part created.[55]

This does not mean that the Christian theologian is forbidden to challenge the inadequacy of the particular language of the Christian myth. Paul Ricoeur has distinguished the *explanatory* function of myth and the *exploratory* function.[56] Because it helps to explain truth, its language can be elevated to a scientific description of reality. As such it can be improved, developed, replaced. Its exploratory character is associated with its mythic language and its mediating symbolic function. Within this function it is neither reducible nor replaceable and always provokes reflection. Indeed it is the matrix of reflection and thought. The responsibility of the theologian is to respect this matrix of Christian reflection, using his own imagination to act on this matrix of thought in order to 'express and make effective the presence of the sacred in such a way as to represent, orient, communicate, and transform existence in the world'.[57] Such an understanding of myth in theology preserves us from reducing biblical statements and stories or conciliar definitions to contemporary human understanding of the sort we encounter in Bultmann's existential anthropology. Likewise it denies any fundamentalist doctrine of literal inspiration 'which entails the absolute suppression of human imagination and intelligence in the transmission of or witness to that revelation'.[58] There is nothing arbitrary in this. It is not a matter of finding a middle way or of creating a spirit of moderation between extreme positions. It springs from the length and breadth, height and depth of the Christian mystery of God in Christ reconciling the world to himself (2 Cor. 5.19). It is the relationship of our existence here and now to this action of God in Church that constitutes the Christian myth, differentiating it from the realm of ordinary stories, tales told for the purpose of edification or with a moral purpose. It functions to create a new existence, a new being in Christ.

Over and above the value of myth for reflection on the mystery of 'life in Christ' there are practical consequences in it for action and mission in God's world. Jennings says:

> Finally, the mythos functions to transform existence. It is in this respect teleological. To assert this of the Christian mythos is to be reminded that there is no severance of *theoria* and *praxis*, of theology and ethics, of faith and obedience, of hearing and doing, of indicative and imperative. Any attempt to

understand the Christian mythos then must involve us in a consideration of its meaning for action in the world.[59]

Far from producing a false asceticism or separation from the roots of human concerns, a true understanding of life in Christ specifically includes the worldly, the secular, the profane 'but precisely as that is engaged by the sacred'.[60] So when we speak of the Christian myth we are speaking of an event that engenders 'not only a faith which remembers and relies upon what it remembers, but a hope which expects and anticipates that which it expects'.[61] This is of prime importance when we come to speak of liberation theology in the next chapter. When we think of the problem of Christian disunity, we have to remember that our efforts to build up a body of opinion that can be expressed in univocal propositions, i.e., propositions with one clear and distinct meaning, can have at best limited success. This is because the basic elements are often in tension with each other in what seems irreconcilable diversity. This would include primary elements such as the significance of Jesus, the bestowal of the Holy Spirit, and the nature of the Church. Thus, in the New Testament we do not find a uniform theology. This does not invalidate our search for visible Christian unity nor diminish the importance of seeking doctrinal agreement. On the other hand it does mean that there are basic tensions within church groups that unity will not eliminate. Any attempt to play these down or to harmonize them could well lead to a distortion of both truth and conviction. The letter of Barth to Küng to which we referred earlier on, serves to remind us that we are divided within the same faith·because we believe in the same Lord. Our efforts to eliminate divisions is based on a common devotion to Jesus and his cause in terms of an essential unity that will express the truth of his message and his will for his Church. And whatever else we shall discover as essential for visible Christian unity will have for its foundation that unity of faith already expressed in the assertion that the full presence of God is in the fully human Jesus. This is the Christian myth and mystery.

The recognition of myth as the way of expressing God's action in the world and man's encounter with God is a way beyond what might seem to be a Catholic–Evangelical impasse. For it requires a joint reflection on the relationship of Scripture, Tradition,

Church as our disposition to be creatively faithful to the good news of God in Jesus Christ. And such fidelity entails a commitment to make the gospel intelligible to this generation of Christians and the world in which it will be announced. 'It is for this reason that the reflection which is founded by the mythos is not simply elaborative (extending and applying to fresh circumstances a received mythos) but also critical (turning to interrogate even expressions of the mythos itself).'[62] Faith will want to seek understanding to avoid the risk of fashioning gods of purely human understanding. The theologian exercises his critical function as a gift of the Spirit for the whole church community. But his critical reflection must be done in dialogue with that community, sustained by essential elements of the Christian myth. And because it is the function of myth to locate the sacred at some point in space and time, or within some sacramental rite in such a way that it binds the community together and identifies it, it is also the business of the whole Church to understand what sort of shift is taking place for a new communal reflection on the effectiveness of the myth.[63]

The reappreciation of the richness and fullness in the notion of myth challenges the Evangelical Christian to discover in rite and symbol a legitimate expression of Christian life. The Catholic Christian is challenged to find anew in the Bible an inspired mosaic of normative expressions of Christian life in the primitive Christian community. The Bible is a paradigmatic account of the story of that community and how it built its life around Jesus the Lord, the Risen One who is yesterday and today and the same for ever. That both Catholics and Evangelicals are reading the Scriptures afresh as an account of the resurrection read back into the life and death of Jesus is a sign of real hope. That Christians are becoming more interested in the thrust into the future as a vital dimension of New Testament thought is no less hopeful for Christian unity. The Second Coming of Jesus is not a doctrinal epilogue. It is that to which the whole of history points as its consummation. It is a genuine expectation that can bring us together in life and work, in faith and order. Rather than interpret this event in an excessively judgemental-apocalyptic way, a kind of threat to hold over the rest of mankind, we are called to reveal Jesus as the unique one in human history. Through him we are able to offer hope to others and work with others for the proper consummation of human history. This forms the conclusion of Professor Moule's work, *The Meaning of Hope.*[64]

> One perfectly obedient life we claim has actually been lived – the life of the absolute Son of God, Jesus Christ. We have already recognized that the supremely victorious quality of that life and death and resurrection constitutes the sheet anchor of our hope. It is clear . . . that this is not merely a historical anchorage in the past, but more organically viewed, a representative principle of obedience at the very heart of things – a cell of life and health at the center of a sick organism. . . . And it is this vital growing point, and its growing Body, the Church, animated by the Holy Spirit, which gives ground for hope of a final redemption and restoration of all things.

This eschatological emphasis on the final redemption and restoration is not a shift away from the immediate demands of Christian discipleship. It is a renewed awareness and appreciation that together we are the Church, the mystery of the fullness of Christ, and that through us this mystery is being worked out, realized as God's plan for the life of the world. Christians are mediators of the message of hope given by God in Christ. The Church is not a principle of mediation apart from the mystery of his mediation whereby he joined the Church to himself. One of the images and models for understanding the Church is that of a primordial sacrament of man's encounter with God in Christ, an initial stage in the plan of God, the mystery to restore all things in Christ (Eph. 1). This approach would seem to be helpful at this stage of Catholic–Evangelical relationships in developing a shared vision of the Church's life and mission.

In writing of a general Catholic–Evangelical convergence as a substantive of Christian hope, it has been difficult to present a clear pattern. In Christian history two distinct patterns of Christian life and thought seem to have developed. Many Christians still see these as irreconcilable and perennially divergent. Others seem satisfied to let the two streams flow separately, agreeing to disagree. While I am convinced that the other substantives of hope which are reflected in this book make both positions impossible, I also feel that this chapter has pointed out a number of areas that form a parameter for Christian dialogue about essential matters of faith that make talk of convergence both plausible and a sign of hope. Because of the lack of a simple, clear pattern with which to end on a hopeful note, a closing summary may prove helpful.

(1) Dialogue is possible. While non-theological suspicions and reservations continue to plague some Evangelicals, many more do want sincere love and openness to dominate their relationships with Catholic Christians. Where the dialogue is conducted in a spiritual atmosphere the most difficult questions can come under discussion. I suggested such an approach, by way of example, when referring to justification by faith alone. Anyway, most dialogues begin with the highest common factor, namely shared life in Christ. Spirituality, for example, is where Roman Catholics and Methodists like to begin.

(2) Devotion to the gospel. Both traditions recognize and respect a real concern in the other to be faithful to the gospel. Devotion is always a desire to give oneself to the cause of Christ. It is the discernment of God's will for the life of his Church as mediator of the good news.

(3) Movement away from fundamentalism. It is recognized more and more that this is bred in immaturity and ignorance. It is a stumbling block to those seeking a mature faith and a scandal to theological sophistication and professionalism. There is a growing awareness that the Bible and many formularies of faith must be read critically as regards their historical and theological orientation. The Bible is not a resource book for solving problems, a kind of I-Ching. The Holy Spirit is given to lead me into the particular truth to which I am asked to respond in faith in my situation in full freedom and with a sense of Christian responsibility. The Bible is the book of promises, promises as relevant to us as to the men of faith in the past.

(4) Openness to the Holy Spirit. There is a growing recognition that neo-Pentecostalism, often called the charismatic renewal movement, has evangelical roots, that it is very much a transdenominational experience with a dynamic towards Christian unity. There is a cautious but growing acceptance of it as a genuine form of renewal by both Evangelicals and Catholics. Over and above this renewal movement the renewal of Bible study and scholarship has focused on the central role of the Holy Spirit in the life of the early Church.

(5) New ways of relating the Bible to the gospel and the gospel to the Church. The Christian myth which expresses the mystery of God among men is produced in a community of faith. This community expresses the event on which it is founded in writings, rituals, and images. As time goes on, the community determines which expressions adequately represent the faith. The authority of these expressions of faith is derived from the Holy Spirit of God. In this sense there is the ongoing task of listening and acting under the Spirit. It is a task in which the whole Church is caught up, not excluding theologians, in order to locate the meaning of Christ in a given period of history. The Christian message is first proclaimed to hearers of the word, then it is written down as a secondary formulation of that proclamation. From this written record of the primitive proclamation the good news of God in Christ is enunciated once more. Both the Evangelical and the Catholic Christian are concerned with the best way of safeguarding the continuity and fullness of the good news.

(6) A renewed understanding of catholicity as fullness and wholeness of life in Christ. This fullness and wholeness expresses itself in the conjunction of word and sacrament. By this union the life of Christ and his saving death and resurrection is transmitted and envelops or integrates the totality of human existence in the Body of Christ across the ages.

(7) Renewed understanding of the Church as a community. That the first disciples of Jesus spontaneously united in a community and spread their lifestyle, albeit in different forms at different times, seems to be renewed in Christians in our time. Just as the miracle of a loving community in the midst of a socially fragmented and divided world happened at the beginning (Acts 4.32–7), it is happening at the beginning of Christian renewal in our time. The many forms of community throw Christians together in a basic experience of their oneness in Christ. The movement towards a renewed sense of the Church as a community merits a special chapter in this book.

(8) Renewed understanding of historically divisive issues, namely justification, scriptural authority, tradition. We are not thinking only of Roman Catholic versus Protestant. As catholicity and its spirituality are explored, these issues are being resolved. Justifi-

cation is being put in the spiritual context of radical discipleship for the sake of Christ's Kingdom. The question of Scripture as the sole norm and authority for Christian life and truth has been opened again through the new hermeneutics. Tradition has been related to the ongoing life of the Spirit in the Church as a community of faith. It is not an independent source of magisterial pronouncements, made independently of the community of faith in its discernment and practice as a body of believers.

(9) Renewed thinking on the meaning of salvation and mission. This has been brought about with the catalytic effect derived from the experience of the Third World. The inductive way of doing theology and the new pluralism in theology have aided this process.

(10) Commitment to liberation and human rights. It is the very climate of the world in which we live. Liberation can make the gospel of Jesus relevant in a way and to an extent never possible before. The Church as bearer of the gospel too often obscures the radical thrust of that message of Jesus. The Church obscures the human face of Christ by a spirituality and morality unrelated to the world of great human concern for radical liberation. The Church is beginning to take up its prophetic mantle and close the hiatus between sacred and secular through a renewed awareness of a Kingdom of God which comes in time to a particular place.

(11) Revaluation of myth and mystery. Myth is neither allegory, illusion, nor edifying story. It is the symbolic transformation of what is given in divine revelation. It is the recognition that this revelation cannot be reduced totally to conceptual clarity, something demanded by the rationalism of the Enlightenment. Theology tries to interpret the symbol of the divine disclosure. This symbolic transformation of the divine disclosure is what we mean by myth. Because the Christian myth is structured by Christian faith it is always susceptible of further clarification and amplification. Christianity moves towards the future disclosure promised by God in Jesus through the Spirit, the final appearance of God among men. This is the Christian mystery which the Christian myth serves.

(12) Renewed understanding of the relationship between the Evangelical and Catholic dimensions of church life. These are

really two sides of the same coin minted for Christian faith. Evangelicalism is fidelity to the gospel. Catholicism is fidelity to seek the fullness of life promised by the gospel and celebrated in the Christian community.

In concluding this chapter I am aware that evidence for Christian hope is of the cumulative kind. It is not immediately evident at every stage in the journey. But the Spirit knows how to work through the explosions of great movements and through the subtle shift from darkness to dawn and daylight. Christians must find a new hope in the Holy Spirit as the 'Lord and Giver of Life'. Faith in the Spirit to lead us where we cannot presently imagine or conceive ourselves arriving will prove to be the genuine 'faith of our fathers'. There is a very real sense in which to forgive is to forget. It is not a forgetting of the psychological order. If we have been separated a long time we cannot expect to feel entirely comfortable in one another's presence. Nor can we expect an easy convergence. Time is gift. Time is grace. The forgetting is best understood in the light of Philippians 3.13: we forget 'what lies behind . . . straining forward to what lies ahead'. It is the willingness to move ahead of where we are at the moment that achieves Christian forgiveness and forgetfulness. *The Nottingham Statement* invites us to a visible unity at the point 'where there ceases to be any concept of "each other" but only a common life of all'.[65]

# 4

# The Christian Liberation Movement

Whatever diminishes, enslaves or negates man is an off-
ence against human dignity; it is also a kind of blasphemy
against God.
*Cardinal Hume to the Church of England Synod*

In the previous chapter an article by the religious affairs correspondent of *The Times* was mentioned with reference to the significance of the Nairobi Assembly of the WCC. In the same article
he noted that the work of the Latin American theologians 'is more
concerned with the role of the Church in the work of political,
economic, and psychological liberation of man'. He also commented that 'the role of Western theologians may not . . . be to
identify . . . with this new theology as it stands, but to adopt its
"way of doing theology" '.[1] When we speak of the liberation
movement we are generalizing on a rather grand scale. It would
be more realistic to speak of liberation movements, since the
range and the differentials of political, economic, and psychological liberation are wide enough to constitute a human phenomenon. Perhaps we are justified in using the singular to identify
the manifold evidence of a new human quest for freedom because
it constitutes a single phenomenon that is rapidly spreading
throughout the world. Not since the movement for political freedom embodied in the French and American Revolutions of the
eighteenth century has there been such an outburst or widespread
phenomenon. Indeed it goes beyond these both in depth and
extension. That Christians should participate in such a movement
ought not to be unexpected. As a community of faith whose inner
law is love and whose inner dynamic is hope it ought to be
expected that some prophetic leadership in the search for human
freedom consonant with human dignity would come from the
Church. And yet it is the prophetic activity and stance of the
Church that has to be articulated for Christians and non-Christians. Because the Church is unrenewed in large segments of its
life it cannot comprehend its own prophetic role as a liberated

and liberating institution. Instead of rejoicing in hope for the human community, a great number of Christians either wring their hands in despair because the Church is going to the dogs or shake clenched fists in angry reaction because it is going to the Marxists. Neither is true and neither is a valid Christian attitude. It is the task of theology to serve and articulate what is valid and implicit in Christian faith, hope, and love. And so we speak today of liberation theology, a theology that is born of experience as well as deductive speculation, a theology that is created to help Christians face new and particular situations that are shaping the human condition – cultural, political, historical, psychological, geographical. When we speak of liberation theology it would be more in accord with the methodology of liberation theology to speak of liberation *theologies*. Much of the basis for these theologies has been established in the theology of hope with its emphasis on Christian participation in the secular task of building a more human world as part of Christian witness to its own faith in the coming Kingdom of God. Both actual Christian participation in liberation movements and the theology which is developed to guide such participation rest on a number of basic presuppositions already developed and to be developed in the following two chapters of this book:

(1) It belongs to the missionary nature of the Church to share the prophetic ministry of Jesus, becoming involved in challenging and changing social values and structures of dehumanization and injustice within a given society.

(2) The power structures of the Church are not exempted from this prophetic scrutiny, and a critical look at them is part of its renewal.

(3) Issues arise in society that force Christians to take a stand in a *prophetic* and *charismatic* way.

(4) Human fulfilment and creativity is a more open notion of salvation and calls into question certain approaches to Christian mission and evangelization.

With reference to this last presupposition one often encounters a bias towards Christian participation in the struggle for liberation among peoples. The objection centres on the issue of reducing the purity and substance of the gospel to the level of an economic power struggle or political goals not immediately seen to be advantageous to the Church. Liberation theologies are political programmes thinly disguised in theological language.[2] But even where attitudes and language do not reach such extremities, many Christians cannot face the right and duty of the Church to be involved in all that affects the life of people, the right and duty to be in the marketplace. For them the Church offers sanctuary, an escape from the harsh pursuit of the realities of life. It is the sacred precinct that opens out to the transcendent existence for which man aspires, a world to come, now separated from the world of political action and decision. This is a profound misunderstanding, if not betrayal, of Christianity as bearer of good news. It is the reduction of Christianity to being a religion rather than a community which anticipates through social commitment the new creation begun in Jesus through the Spirit, a Kingdom already in our midst to which everyman is invited, a Kingdom of justice, love, and peace. Even where there is some sophisticated recognition that social, political, and cultural factors are forces affecting our theologies, all too often the principle that the whole human condition is the proper subject matter of Christian theology and life is not fully acknowledged. Closer to our own political life it is absurd to think that the British and Irish Churches have neither responsibility for nor anything to say about the whole situation in Ulster.

Out of these presuppositions there is a growing commitment by the Church to various dimensions of the liberation movement. As a part of this commitment Christian theologians are more and more exercised by their responsibility to formulate and articulate the Christian reaction to man's contemporary struggle towards a new level of human dignity and freedom. The names of Juan Luis Segundo, Hugo Assman, Rubem Alves, Beatriz Couch, Enrique Dussel, José Miranda, José Bonino, Gustavo Guttierez, Paulo Freire and Ivan Illich read like an ever growing litany of spokesmen, theologians, and educators of the new call to freedom and justice for all. While these in the main speak from a Third World context, e.g., the Latin American experience, there are others like James Cone and Deotis Roberts who would speak to the North American context of liberation, e.g., freedom for ethnic minorities. Someone like Rosemary Reuther would speak to the areas of class, race, and sex discrimination in this context. Yet these do not exhaust the growing number of liberation theologians who are beginning to speak out of their national and cultural contexts. If I concentrate on the Latin American theologians it is because I feel they have developed liberation theology in a significant way. Moreover, they do theology in a context that highlights the universal struggle for freedom and the actual role of the Church in that struggle.

Liberation theology rests on a refusal to accept the world as it is. It is destined to be different. This theology rejects older theories of truth that would define truth as the conformity of the mind to a given object or reality. Such a theory only confirms and makes legitimate the world as it now exists. For liberation theologians the world is an unfinished project which is being completed by the people who make it up. Its reality depends in part on what people think and do. Knowledge is one dimension of this world-building process. But knowledge is important, for our perception of society affects our behaviour and the actions and decisions that enter into the making of our future. The norm of truth is taken from the kind of world our human knowledge helps bring into being. If our thinking helps an evil world to endure, such thinking cannot be said to be true. But if our thinking enables us to perceive present oppressive structures and discover new trends in history to transform and overthrow such structures, then this is truth, this is true knowledge, this is science. This is the process whereby the world becomes more truly human, a place where truth and goodness are inseparable. The corollary of such a thesis for the Christian theologian could be stated thus: Christians have to listen to God's word addressing them from within their historical, concrete situation, listening in terms of their own collective struggle. God's truth is shaped by a divine message uttered to men over the centuries. But the truth lies in the discernment of present evils, of decisions to be made now, albeit subject to the central terms of the biblical message of Jesus and the prophets. But its truth consists in the discovery of the redemptive movement in history, the activity of God in human affairs which is promised in that ancient message, old yet ever new. Such discernment and discovery involves the whole community. Christian communities have to 'do theology' in this respect. This means that practice (*praxis*) and truth (*theoria*) interact. This interaction between what we know to be true and practical decisions and judgements to be made in the immediate situation is guided by the vision of God's mighty acts in history and his promised reign. It is also guided by faith in the forward movement of history guaranteed by the passover of God's people and the resurrection of Jesus. Paulo Freire says: 'This Easter, which results in the changing of consciousness, must be existentially experienced. The real Easter is not commemorative rhetoric. It is praxis; it is historical involvement.'[3] I have mentioned that it is more precise to speak of liberation theologies. Liberation theologians would prefer this because, as they see it, oppression can be pretty extensive, e.g., class, race, sex, economic, political oppression. These are historically different in different societies and cultures. For a given society economic oppression is central, while race or sex may be the principal element of oppression in another society. These theologians also recognize the value of examining secondary forms of oppression in relation to what is the central form of oppression, the better to understand how to transform the historical dehumanizing structures into liberating structures. For example, the USA negro will see oppression primarily in terms of racism. For him economic oppression is secondary. The Latin American worker is concerned with a critical analysis of the economic system as the root of his oppression. For him racial oppression is secondary. The negro sees that racism is related to economic exploitation and class identification. He would not see the basic issue of black freedom as one of economic oppression. In a sense theologians of a dominant culture, e.g., white, Anglo-Saxon, Protestants, are unable to produce a liberation theology, though they can opt for solidarity with marginalized sections of society. They can free themselves from identification with power structures. Just as churches, dioceses, and religious orders can question the investments of the corporations in which they hold shares, so theologians of the dominant culture can develop what Rubem Alves calls a 'theology of captivity' whereby they are able to come to a deeper Christian understanding of society and reread history from a viewpoint of oppressed peoples.[4] Liberation theologies are not the product of single intellectuals. They are the reflections of communities involved in a struggle for freedom from oppression.

These are the general characteristics of liberation theology. To the extent that we are to speak of this theology as a singular method of doing theology we also have to remember that its method is tightly bound to the general educative process. Education is an important, a vital dimension of liberation theology. When I speak of education as a dimension of doing liberation theology, as part of its methodology, I want to be clear that there is a danger of which Paulo Freire warns us; that of turning education for liberation 'into a purely methodological problem' which would make it 'something purely neutral', removing 'all political content from education, so that the expression "education for liberation" no longer means anything'.[5] Precisely as part of the theological method, however, it is necessary to look at the meaning of two significant terms. I am speaking of the notions of *conscientization* and *deschooling*. The first has come to be associated with Paulo Freire, a Brazilian educator; the second with Ivan Illich, educator, prolific author, and co-founder of the Intercultural Centre at Cuernavaca, Mexico.[6]

## 1. *Conscientization*

If it were expressed in theological perspective, it operates on the paradigm of Exodus, i.e., passover and resurrection. Salvation is something to achieve in history and not simply as something to be hoped for in a distant heaven.[7] It challenges our conscience because it shows us that God wants us to act and to move out. The peace God offers is one that has to be lived by commitment to people and their liberation through the transformation of the structures that are dehumanizing them. Within a philosophical perspective it is a process of becoming aware of all that it takes to be a man, to look at all human relationships with and in the world. This process takes us beyond a simple, spontaneous, naive apprehension of ourselves living in the world to a critical reflective stage where we can explore our reality and probe in depth in order to come to a deeper understanding of what it means to be human in our particular situation. Within an educational framework the word means an awakening of consciousness, a critical awareness of individual identity and situation. It means the ability to make responsible decisions that will affect the person involved in a particular situation. Essential to this process is what is called *praxis* which involves both *reflection* and *action*. There is always a unity between these two. So Freire's concept of praxis includes what he calls 'theoretic praxis' and 'accomplished praxis'. Both forms are constructed, shaped, and reshaped by a constant movement from practice to theory and back to practice. This educational theory is not drawn from textbooks but from an ideological commitment to abolish élitist and privileged forms of leadership. So reflection and action have their sources in language, culture, the problems of illiterates, philosophies of knowledge, the context of history, an analysis of Latin American underdevelopment. Development is what people do for themselves, with or without outside help, to enable themselves to take part in the decisions that will affect their lives. This will involve them in political action of all kinds in order to change the structures of power that oppress them and eliminate the systems that support these structures of injustice. To teach a man to read in such a way that he is aware of himself as man with a power of freedom is a liberating act and one that is political as well for it prepares such a man for political decisions. As such this can be very threatening to powers and principalities in high and dark places. Conscientization distinguishes carefully between *modernization* and *development*. Modernization is a concept of social planning through technology and industrial development on the part of an inherited élitist class superimposed on the masses. Development on the other hand is liberation at two levels: liberation from imperialism and liberation of the oppressed social classes from an oppressive élite. Conscientization is an analysis or an analytical approach, a general method of working out problems and contradictions related to authentic human development. Conscientization operates wherever there is a *Third World*, be it in Europe, Africa, Latin America, Britain, or North America. It empowers the powerless to act together effectively in the decision-making, participating process. This means more than five minutes in a polling booth once every few years.[8] 'Conscientization, then, is the most critical approach to reality, stripping it down so as to get to know the myths that deceive and perpetuate the dominating structure.'[9]

## 2. *Deschooling*

This notion advocated by Ivan Illich is a way of conscientization. We have to unlearn by uncovering the myths of our society wherever they are operative and counterproductive in the lives of ordinary people. This may take one into education or medicine, politics or economics. But its main target is education. Ivan Illich puts it this way in his book *Celebration of Awareness:*

> Logic would seem to require that we do not stop with an effort to improve schools; rather that we question the assumption on which the school system itself is based. . . . A second look reveals that this school system has built a narrow bridge across a widening social gap.[10]

In a graduation address at the University of Puerto Rico Illich referred to schooling as a sacred cow, saying that the 'age of schooling' began about 200 years ago and became an idea that schooling was a necessary means of becoming a useful member of society. 'It is the task of this generation to bury that myth.'[11] Paulo Freire does not believe that institutionalized educational systems can really conscientize or liberate. To separate education and politics is to detach theory and practice, to remove education from the reality on which it ought to be feeding – the life of the people. Education so organized becomes a realm of abstract ideas and values, a repository of behaviour patterns for an élite society. Education can never be neutral.[12] Therefore it is necessary to hold three interacting strands of education together:

(i) Religious – theological assumptions about humanity, e.g., how free are we to take an active role in the choices that shape our individual and social lives?;

(ii) socio – economic assumptions, e.g., to what extent do present structures support some and victimize others?;

(iii) educational theories related to these two sets of assumptions, e.g., that teaching and learning are always interactive components in one humanizing process.

In both conscientization and deschooling we find the general features and perceive a method and ethos for doing liberation theology. Yet it remains to be seen how effectively and wholeheartedly theology will incorporate these features into itself. And it must be said at once that liberation theology lives with the provisional because the Christian faith it serves involves a firm commitment to eliminate poverty and bondage in the situation of our present age. It is a new quest to reach a new level of freedom and human dignity for this generation. Some of the liberation

113

theologians are chary of others who seem tempted to make this theology so abstract and absolute that it will evacuate the provisional, historical, concrete character of it in handling the real conditions of poverty and oppression.[13] They are afraid it will become a theory without praxis. Theologians like Guttierez see liberation theology on a wider horizon of the secularization process we spoke of in the first chapter.[14] Moreover, he speaks of a spirituality of liberation and says that 'theological categories are not enough'.[15] Whether this would keep his Latin American fellows happy is doubtful. But it is clear that he stresses the spirituality of liberation because 'we need a vital attitude, all embracing and synthesizing, informing the totality as well as every detail of our lives'.[16] This spirituality rests on an awareness of the dominion of the Holy Spirit and is defined as 'a concrete manner, inspired by the Spirit, of living the Gospel'.[17] This spirituality is one that centres on *conversion* to the oppressed, exploited, and despised. In this spiritual ethos life and freedom are seen as God's gift, as *gratuitousness* to all. It is the source of *joy*, a 'joy born of the gift already received and yet still awaited . . . expressed in the present despite the difficulties and tensions of the struggle for the construction of a just society'.[18] The spirituality of liberation finds expression in the Magnificat with its tones of liberation, of promises to turn things upside down in favour of a future for the poor and the oppressed. Guttierez says that 'living witnesses rather than theological speculation . . . are already pointing out the direction of a spirituality of liberation'.[19]

When we turn to a theologian like Juan Luis Segundo the provisional character of liberation theology is by no means a superficial thing or a passing fad. In his introduction to *The Liberation of Theology* he says:

> It is my opinion that the 'theology of liberation' . . . represents a point of no return in Latin America. It is an irreversible thrust in the Christian process of creating a new consciousness and maturity in our faith. Countless Christians have committed themselves to a fresh and radical interpretation of their faith, to a new re-experiencing of it in their real lives. And they have done this not only as isolated individuals but also as influential and sizeable groups within the Church.[20]

Segundo wants to explore the epistemology and precise theological method inherent in a theology that claims direct connection with the whole process of human liberation. While conscientization and deschooling are vital components of the method and without wishing to turn liberation theology into a methodological problem, he wants to establish the conviction that 'liberation theology is not provincial or fundamentalist'.[21] It has to break away from the deductive way of doing theology that has been so much a part of European and North American theology, a theology that provided pat answers for complex problems and transcendent principles for human misery. I feel that Segundo's work is invaluable, not only because of its fidelity to conscientization and deschooling, but because it calls into question the provincial dialogue of the Western Church. It has the potential to accelerate the pedestrian methods of ecumenical theological dialogue, break the chains binding interchurch relations, and get us beyond the history of the last 400 years. It does this not by opting for complete discontinuity with the past, but by going straight to the ideologies and struggles of the present, acknowledging its dependence on contemporary sciences. In all this it discusses the word of God as it is addressed to us now – 'thus saith the Lord'. For this very reason it combines the disciplines which throw light on the present with those that open up the past to our understanding. According to Segundo this is necessary to avoid a new form of oppression, one that would 'incorporate the idiom of liberation into the prevailing language of the *status quo*'.[22] The common concern of these theologians and educators is to prevent the liberative function attached to their approach from being neutralized, i.e. theory separated from praxis and the life of the oppressed. This means there has to be an interpretation of each new reality or situation as it presents itself. For the Christian this means a continuing change in our interpretation of the Bible within the community of faith. In the light of the Scriptures we struggle to transform the real situation. This brings us back to a reinterpretation of God's word again. Broken down into stages this means:

(1) the experience of reality and the calling into question of an associated ideology;

(2) the application of this suspicion to theological ideology;

(3) a new experience of theological reality that questions whether

115

a prevailing interpretation of Scripture has taken certain data into account;

(4) a new hermeneutics (method of interpretation) is developed with which to interpret our faith according to the Scriptures.

The better to understand this interpretative process Segundo turns to a black liberation theologian, James Cone, to provide an example.[23] Let us follow the four steps again with Cone's theology providing content – a content with which we may or may not be in agreement:

(1) God is active in the world for the community of the oppressed and this is the gospel of Jesus Christ. We are not to be concerned with abstract principles of the right or wrong course of action. There is only one principle: an unqualified commitment to the black community as it defines its existence in the light of God's liberating action in the world.

(2) God is not colour-blind and a theology purporting to be so is an ideology that ignores the cause of oppression, namely colour. People suffer precisely because of their colour. If you ignore this, it is impossible to translate biblical liberation into the concrete struggle of black versus white here and now.

(3) White theology is to be denied as a proper way to articulate human existence. Black theology is to be affirmed because it is the black community which is searching for ways of talking about God that will enhance and enrich their understanding of themselves.

(4) Black theology questions what God's love is for the oppressed. God shows up in a different light when people find themselves in different historical conditions and the truth about God is also different. This is a way of saying that orthopraxy leads to orthodoxy and not vice versa.

In using this example of Cone's theology Segundo wants to make clear that the Bible is not discourse between a universal God and universal man.[24] He says of this way of interpretation: 'When it is accused of partiality, it can calmly reply that it is partial because it is faithful to Christian tradition rather than to Greek thought.'[25] That this is the exercise of a radical interpretation of Christian life may seem frightening in the sense that there is no telling where it may lead. This is not alien to Christian hope. We go on talking about renewal and Christian unity without very much progress being made. We neutralize the radical nature of renewal and we defer decisions on Christian unity. Liberation theology is not afraid to make judgements.

> Despite theological disagreements about the nature and essence of the sacraments themselves, the use of the sacraments in many Christian Churches represents a substitute for the security that should come from our committed efforts to transform and liberate history . . . The real problem of Christian unity . . . comes down to this: When will we manage to break that conservative, oppressive, undifferentiated unity of Christians in order to establish an open dialogue with all those . . . who are committed to the historical liberation that should serve as the basis for the 'service of reconciliation' in and through real justice?[26]

The Latin American theologians insist on a prior commitment to liberation before attempting any specific contribution. Social praxis precedes evangelical values and proclamation. The historical relevance of the gospel can only be determined through social praxis.[27] A political option for liberative change is itself an intrinsic element of faith. 'We can only have an authentic faith . . . when we have committed ourselves to an authentic struggle that opens our eyes to the new possibilities and meanings of God's word.'[28] The commitment to the struggle is not to be equated with the adoption of an ideology. As Segundo notes, there are ideologies in Scripture because it is a record of responses learned in specific historical situations. Faith is 'the total process to which a man submits, a process of learning in and through ideologies how to create the ideologies needed to handle new and unforeseen situations in history'.[29] It is the concrete historical response in faith that constitutes an ideology – not vice versa. Whereas faith is absolute, ideologies are relative. They serve faith, for faith takes the truth revealed by God and places it in the service of historical problems to be solved. The solution is worked out through and in an ideology. There is nothing arbitrary or unconditional in the way we adopt ideologies. They are meant to serve faith and hope and love. In this way liberation theology is feared as another major crack in the mighty fortress of Christian faith because it relativizes all ideologies, making them subservient to faith as absolute obedience to God. Some might wonder if this is not to relativize the use of means and ends, i.e., ends justifying any means. Would this not create a situation ethics that asks simply: What does Christ's love require here and now? Are we not opening the door to an instrumental adaptation of Marxism? Do we not unleash the furies of violent revolution? These are the anxieties and fears that surround the whole liberation movement throughout the world. If the liberation movement and its attendant theology is to be proposed as a substantive of Christian hope, it must answer these questions, assuage normal fears and anxieties, and provide an account for the hope we put in this movement and theology. Above all, Christian hope must contain in itself genuine Christian faith and love.

## Means and ends

To come down with an absolute choice for either means or ends is to opt either for legalistic moralism (this must never be done) or for the premiss that the end justifies *any* means. There is middle ground here. The means to be used are affected by the situation itself. Thus J. G. Davies, a British theologian, says: 'There are no such things as means *per se*. There are only means conditioned by a situation. To seek to define the sanctity of ends and the purity of means is to be guilty of an abstraction.'[30] And he quotes Hugo Assman: 'Anyone who always know *a priori* how to act in a situation which does not yet exist takes an immoral decision precisely because it is abstract and non-historical.'[31] It comes down to choosing *just means* to attain *just goals*. There is pseudo-radicalism in a lot of protest movements. There is no point in surrendering to irrational forces without a programme and an alternative vision of a new order in a given society. Associated with the new order is the concern for the establishment of peace and reconciliation, the sign of God's Kingdom. So, we are not speaking here of liberation movements committed to a goal without any reference to the justice of the means employed. Davies asks for a recognition 'that there has to be a proportionality of means to end and also a discrimination between means'.[32] Thus whatever means of force are used, 'elementary rules of humanity have to be

118

observed' and 'force is to be undertaken and only exercised within an action that is obviously inspired by justice and peace'.[33]

## Violence

The Christian ethic of liberation with its tension between justifiable violence and absolute pacifism remains unresolved. This stems from an inner tension in Christianity itself. No amount of moral synthesizing in the name of justice or of declarations on pacificism in the name of the 'pure gospel' can dispel it. As Paul Oestreicher has pointed out, Bonhoeffer 'accepted without illusion the unresolved tension between discipleship and political responsibility'.[34] The New Testament certainly carries on the tradition of concern for seeking and establishing the justice of God among men. It also constantly points to the realm of life called the Kingdom of God where justice and peace meet and man is in communion with man in God. It provides man with an ethic and lifestyle which anticipates this blessed life of the Kingdom. Such anticipation makes possible a way of expressing the unique love of God among men. It is wisdom with God, but foolishness with men. Christ, the Wisdom of God, exposed the oppressive ideology of his time and place and paid the price for it by accepting death, death on a cross, praying for his executioners and enemies. He preached non-violence, forgiveness, the defeat of evil with goodness, and access to power through weakness. It all adds up to a lack of common sense. It is an option based on the conviction that the peace and reconciliation which are perfected and fulfilled in God's Kingdom can somehow be realized even now. Moreover, the dynamic of love that is operative in the search for peace and reconciliation is effective in promoting justice among men in the present age. This is prophetic in an eschatological way, i.e., in a way that anticipates the life of men together with God. That Jesus chose this way of life and witness seems to be indisputable. This is not to portray him as 'gentle Jesus, meek and mild', something that amounts to a caricature of the personality of Jesus, a product of romanticism, a sentimental sop to weak ineffectual temperaments.[35] Jesus was singleminded and toughminded, a radical reformer, intent upon a revolution that would begin in the heart of man, requiring a radical transformation of his outlook. The wrath of God, the singlemindedness or steadfast fidelity of God, all that indicated the reality and seriousness of the covenant relationship were expressed in him and through him. He fulfilled both the Law and the prophets. To say that he chose the way of non-violence is not to condemn his followers who have had to reflect on the possibility that a certain situation could justify the use of violence in some sense of the word.[36] Jesus chose his way in terms of his vocation and mission to manifest prophetically and in fullness of perfection the life of man in the Kingdom of God. Just as some men and women undertake a life of celibacy for the sake of the Kingdom and in response to a call they feel from God, so some Christians work out a commitment to peace and reconciliation through non-violence. The celibate vocation does not condemn Christian marriage nor diminish its witness to the loving fidelity of God. Neither ought the way of non-violence to condemn those who work for human justice by means that seem to clash with the way Jesus chose to manifest his mission. Because they are in an historical situation no less than Jesus where it is vital to bear witness to the freedom from oppression proclaimed by a loving liberating God to the dispossesed, the oppressed, the poor, the rejected, on whom Jesus built his Church and through whom he proclaimed God's Kingdom, can we say that the decision to use some measure of violence is at variance with the overall message of the gospel? Is it not possible that there is another way thrust upon some Christians to witness to the serious purposes of God in the affairs of men, another way of manifesting God's love and care for the *anawim*, the lowly and dispossessed and vulnerable, those in any way disadvantaged? Faith and fidelity towards God in Christ has to be interpreted in differing situations. This is the hermeneutics of some liberation theologies. Risky? Yes. Radical Christianity has always been so. Without denying the ethical risk and tension such choices bring with them, it seems to me that Christian prophecy admits plurality – an honest choice of honest ends through honest means to bear witness to God's promise of new life for all men. The choice must arise from a heart that is honest before God. Blessed are the pure in heart! Such a decision comes from an agony that wants the cup to pass, though not at the expense of disobedience to God. And such choice must be rooted in faith in the Easter event, the total paschal mystery of resurrection through the power and paradox of the cross. Perhaps a new respect for pluralism among Christians in their witness in the decades ahead will take all this into account. Christians will take two different paths on the pilgrim journey to God's Kingdom of justice, peace, and reconciliation. In Alan Richardson's *The Political Christ* he points out that the Christian Church is a new kind of society without parallel in the history of religions. In support of this he says 'that there was no distinctively Christian ideology or ethical system or political programme'. And he adds: ' . . . if, all too often, Christian Churches have conformed to the ideological presuppositions of their environment, this does not mean that Christianity itself is ideological in essence.'[37] To argue for a pluralism of Christian witness is neither new nor a vain attempt to create the quality of comprehensiveness that inadequately reconciles extreme positions. If we argue the case here for a responsible liberation theology that does not exclude armed struggle in every situation, it is equally possible and emotively easier to argue the non-violent approach. Paul Oestreicher says:

> . . . Christians, whether black or white, aspiring to accept the radical demands of Christian freedom should not fear to see the liberation struggle through New Testament eyes and to support those fools in the struggle who for Christ's sake are prepared to put to the test the liberating example of strength through weakness.[38]

The prophetic dimension of Christian life and ministry comes up often in the context of liberation theology. It is important to mention therefore that the prophetic dimension is more than a counterweight to the institutional dimension of the Christian community. I am referring to the common life and ministry of all the disciples of Jesus. It is the prophetic element of this common ministry that prevents an unhealthy cleavage between lay and clerical Christians, enabling the Church to be seen as a prophetic community in life and mission. This dimension brings Christians to take a critical look at the implications of Christian love in relation to concrete historical situations. It takes into account hidden motives and ideologies, unconscious desires and anxieties, limiting irrational complexes. Love is the power of discernment poured into our hearts by the Holy Spirit. In this respect the claim of Christian love is unique. It is a power that transcends any one of its expressions to point out the redemptive possibilities in each specific situation. The image of the prophet as a raging, wild-eyed, semi-madman is most certainly a caricature and false to the theology of prophecy in the Judaeo-Christian tradition. God has put the burden of his brother on a man, has made him his brother's keeper, left him bowed and broken before human greed and hypocrisy, left him in terror at his brother's agony. Thus:

> Prophecy is the voice God has lent to the silent agony, a voice to the plundered poor, to the profaned riches of the world. It is a form of living, a crossing point of God and man. God is raging in the prophet's words. Thus prophecy protests the degradation of man, the anonymous levelling out of human existence. . . . Present prophetic hopes must be proportioned by a keen discernment of modern man's anguish, his terrible feeling of emptiness, his awareness of having come to a spiritual standstill, a moral dead-end. Concrete measures will be dictated by the nature of the challenge; they will be elaborated in view of the ideals of love and justice that must and can, in the new context, raise up the heart of man. It pertains to the Church's prophetic mission to encourage the boundless aspirations which drive humanity in search of deliverance and salvation. . . .[39]

Liberation theology attempts to articulate such prophetic faith, to renew it in the Church's consciousness and commitment. The Church can be itself most truly when it commits itself to the struggle to liberate the poor and disadvantaged after the pattern of Jesus Christ. The 'third world' can be found somewhere on the map in every country. And as Mother Teresa of Calcutta has reminded us, the rich have their own special kind of poverty. The need for liberation exists at every level of society. But there are priorities and a sense of urgency in favour of basic needs and fundamental human dignity for millions right now. The Christian community will do a disservice to the Kingdom of God if it procrastinates. The crude facts are that a third of the world's population makes use of two thirds of its resources; two thirds are able to make use of only one third of these resources; one third of the world's population controls two thirds of the world's wealth; and one third of the world's population consumes two thirds of the world's food. This is but a fraction of man's tyranny over man. The prophetic ministry of the Christian Church must once more authenticate its ministry of word and sacrament. Without a prophetic ministry, whatever measure of ecumenical agreement on their nature or essence, 'the use of the sacraments in many Christian Churches represents a substitute for the security that should come from our committed efforts to transform and liberate history'.[40] On 25 June 1965 Camilo Torres, writing to the Cardinal Archbishop of Bogotá, Colombia, requesting lay status in the Church, said:

> In the present structure of the Church it has been impossible for me to continue my priestly duties in the aspects of external cult. However, the Christian priesthood does not consist only of the celebration of external rites. The Mass, which is the final object of the priestly action, is fundamentally a communal action. But the Christian community cannot offer the sacrifice in an authentic form if it has not first fulfilled in an effective manner the precept of 'love thy neighbour' . . . . I sacrifice one of the rights that I love most dearly . . . in order to create the conditions that make the cult more authentic.[41]

It might seem that too much stress on the prophetic dimension of Christianity could produce an indifference to the ministry of word and sacrament. Apart from its presence as an authenticating factor for Christian life, and apart from its intrinsic pluriform witness to the love and justice of God, it enables us to look at the Church from a new ecumenical vantage point. The Protestant liberation theologian, José Miguez Bonino, makes a point of this.[42] He relates the question of pluriformity, e.g., violent–non-violent revolution, and other options made in fidelity to what we conceive in faith as true discipleship of Jesus in the proclamation of God's Kingdom. While western churchmen speak of visible unity, without implying uniformity in church order and discipline, they do work for a unity that is a genuine unity of faith, even though they may differ as to the essential content of Christian faith. If I understand Bonino correctly, he takes the line that you cannot get to orthodoxy in the Church's faith apart from orthopraxy. His theology of the Church consists in an ongoing struggle to become the true Church through an option to enter a concrete historical praxis in fidelity to Jesus Christ. 'A Church becomes a community of faith in decision. And this decision places it for or against Christ.'[43] He would seem to view confessional conflicts in the light of concrete historical issues rather than in the light of doctrinal issues, such as authority, ministry, sacraments, and the like. He says that 'the true quest for unity is not therefore to be found in the negotiations of ecclesiastical bodies – which are only a field, not the real contenders – but in this conflict and encounter which takes place within and across them.'[44] Whatever reservations such an approach to ecumenism evokes, it does bring western theologizing back to its task of uniting a Church for mission. It is the renewal of a sense of mission that makes the Christian community indebted to liberation theology. This theology renews prophetic activity in the Church. It reminds the whole Church not only of the radical demands of Christ's love – but of his sense of justice as well. Securing justice is of the Church's essence and life. Abraham Heschel says that 'justice is as much a necessity as breathing is, and a constant occupation'.[45] He continues:

> Justice is not an ancient custom, a human convention, a value, but a transcendent demand, freighted with divine concern. It is not only a relationship between man and man, it is an *act* involving God, a divine need. Justice is His line, righteousness His plummet (Isa.28.17). It is not one of His ways, but in all His ways. Its validity is not only universal, but also external, independent of will and experience.[46]

It is this prophetic and radical sense of justice that has to be renewed if we are to respect Christian differences in the demands it makes on conscience regarding the best means to achieve justice and express self-effacing love.

## Christians and instrumental Marxism

Among the questions raised by liberation theology none is more vexing, pressing, and contemporary than the matter of how Christians and Marxists collaborate. It provides a concrete historical relevance to the discussion of means and ends, of violent and peaceful revolution. No other factor creates the host of suspicions surrounding liberation theology to the extent that this association of Christian and Marxist aspirations does. Instrumental Marxism has no simple definition. It is a method of critical analysis of the social and economic factors which oppress and hold people in degrading poverty below the basic standard of human dignity. In this method Marxist categories of thought are freely used. An instrumental use of Marxism implies picking and choosing from the Marxist tradition. It recognizes a pluralism within this tradition. There are brands of Marxism. Be it in China, Russia, Cuba, Chile, Yugoslavia, Italy, France – Marxism has diverse cultural and social contexts. This corresponds to the very nature of liberation theology which holds as a first principle the need to adapt (praxis) to differing historical and cultural patterns. Often instrumental Marxism amounts to taking a stand against imperialism, colonialism, or racism that has become the inheritance of the Third World. Camilo Torres is the popular figure of such a stand. Born into a rich family he sacrificed security, the privileges of family and priesthood at thirty-six to join the revolutionary forces within Colombia where two thirds of the rural population are landless workers. He took a stand in conscience without denying his identity as a Christian patriot, priest, and sociologist. Yet he was prepared to fight alongside the Marxists for common goals in opposition to the national oligarchy dominated by American interests, in order to restore dignity and self-determination to ordinary people.[47] An Italian Christian Marxist, Giùlio Girardi, would bypass the whole question of compatibility between Marxist and Christian ideology. He would see no need to raise questions of this nature. Marxists and Christians have been thrown together in a common struggle. He presses for a distinction between the dogmatic Marxism of institutions and the personalist Marxism with a human face. Roger Garandy was an early advocate and dialogician of the Christian–Marxist attempt at rapport and integration of purpose. While he never respected the uniqueness of Christianity he maintained that the two ideologies could be synthesized in an existential and prophetic way.[48] But as Peter Hebblethwaite has noted, we are left always with the question: which brand of Marxism and Christianity is being synthesized?[49] A much clearer line of approach to the question of the Christian–Marxist synthesis is to be found in the movement called Christians For Socialism (CFS) which came into existence in 1972 at a meeting of 400 Christians held at Santiago, Chile. Bonino has described this meeting in the introduction to his *Revolutionary Theology Comes of Age.* As he said, 'we did not expect to depart carrying a mere set of well-meaning resolutions but an adequate instrument for the struggle'. CFS openly espouses Marxist ideology as a critical theory that is open-ended for genuine development. It has a prophetic function within a Church which allies itself with capitalism. As a Christian body CFS would regard political commit-

125

ment and involvement as a service to the Church. In dissociating Christianity and capitalism the argument does not confine itself to pointing up the incompatibility of these two forces. CFS argues that Christianity is less incompatible with Marxism. CFS has developed branches in Spain and Italy. In these countries CFS is fully committed to the creation of a socialist society and the extirpation of capitalist society. The inner motive is in terms of Christian faith in the resurrection of Jesus. This newness of life promised in that event is realized when man ceases to exploit man. Marxism can contribute to this process. The contradictions between Marxism and Christianity will be overcome in the actual struggle for liberation. There is an inherent fundamental agreement between the imperatives of Christian faith and those of Marxist revolutionary commitment. These Christians would say that we have to revise our notion of God as a God of peace and reconciliation *without struggle*. The God of the Bible is the Lord of Justice who fiercely vindicates the oppressed. The Magnificat is the anthem of Christian revolution. In an article in *The Month* Peter Hebblethwaite says that 'the line from the "theology of liberation" to CFS is direct and continuous' and 'not, as the right wing imagines, as a result of some fiendish plot, but because sincere men have become convinced of its truth'.[50] However, there are Christians like Hebblethwaite who question the possibilities for success in this attempt at a synthesis of Marxism and Christianity. They wonder if we can use Marxism instrumentally, putting brackets around its materialistic atheism, and still come up with the answers to the burning social issues of our time. Can we really treat Marxism as little more than a practical system for allowing social change to take place? Will we not have to take the risk of a more subtle convergence? Hebblethwaite suggests that it might be Christianity that is being used instrumentally as well. In fact he does not see how such a synthesis could be achieved apart from a mutual recognition of instrumentality for a common goal, the liberation of man. He further suggests that the way some exponents advocate the synthesis amounts to the disposal of Christianity when the crunch comes. It is Christianity that has to go.[51] Some, like Bonino, would argue that we must not approach the question as one of conversion, 'as if Marxism were a religion or Christianity an ideology'.[52] By putting Marxism in a Christian context and against a different horizon it is inevitably modified.

He accepts the distinction Guttierez makes between the level of political action which is rational and scientific and the level which is utopian, i.e., a vision of new men in a new society. Taken together these two levels open up new fields of human fulfilment. With Guttierez, Bonino believes that faith which is neither scientific nor utopic – but a living relationship with God and man – relates these two levels by stirring the utopian imagination towards political and technological activity that stimulates a sense of responsibility for creating a just and integrated society. I mentioned this in the first chapter when speaking of the relationship beween Christian hope and utopia. Because faith is the matrix of hope, just as hope is the dynamism of faith, it bears a relationship to these rational and utopian projections by giving a vision of the Kingdom of justice and peace promised by God. It is living and real only when it is actively engaged because the living relationship between God and man which defines faith is a mutual relationship based on the freedom of God and the freedom of man, though it is a covenant relationship initiated by God. Social utopianism, together with political theory and the scientific tools for social analysis, along with economic and ecological planning, can provide that indispensable active engagement that makes man's response to God an authentic, free, living relationship. It is determined only in the sense that it is guided and motivated by God's purpose in establishing a realm of justice, truth, peace, and love. This argument assumes that the general aim of Marxist ideology, the elimination of human exploitation, is in accord with the general purposes of God in history and beyond history in terms of human destiny. Alfredo Fierro pursues this argument in his work *The Militant Gospel*.[53] He says:

> Today Marxism is the broadest and most comprehensive of the theoretical approaches to human historical reality. . . . We are living in a period when the historical-materialist line of reasoning holds sway. . . . In such circumstances it would be foolish and unreasonable to theologize while turning our backs on the Marxist hypothesis. It is not that theology can rest content with considering only that particular theory. The point is that theology certainly cannot be complete if it does not consider and adopt that theory as a hypothesis.[54]

This line of reasoning is in accord with the nature of liberation theology, namely, to work from social praxis to give meaning to our theology and our proclamation of the gospel.[55] The argument presupposes a genuine political, rational, utopic context for the exercise of faith wherein faith discerns the context as valid or not in terms of how it understands what God is asking in order to live according to the norm of love that pursues justice for all. Faith summons us to live beyond ourselves, but it does not thereby make any person or generation of persons expendable. José Bonino says:

> Every generation . . . is at the same time means and end, the bearer of sacrifice and the inheritor of hope, called to realize as fully as possible all the human possibilities open to it (politically, socially, economically, spiritually) and called to suffer and to toil for new and greater possibilities for future generations. No really human achievement can be obtained through the denial of the humanity of some men or of a generation.[56]

The best approach to the question of instrumental Marxism seems to me to view it as part of a greater quest for the purity and wholeness of faith and a way of exercising the inductive method of liberation theology. Christian participation in the liberation movements is both necessary and hopeful. It does mean that Christianity will disengage itself from a particular ideology, leaving Christians free to discern relevant social values in a given praxis that expresses faith. It implies the openness of obediential faith that is formed and developed by genuine signs that point to the formation of a new humanity in a new creation. That this openness includes a critical adaptation of certain Marxist values ought not to be ruled out by ideological bias. Religion itself must be adapted critically and freed from ideologies that no longer serve faith. The Church in this sense too must always be open to reform and renewal. Christianity is not a new religion. It is about the new creative act of God in Jesus Christ, fulfilling an ancient promise to create a new heaven and a new earth (Isa. 65. 17–25). It is about obedience to the word of God that this work shall be completed and its first fruits anticipated and enjoyed by all God's people on the earth. In this sense the religious and profane dimensions of life are subject to what God is doing in the world. It is just as impious to turn Christ's Church into a pious institution as to turn God's world into a labour camp. The earth he has given to the sons of men (Ps. 155). The Church is the place where God is to be worshipped in spirit and in truth (John 4.23). The Church like other institutions must formulate politics. But it must be sufficiently self-critical to question its presuppositions, the ideologies to which it has attached Christ's cause. What the world will call a *volte-face* may well be an act of repentance in obedience to the Spirit. The Church is God's creative act begun under the Spirit for renewing the face of the earth and the hearts of men. When the Church is free enough and purified sufficiently in its faith, it need not fear any ideology, any new decision to be made, any new act of discernment to be undertaken in the name of the promised Kingdom of God. Newness of life is the Christian way of life (Rom. 6.4). This newness of life is indeed revolutionary. In a given time and place it may demand a revolution or participation in one. But it is a quality of newness that demands change which is honestly associated with human development. Whatever Christian conscience dictates in co-operation with and adaptation to certain aims of Marxism, it most certainly dictates commitment to political and social liberation, to human development and progress. Liberation theology in its articulation of the liberation movements must be open to all authentic options that express its commitment to Christ's mission of liberation that is consistent with the historical incarnational nature of that mission.

## Liberation and development

Liberation theologians and educators have mixed feelings about the notion of development. They tend to reject the concept as inadequate for creating a new social order. Too often it is considered an umbrella term for halfway and halfhearted measures and methods of liberation. It is an emotive word that may signify peace at any price or some other alternative to violent revolution and protest. It gets confused with *modernization*.[57] It is negative in the sense that it contrasts starkly the rich countries with the anguish of the underdeveloped poor countries. It can be synonymous with economic growth or with a *total social process* in which a country takes responsibility and control of its own destiny. Guttierez could call this total social process 'liberation'.[58] Both terms cover a commitment to a total social process that liberates men and women from social manipulation, from poverty and ignorance. It may well be legitimate to use one or other of these terms in differing situations without one excluding the other. To talk about liberation in Britain might seem exaggerated or foreign, probably because of associating such a term with violent revolution. To speak of development in Chile or Uganda could be obscene, at least meaningless. In a general sense the Church has preferred to talk about development. It is beginning to talk about liberation. The language of militancy and revolution makes good rhetoric when radical Christianity is discussed. In fact the Church fears the possibilities behind this sort of language. At present the language and concepts of liberation and development overlap. We must learn what is appropriate for particular social conditions. However, in the general vocabulary of Christian thought it is now time to grant parity to the language of liberation with the language of development. Guttierez, reflecting on the language of development in Roman Catholic documents, namely the *Mater et Magistra* of Pope John XXIII, the *Gaudium et Spes* of Vatican II, the *Populorum Progressio* of Pope Paul VI, indicates the reluctance to talk the straightforward language of liberation. He says of *Populorum Progressio*: 'The outright use of the language of liberation, instead of its mere suggestion, would have given a more decided and direct thrust in favour of the oppressed, encouraging them to break with their present situation and take control of their own destiny.'[59] That the Roman Catholic bishops tried to do this in their 'Pastoral from the Third World' (1967) and at the Medellin Conference (1968) must be construed as a hopeful sign.[60] We can begin to hope that more Christian leaders will use the language of liberation unequivocally in obedience and fidelity of the Spirit who extends the mission of Jesus through the mystery of the Church in the world. Both Bonino and Miranda have stressed the fidelity of liberation theology to a renewed understanding of the message of the Bible.[61] There is much more involved in all this than a new social pastoral activity or missionary strategy. A theology of events or signs of the times is renewing the whole corpus of theology. This is a sign of health for theology itself for it squares with Christian experience. Salvation is a public act of God. There are not two orders of reality, natural and supernatural, an order of creation and an order of redemption. There is only the existential order. The world is mankind itself and all authentic life is life in Christ. The Church is the community consciously affected by the power and presence of God in Christ.

As such the Church must respect the autonomy and inner dynamics of all temporal affairs. The truth and love and justice we now seek for all men will be made perfect in God's Kingdom. But we must seek the Kingdom now through the pursuit of these values as the deepest human values. Failure to do this is sin. Christianity proposes itself as a way of life with an essential meaning for society as well as for the individual. Consequently, underdevelopment is more than a lack of development. It results from sinful oppression and cries out for the liberation of man from man's sinful failure to pursue these basic values. All our actions are directed towards this goal. The very diversity of our activity, be it social, pastoral, liturgical, educational, points up the many areas where man waits to be liberated from internal and external oppressions at the very heart of life. So, whatever the appropriate term, wherever the appropriate emphasis, it is necessary to think of development and liberation as mutually related and intertwined. They can never be dissociated. The liberation movements with their attendant theologies have a role to play wherever there is a lack of participation, a lack of wholeness on the part of any segment of any society. Modernization and consumerism create a situation of enslavement just as truly as sex and racial discrimination do. Liberation tears away the mask of development and progress that hides all kinds of tyrannies and oppressions. Just as a certain level of development is needed in the Third World, so a kind of liberation is needed in Europe and North America to cope with the problem of *overdevelopment* and unlimited material progress as a way of life. We seldom think of overdevelopment as a threat to our freedom and the freedom of others.

If underdevelopment means that there is some sort of failure in realizing certain possibilities for genuine human development, overdevelopment is a kind of growth that has advanced too far *in relation to the culture as a whole.*[62] Bob Goudzwaard believes that the word of God is present in our western society as a *detecting* power for the troubles, miseries, irrationalities, and forces of death in man. But it is also a *liberating* and *directing* power. The former prevents our deepest human-spiritual convictions from being manipulated by practical economic goals; the latter effects a responsible personal choice between obtaining our own luxuries and providing for the hungry and naked. In a very real sense of the word men of good will and those of the Judaeo-Christian tradition in particular are called to discern possible ways of witness to the coming of God's Kingdom, to allow themselves to be 'conscientized' in this whole matter of liberation from overdevelopment, to learn to live simply so that others may simply live. Goudzwaard says:

> A basic rule of that Kingdom is that happiness lies more in giving than receiving, that a man can become rich in Christ by giving away his treasures. In that community social, economic, and racial differences, rather than causing separation, have to intensify genuine communion and solidarity, transforming that community into a real and substantial healing for all who are hurt and broken by an idolatrous culture. Thus we may live today in the perspective of the great day of our Redeemer, a Redeemer whose distant footsteps can already be heard amid the noise of our present society.[63]

It would seem, then, that the dominating theme of our new social consciousness ought not to be oriented towards either underdevelopment or overdevelopment. I would go as far as to say that most Europeans and North Americans have developed a social conscience towards the Third World that is a false conscience. They fail to see that the roots of the Third World problem are deep in their own culture of overdevelopment. Until we see that the concept of development is subordinate to that of liberation, until we see that liberation applies to western and Third World cultures as does development, the booming, buzzing, frenetic charades of institutional charity will continue. So will the ferment of frustration, manipulation, and oppression. Each society must be self-renewing to some extent. This means it must criticize its values and perspectives. The Roman Catholic Church undertook this task in the 1960s. In the same period the United States was torn by radical demands for total change. In both these institutions a period of contemporary demoralization has led to a breakdown in the relationship of the individual to the institution. This is both the risk and hope of any genuine renewal. In a world of larger and more inclusive organizations the individual purpose becomes part of the system's waste-product. Even the leaders of the institution are caught in the system. The queen bee is as much a prisoner of the hive system as any other in it. To solve this very serious problem throughout society at large the concept of liberation for the creative prophetic voice to direct institutional leadership and create the social framework where the common good and individual personal growth are reconciled, however imperfectly, is a basic need in society today. John Gardiner once said: 'Traditionally, we have spent enormous energy exhorting the individual to act responsibly, and very little energy designing the kind of society in which he can act responsibly.'[64] The words of the prophets can be found on subway walls and in tenement halls. There are signs and prophets everywhere. And there are major prophets. They are living voices and signs, directing and pointing our institutions out of the vicious circle of self-perpetuating and self-justifying value systems. Such a major prophet was Ernst Schumacher. He did not pity the Third World or the developing countries. He knew that they have their own technique for survival, something right in their cultural roots. He pitied the West more because western economics seemed like an express train hurtling at ever increasing speed towards an abyss. He recounted a visit to a communist country where this image was applied to the West by his hosts. And then he recounts that there was a short pause followed by the assurance, 'But we shall overtake you.' Schumacher laconically added: 'That is the automatism of progress.'[65] On the same occasion he said: 'If you want to be a good shoemaker, it is not enough to make good shoes, and to know all about making good shoes. You also have to know a lot about feet.' There is a general horror in reaction to any talk of revolution. People associate it with violence. Yet we go on singing the praises of technology, forgetting that a lot of it has become what Schumacher called 'violent technology'. If we practised more appropriate technology, the danger of violent revolution would be greatly reduced.[66] Affluence pursued for its own sake in the name of an abstraction called the 'good life' or 'the great society' does not do much for human life except create more wants than needs. More and more people are talking about an 'alternative society', new lifestyles, a new quality of living, life that depends less on consumption and more on sharing. It accounts in no small part for the community movement of which we will be speaking in the final chapter. For Christians and others the spirit of the Beatitudes (Matt. 5.1–10) becomes an alternative lifestyle, the ethic of the Kingdom of God. The Beatitudes turn possession and temporal security into freedom and simplicity, and open life up to enjoy the wholeness of life shared with us by God, as having nothing, yet possessing all things (2 Cor. 6.10). It is this wholeness of life available for each man and all men everywhere that constitutes development. This notion is related to the biblical concept of justice promoted by the prophets. It is something that goes beyond good sense, or good will, or good order. It is the quest for the radical meaning of peace, of universal shalom. Development which is the search for peace is preceded by liberation which is the search for justice. And so it is in our time. If we are to escape from political rhetoric, we have to continue the ancient quest for justice and peace under new names – liberation and development.

## The mission of the Church

The Christian Church is an evangelizing Church. It believes it has a message of good news for everyman. Liberation and development are essential to that message. The concept of mission, like that of 'Third World', cannot be identified strictly geographically, though it has become a label we put on certain parts of the world. The same may be said of Christian mission which we think of as a movement from one part of the world to another where the Christian Church, its method and ethos, have not yet been established. The shifts in history are subtle, created by new situations and creating them. The Church tends to develop policies and ideologies rather than discern the subtleties of history. A hundred years ago Europe was the nominal centre of Christianity, especially Roman Catholic. This tradition was deeply enshrined in European history and culture. Post-Reformation Christianity, *sui generis* in Britain, left its own Christian culture. That this vestigial Christian culture was able to create the illusion of a contemporary Christian people is all too evident in continental Europe and insular Britain. Moreover, it is a fact that a history of Christian mission has been part of the story of colonial expansion. The great missionary outreach of the latter half of the nineteenth century and the first half of the twentieth has dramatically altered the Christian centre of gravity due to the reception of Christianity in the Third World and its population explosion. The revival of the Church in Latin America since Vatican II can only be described as remarkable. In his impressive work *The Coming of the Third Church* Walbert Bühlmann describes this shift. And though he does not do so primarily in geographical terms, this factor does enter his thesis. The Third Church is made up of the nations which have received their independence since the Second World War. Working on the 1960 Roman Catholic population figures, a little more than half were in Europe and North America. A little less than half were in Africa, South America, Asia, and Oceania. If this trend were to continue, 70 per cent of RC Christians would be in the southern hemisphere by the end of the century. While some of his statistics and projections cover very broad geographical areas and could be subjected to critical analysis, his main point, that the centre of Christian witness and life is shifting, seems valid.[67] As missionary churches become mature local churches, Christian missionaries have to reassess their role and the nature of their mission. The April 1975 issue of the *International Review of Mission* was devoted to the idea of a moratorium on personnel and finance from the western world. However unreal such a proposal may sound, it signals a time to understand what lies behind such a proposal. There is the rejection of the assumption that only the West has the right to evangelize the Third World; that western missionaries have a superior understanding of Christ's teaching and the meaning of salvation. There is the desire for theological and ecclesiastical liberation from the oppressive paternalism of some western missionaries. R. Elliott Kendall of the Conference of British Missionary Societies notes that a moratorium would be a distinct advantage to the Church in Britain because 'it would be a means of arousing Christians in my country to a new attempt to understand and be involved in Christian mission in Britain'. He also thinks that a moratorium 'would help us educate Christians in the congregations to the new situation in the world'.[68] Dr Emilio Castro of the WCC Commission on World Mission and Evangelism sees the purpose of the moratorium as 'a recovery of respective identities in order to achieve more effective missionary action at the local level and more mature relationships among partners in mission'.[69] The suggestion of such a moratorium has meaning for the Ecumenical Movement. On the assumption that it does not represent a retreat into cultural ghettos or enclaves or into denominationalism, it represents a new phase of ecumenism. The older phase had as its aim the reduction of alienation between churches on doctrinal grounds. The newer ecumenism represents a new evaluation of how a diversity of cultures, economic interests, and political ideologies form a part of the mystery of unity in Christ. How that mystery uniquely allows men to have communion with other men *as other* must have its proper witness through the Ecumenical Movement. Ecumenical life is not a levelling experience begetting mediocrity and uniformity. It is a fulfilling and enriching experience in communion with others. Because of its intimate relationship with mission, indeed it is *for mission*, this entire review of missionary motivation and method is vital for a healthy Church. That it is taking place is a sign of hope for ecumenism and the vitality of the Church. We need a pluralistic life and not simply a pluralism in theology. The Churches of Asia, Africa, Latin America and other Churches are looking at things from viewpoints quite different from those of us in Europe and North America. As John Taylor noted in the Church Missionary Society *Newsletter* of November 1974, in which he described developments in the WCC, 'the old interdenominational ecumenism has been overtaken by an immensely wider and more problematical intercultural ecumenism'.[70] This cultural ecumenism takes into account questions of 'selfhood' and 'identity' of which Emilio Castro speaks. Any united Church of the future has to reflect the diversity of gifts associated with the one Holy Spirit. It is not at all ridiculous, though we westerners may be tempted to smile, that a theologian should write a *Waterbuffalo Theology*; that there should be a 'black theology'; or that a book could be written entitled *India and the Latin Captivity of the Church*.[71] These are some of the many signs of this new phase of cultural ecumenism. All this involves more than the mastery of halfway measures in the revision of missionary methods. There is more than adaptation to cultural differences, more than the ability to achieve facile intercultural communication. John Taylor reminds us in the same CMS *Newsletter* that 'we should remember that it is not only a people's ideas that are rooted in a particular culture but the people themselves . . .'. At the same time the quest for identity and selfhood is not a disintegrating development within ecumenism or mission. It is about self-knowledge which leads to the freedom of self-giving and self-dignity. It creates fully equal partners in the ecumenical dialogue and in the common task of evangelization. Cultural ecumenism prevents a vacuum developing in the course of any kind of future moratorium that might be declared. Cultural ecumenism insists on pluralism in unity, identity with mutual recognition, openness, forgiveness and reconciliation. It expresses the Church's life as a community of sharing more than ever before and on a more universal scale. The value of this witness to the rest of the world, the *oikoumene*, is incalculable. Cultural ecumenism is bound to affect the ecumenical dialogue of Europe and North America. Ecumenists have talked a great deal about the non-theological factors in interchurch dialogue. Our Churches *as they are* are the products of history and culture. History is about the past as it lingers on and lives in a collective memory. Culture is about the present context of life, nourished by the past that has entered the very soul of a people. It is easier to leave history behind than to extirpate a culture. The former is necessary, the latter dangerous and undesirable. So when we talk about non-theological factors we are speaking of factors which 'are often the most permanent because they are the stuff of humanity itself'.[72] Our western efforts to rediscover and make visible our Christian unity will be successful to the extent that we are willing to let our history find its place *as past*. But we must go on respecting and sharing our cultural differences *as alive and active and mutually nourishing* the Body of Christ. With a new openness to the Holy Spirit as Lord and Giver of Life we simply go on discerning what really divides us as Christians, not what we feel or imagine divides us. And in this subtle interplay of history, culture, and doctrine under the tutelage of the Spirit the Church will not only be united but renewed for real mission to the world.

It may seem that we have talked about the general characteristics of the liberation movement rather than justifying and substantiating its contribution to contemporary Christian hope. This seemed necessary because of the complexity of the issues involved and the consequent ease with which the movement lays itself open to misunderstanding. Extreme situations beget extreme reactions. This often happens when a moment of history indicates that it is time for an idea to be born or is overdue or an action is simply the result of the fullness of time (*kairos*). South Africa and Rhodesia bring one to the brink of such a reaction. This has already been experienced in the liberation of blacks in the United States. It is in motion among the poor and oppressed of Latin America. There are the undertones of frustration and the overtones of rage in the liberation movements that find their way into corresponding theologies and upset the more respectable and established among

137

the theologians. It is hardly the time or place to plead moderation. The prophets were hardly moderate. Who could be moderate when the shacks of poor workers are bulldozed as part of the preparation for a multi-million-dollar football spectacle in Argentina, truly a place of the shirtless ones, oppressed and manipulated, participants in one of history's grand spectacles? Through the liberation movement the Christian Church has an opportunity to manifest its prophetic nature and its fidelity to the ministry of Christ. Liberation theology and the movement it expresses rests on a refusal to accept the world as it is, as less than it is destined to become. This theology rests on doing the truth in genuine love. By its mutual inclusion of biblical exegesis, sociological analysis, and practical engagement, it brings the Church and world into a living relationship of the sacred and the secular, the religious and the profane, the unity of creative and redemptive forces which is the fundamental of Christian hope. The unity of mankind, the true *oikoumene* or family of God, is the object of this hope. It would prove a dangerous imbalance if the Christian witness and participation were missing from a movement of expanding awareness that is spreading over the globe in a first wave of protest and liberation and deschooling. Theology will modify its own abstract nature, taking on a pastoral dimension that puts it in the service of the life of faith as it actually resides in people in concrete life situations. Theology as such is a gift of the Spirit who is able to direct and establish the proportionate act of faith that God may be asking of his people in a particular time or place. It is in this sense that liberation theology serves faith. Because of the issues which form its subject matter, liberation theology directs Christians to a response of faith that is proportionate and adequate to achieve certain goals which are aligned with the establishment of his Kingdom. Christians make their response of faith by exploring the immensity of the universe and the secrets of the heart of matter. But they also must face the immensity of moral problems unleashed by knowledge and *technē*. Their proper concern is human existence and the human capacity to create the conditions of love and self-sacrifice that will correspond to an almost universal awareness of situations that need to be redeemed and transformed. It is a utopic capacity created to dream and hope for new ways to live together on the earth. It is the urge to say 'why not' instead of 'why' to all that promises a future for man and a future for God's ways with us on the earth. Now the point in saying all this is to stress the need for a faith and a spirituality that effects a vital attitude, a searching spirit committed to bring everything together. Liberation theology with its insistence on the mutual interaction of theory and praxis keeps the great truths about man and his world alive in the hearts of those who are committed to make and find the fullest measure of truth about man and his resources.

The notion of real commitment which is so vital for faith and which makes hope real undergirds the theology of the liberation movement. We are so used to associating faith with intellectual assent or with psychological conviction that we tend to forget it is the response of the whole person. Faith engages the energetic response of the whole person, and eventually the whole community of faith. Liberation theologians and educators and participants allow for nothing prior to a commitment to human liberation. Only then can we really talk about social praxis and the gospel. So very often we confuse the act of faith with subscription to an ideology. Faith makes a total commitment that creates an ideology provisionally, i.e., a vision that expresses and embodies our faith in the particularity of the present circumstance. This commitment cannot be intellectualized or tamed as soon as it is made because it is immediately put in the context of a choice for the right means to attain those goals that represent liberation and development, the first fruits of the Kingdom of God. It seems to me that by a more immediate relationship of means and ends the danger of turning the gospel into middle-class ethics, an ethics of self-righteousness, is reduced. More important, however, Christian moral theology cannot be reduced to a speculative science which focuses almost exclusively on the rightness or wrongness of human acts in themselves without proportionate emphasis on how these human acts are situated in the wider context of life and relationships. Contextual moral theology brings both a necessity and a dignity to moral decisions, making such decisions also an act of faith. In line with this liberation theology the eschatological character of Christian moral theology is renewed. The Kingdom of God is to be anticipated by a life of contemplation and struggle. This anticipation is often witnessed to by a commitment that affects our lifestyle profoundly. The decision of one man and one woman to live in a unique, covenanted relationship with each other certainly does this. The decision of some men and women to live a celibate life, despite the human problems that such a decision may involve, requires a deep Christian spirituality to sustain such a decision. Such spirituality can make the Kingdom of God that much more real if it is genuine. In a world in which the Kingdom has not yet come there are doubts, difficulties, ambivalence, and ambiguity attached to all moral-eschatological decisions. It is not all nice and orderly and clinical as hagiographers and ultra-spiritualists would have us believe. There is always the struggle and the possibility of failure attached to any commitment. Human life is fragile and if it is lived for others it can bring us close to the brink of personal disintegration at times. It may seem that we are in danger of counteracting the ideals and values espoused for the sake of Christ. These personal decisions are more than decisions about marriage and celibacy, however. From all sorts of backgrounds Christians may be faced with decisions of how best to promote God's Kingdom of justice, peace, and love. It may be a decision to take part in an armed struggle for liberation as a tragic necessity in a particular situation. Or it may be the even more painful decision to make a non-violent protest, living with all the consequences. Such Christians bear witness both by their commitment and their struggle that the paschal mystery is one of light and darkness, life and death, justice and love, that it is the central mystery and paradox of Christian life, one not only to be contemplated but to be lived. Our Christian witness to the coming of God's Kingdom is not an undifferentiated faceless witness. It is pluralistic and personal, differentiating communities themselves, calling for a variety of works, ministries, and charisms in a spectrum of human situations. The pluralistic nature of liberation thinking contributes to the development of the theological method. But its greater value is the reality it brings to our Christian commitment to justice and peace. We cannot talk about building a civilization of love without engaging in rhetoric if our commitment is in any way removed from the true situation of men who have to live in conditions far below basic human standards, far removed from ordinary standards of justice and dignity. The Christian commitment is to shift priorities in such a way that the promised reign of God with its fullness of justice, peace, and love is somehow already experienced as present among men. The great merit of Christian witness within the liberation movements is the capacity to provide a living experience of the biblical understanding of the centrality of justice. The practice of justice is the only norm we have for making the love of God meaningful and incarnate in a human expression. We have read the Old Testament for so long as a promise to send a saviour in the transworldly sense of the term that we forget he came to save us *from* our own narrowness and selfishness. He saves us through self-sacrifice and suffering. This is God's way of justice – not a comfortable balance of shared material goods, but an equal opportunity for all the members of a fully humanized community to live beyond themselves for others. Such an ideal is unrelated to the real order of things apart from a commitment to suffer and struggle for fundamental justice, to bear one another's burdens and so fulfil the law of Christ. The law of Christ is love. His teachings show us how we will have to live together eventually. That this life can be anticipated prophetically is the meaning of Christian life itself. Yet the participation will bear the marks of our present human limitations and sinfulness.

This renewal of biblical understanding concerning the centrality of justice in the gospel message is the basis of hope for a renewed sense of mission and renewed structures for mission. This does not mean a switch to setting up humanitarian 'front operations', of substituting tractors for tracts, as Professor Hollenweger puts the option in *Evangelism Today*.[73] The insight of liberation theology is that liberation and development belong together. In the last analysis mission is not what we bring to a people, or even what we get from them. It is what we do among them in the name of Christ for the common good of a particular people. This demands discernment to match fervour. Speaking of the people of Madagascar, Professor Hollenweger asks what the point is in providing tractors to build stone monuments to appease ancestral spirits, leaving little time or energy to set up workshops to train mechanics. Is it not a prior task to liberate them from this fear of ancestral displeasure so that real human development can take place? And this development can take place only by breaking an ancient caste system by demonstrating that this people can be educated *together*. Mission is always something that happens within a community of people *from within*. The work of the Evangelist is to discern where the genuine need for liberation and development lie. As animators of such liberation and development, Evangelist missionaries become fellow workers with God in creating a land of freedom and humanity prepared to receive the seed of God's word for a new birth of freedom and humanity (1 Cor. 3.9; 2 Cor. 5.16–20; 6.1–3).

Someone has suggested we think big and act small.[74] He means that we need a large view of the world that will match the dignity and grandeur of God's calling and purpose such as we find expressed in the first chapter of Ephesians. We need a quality of caring that is particular and close to the earth. We need a caring, an outreach that takes into account the needs of those closest to us, within our homes and communities, joined to a vision of the dispossessed throughout the earth. I would suggest that we learn to hope big and expect small returns, but steady returns. By this I mean that we must not set limits to what God can do in our world if we lend him our commitment to pursue peace and justice. He is greater than our hearts (1 John 3.20). But he is also gracious and humble and works with our limitations and within our capacities. He makes our future his own. Our expectations are never met on our terms for we set limits to the love of God poured into our hearts and therefore to the possibilities of life. But with the gifts of faith and love he gives us hope that carries us beyond the despair and discouragement of the moment to the next particular human insight and commitment. And somehow we know that this present human effort stands for much more than an impossible dream, a quixotic adventure. For it assures us of a future when all manner of things shall be well and the fire and the rose are one. In the meantime we live with another truth that must be borne: Nothing so resembles the human epic as the way of the cross.[75]

# 5

# The Neo-Pentecostal Movement

*The Holy Spirit is at work in our society, and the effect may prove to be as disconcerting and unexpected as it was for the apostles.*

**Cardinal Hume to the Church of England Synod**

Going from the liberation movement to the neo-Pentecostal one to substantiate Christian hope may seem to be a leap rather than a simple progression. Yet, both movements are about freedom. One explores the meaning of freedom for man in society; the other explores the meaning of freedom for Christians in their community of faith. One is about freedom from external bondage of many kinds in order to free men to live creatively and with dignity, to become more fully alive, more fully human; the other is about freedom from interior bondage so that Christians may be free to express the fullness of life God shares with men and women in anticipation of his coming Kingdom (John 3.8). Using the image of depth we could say that one is a movement from the external life of man to a deeper personal centre of his existence; the other is a movement from the centre of inner life to a manifestation of the praise and liberating activity of the Holy Spirit in the depth of the human spirit in its orientation towards God, and in its search for communion among men. The neo-Pentecostal movement witnesses to the freedom of the Holy Spirit to renew the wonderful works of God in our midst at this time in order to renew the credibility of the Church's holiness and mission. The Christian vocation is to make the presence of the risen Christ manifest in its own life and in the life of the world. This must be a transforming, liberating presence. It must provide a sense of solidarity that is nourished by hope, courage, and vision to build the city of man where God will eventually choose to live (Rev. 21). As the movement matures it seems to me that we will discover a dimension of Christian spirituality that is experiential and life-giving to such an extent that the praxis of liberation, the exercise of freedom, is preserved from the danger of confusion with any humanistic ideology. The liberation movement will be preserved from being neutralized and sterilized by excessive theorizing and intellectual abstraction.

There are various ways to refer to the neo-Pentecostal movement which embodies religious experience and expressions of New Testament spirituality. There is no one experience or name that can be attached that will keep everyone happy. The virtue of choosing one name for the movement and sticking to it in a particular discussion lies in the clarity and simplicity it brings to the discussion. Over and above this I find that the use of the adjective 'charismatic' to describe the movement is subject to inflation. Also I prefer to relate the term 'charismatic' to Christian life and spirituality in a wider, more comprehensive meaning that takes into account a fundamental recognition that there is a vast spectrum of God's gifts to the Church in the one gift of the Holy Spirit for its life and mission. These gifts may be differentiated as sensational or unsensational, ordinary or extraordinary, usual or unusual.[1] They range from miracles to good teaching, to administration. God's gifts always respect human nature and talent. But the reality of his grace is much more than the simple embellishment of either. It is 'gift' and as such creates in those who receive it such a new depth of faith, love, and service, such a new docility to be led by the Holy Spirit that it represents a newness of life, indeed a new creation.

Therefore I shall be referring to the movement as neo-Pentecostalism. I do this to distinguish it without separating it from other spiritual movements which are of the Spirit and also involve the reception of spiritual gifts. Indeed, the institutional life of the Church is a gift of Christ (Eph. 4. 7–16). Secondly, I use the term for historical and ecumenical reasons. It has to be related to the Pentecostal movement dating from the turn of the century. It is often associated with events in American Protestantism such as those of the Methodist Bible School at Topeka, Kansas in 1901 and the Azuza Street revival in Los Angeles in 1906. These Pentecostal groups grew out of the holiness movement in the latter half of the nineteenth century in the United States. Today we refer to them as classical Pentecostals.[2] When we speak of a neo-Pentecostal movement, we are indicating a manifestation of some of the characteristics of classical Pentecostalism. This is not to identify the two movements in such a way that one appears to be simply the revival of the other. Neo-Pentecostalism is wider in the range of the spiritual experience it seeks to incorporate and much more comprehensive in the theological traditions which articulate this spiritual experience. Thirdly, neo-Pentecostalism refers to that 'new Pentecost' for which Pope John prayed for the success of the Second Vatican Council, a Pentecost that is happening within the Christian Churches. It is the renewal of radical Christian living in all the Churches as a result of experiencing an outpouring of the Holy Spirit. This outpouring is paradigmatically presented in the account found in the Acts of the Apostles. The Acts of the Apostles is an account of how the early Christian community developed through that outpouring of the Spirit, of how it came to understand its life and mission. It is also an account of how the power from on high was exercised to confirm the truth of the gospel of Jesus as a proclamation that the Kingdom of God had already been established among men. The Acts of the Apostles does not attempt to circumscribe the actual process of how God works among men. But it does remain open to the mighty acts of God that proclaim his Kingdom. And it speaks of the manifold ways of God's action and the possibilities of new life in a new creation, e.g., the cure of a lame man (Acts 3. 1–10). Therefore Acts is about the nature of the Church and its mission. The Church is a community of faith living out the dynamic of God's love and power given to it at Pentecost 'that the world may believe' (John 17.21). Renewal in this sense is always about Pentecost – not as past, but as promise, fulfilled in every age. Through the activity of the Spirit the life of God manifested in Jesus is made available now and in the future. If the Pentecostal theme of Acts is invoked and repeated, it is not because neo-Pentecostalism is trying to revive and repeat a pristine, golden age of the Church. Such an amateurish re-enactment of Acts would be both romantic and dangerous. Neo-Pentecostalism is a response of faith in Pentecost as an ongoing event of Christian life and mission. It is as much about the present and the future as it is about the past. In fact it is more about the future because when we study the New Testament 'we should always have in mind . . . the futuristic aspect of the Church', since 'it does not yet appear what the Church shall be', for we know that the Church 'anticipates in hope the life of the age to come'.[3] Consequently, neo-Pentecostals need not get all mixed up with fundamentalism or literalism in their understanding of Acts. They read the Bible and love the Scriptures as a precious gift of God to his Church. If they look to an apostolic age, it is because they have become aware that events and experiences are interwoven as a paradigm to interpret the events and experiences of contemporary Christian life. The same Spirit is at work now. Consequently many of them speak more of renewal than they do of revival. Revival has undertones of a kind of artificial spiritual respiration or of resuscitation of former life. Renewal is about making something new in a new way, in a way that has not happened quite the same way ever before. Renewal is about continuity, not repetition. Both terms can be used to signify a new act of obedience to God. But renewal, making all things new, is the promise of God himself (Rev. 21.5). This is the promise inherent in a 'new Pentecost' in any age. Christians who claim the promise and appropriate it in faith for the building-up of the Church need not be ashamed to have what is at present a movement within their Church described as neo-Pentecostal. 'The neo-Pentecostal movement challenges the Church to accept by faith that which has already been granted by grace.'[4]

As with the liberation movement, so with the neo-Pentecostal movement, one encounters strong bias against the movement. The bias is rooted in misunderstanding. And while it is not my purpose here to justify the movement, if it is to be seen as a sign of hope for the Christian Church, some of the misunderstanding will have to be cleared up as we move along. Since the neo-Pentecostal movement dates from the late 1950s and early 1960s, we are just now at a stage where preliminary evaluations can be made, where the light of self-criticism can be turned on, where the disciplines of sociology, psychology, and theology can be employed through their interaction to help Christians come to a charitable and fair assessment of neo-Pentecostalism. Kilian McDonnell has contributed a valuable work, *Charismatic Renewal and the Church*, from which I have already quoted. His work is critically drawn from the findings of these various disciplines. I would share with him the conviction that the neo-Pentecostal movement is central to the renewal of the Church. It is not in any sense peripheral or optional, for it is a major movement of the Holy Spirit renewing the Church in an essential understanding of its life and mission. Moreover, it is related to the other major movements of the Spirit of which we are speaking in this book, not least the Ecumenical

Movement. In 1972 I suggested in a more or less tentative fashion that the new wave of Pentecostalism was of significance for the Ecumenical Movement.[5] It has now become a personal conviction of mine that it has an essential role to play in ecumenism. For that reason I must confess to moments of anxiety over Roman Catholic participation. The RC contribution is so substantial that I fear it could form a separate current in the movement, apart from an intense commitment to the cause of Christian unity.[6] Kilian McDonnell has done his work on an ecumenical basis. He says that 'in all the denominational expressions there is a deeper concern for rooting the movement in the theologies of the respective traditions while at the same time rejecting a narrow denominationalism'. And he adds: 'The charismatic renewal in the historic Church is *de facto* ecumenical.'[7]

There are two main contentions that come up in more sophisticated circles. These are theories which attempt to explain why the neo-Pentecostal movement happened at all. First, it is explained as the result of a breakdown in society or as the result of economic or social deprivation. McDonnell has shown how neither of these theories really stands up to the test. He would not deny that they are totally unrelated to the movement, that they facilitate the rise of such a movement. But he would deny that they are the real causes of the movement in the sense that they *determine* it.[8] Second, it is explained as a phenomenon constituted by marginal people among whom there is a great deal of abnormality. Again McDonnell illustrates the inadequacy of the scientific research to demonstrate such an hypothesis. In looking at the developments within the movement over a period of eight years he found that 'diversity of every kind is typical of the Pentecostal-charismatic movement: social, economic, educational, religious, and psychological'.[9] A survey of relatively recent studies likewise feeds into a growing consensus that neo-Pentecostals are not abnormal people. While McDonnell acknowledges that further psychological research into the movement is warranted, he says that the period from 1967 to 1975 ends 'not with complete psychological vindication . . . but with elements which might, in the future, issue in a consensus'.[10]

In the beginning of the movement much more was heard about how divisive it was. A frequent objection to it was that it developed an attitude that those who had had the neo-Pentecostal experience were more fully Christian. It created a kind of first- and second-class church membership. There is no doubt that one can find such an attitude. It comes from either theological error or spiritual immaturity. In the earlier years of the movement there was a closer dependence on classical Pentecostalism with its stress on 'baptism in (of) the Spirit' strictly conjoined to the gift of tongues (*glossolalia*). In many cases the theological language of the classical Pentecostals was taken over uncritically by the neo-Pentecostals. The latter had learned to express their very real spiritual experience in this classical Pentecostal idiom. As the movement matures and theological understanding develops, there seems to be a lessening of this sort of dependence and the charge of divisiveness diminishes. But this does not mean that the move-ment has ceased to be either an explosive or a divisive issue. Both spiritual immaturity and theological misunderstanding, as well as theological differences, part and parcel of church life, are sharply focused on and within neo-Pentecostalism. However, differences could be resolved with greater success were there a greater open-ness and spiritual understanding operative in Christian spirituality in our church traditions, less defensiveness and self-satisfaction, less bias towards immediate religious experience, a greater appreciation of the charismatic nature of the Church. The fault does not lie on one side only. If the Churches continue indefinitely to be content to let neo-Pentecostalism remain a movement, it could well become divisive, dangerously divisive, within the Church and among Christians. This could well happen were we to continue with the attitude that the charismatic dimension of church life is separate from or peripheral to the institutional life of the Church. It seems to me that the process of renewal ought to move from a definite Pentecostal experience ('baptism in (or of) the Spirit', for want of a better term), accompanied by some of the Spirit's gifts that manifest it, towards a charismatic spiri-tuality that reflects the very nature of the Church as an institution born of God's Spirit, differentiated from the institutions of the world, and prophetic of the 'invasion' of the Kingdom of God. We ought to stop talking about a charismatic dimension which can be opposed to some sort of institutional dimension, as though these were somehow in tension and competition with each other.

I think it is important to remember that neo-Pentecostalism is a movement. Like other movements it focuses attention on forgotten or half-remembered truths. As movement it is meant to cease and find its meaning in something larger and more unifying, more related to the intrinsic nature of things. For this reason I prefer to speak of a narrow Pentecostal experience which stresses 'baptism in the Spirit' as a second call or vocation to a life of Christian holiness and wholeness. By this I do not mean a second spiritual baptism in contradistinction to a first sacramental baptism. I refer to a new manifestation and experience of the Holy Spirit which opens the heart of the believing Christian to a new beginning that enables him to live with a radical openness to God as the present living source of spiritual love and power. The experience is one either of release that comes from the activity of the Spirit within one's self or of an infilling of the Spirit from beyond one's self. The manifestation is effected through *charismata* or gifts. These may be the gifts of tongues, their interpretation in Christian gatherings, prophecy, healing, discernment of spirits, exorcism, teaching, and others that contribute to building up personal spiritual life and the lives of others *as members of the Body of Christ*. I have mentioned these few by way of example. These gifts or *charismata* witness to the renewed activity of God in the individual and within the community of believers. They witness to the reality of the divine presence and power among us. This experience enables us to understand that the life of the whole Church is a gift of God. This leads one to speak of a wider charismatic renewal movement. This is concerned with *the whole range of God's gifts* for the Church. These gifts include those of a more permanent institutional nature such as sacraments and ministerial offices. In this context the Scriptures are his gift to the Church. Then, in varying degrees of value and function for building up a Christian life of love for others and friendship with God, come those mentioned in connection with the Pentecostal experience of Acts or in relation to a community such as the Corinthian Christians or those at Rome for whom Paul mentions certain gifts. Those gifts mentioned in Scripture need not exhaust the creative activity of the Holy Spirit. The variety and number cannot be limited because the Spirit cannot be limited as he works in each age of faith. This wider charismatic spirituality reduces the danger of creating two levels of Christian life and witness. It prevents the introduction of a fundamental divergence of prophetic witness from ordinary witness in the life of the Church. This makes the charismatic element an element of renewal by focusing attention on the fullness of life in the Holy Spirit, a fresh opening to the operation of the Spirit which can lead to deep contemplation and a dynamic missionary movement towards the world. It enables Christians to manifest the charismatic nature of the Church as an institution prophetic of the coming Kingdom of God. The Church extends the anointing and consecration of Jesus by the Holy Spirit for communion with God and as a vibrant sign of the Father's loving care for the world. There is no doubt in my mind that the neo-Pentecostal movement has helped Christians to a better understanding of what church membership means, namely sharing, reflecting through the Scriptures on the life of faith, and reaching out to others in word and deed with the good news of God in Christ. Charismatic spirituality assures us that the Pentecostal experience is an ongoing relationship with God, not an isolated experience. It is a new relationship with the Holy Spirit inasmuch as one listens to the gospel with new sensitivity and obedience, with a new orientation of one's life to Christ as Lord. The neo-Pentecostal movement leads to new efforts to build Christian community as an essential aspect of church life. But I should like to stress charismatic renewal as *the development of a spirituality*, as something wider than a movement and more ongoing than an experience, something that grows out of a central experience called 'baptism in the Spirit' with its extraordinary experience of God's active presence through the manifestation of certain gifts of the Spirit. Charismatic spirituality which ought to be part of ordinary Christian spirituality is renewed by the neo-Pentecostal experience. Yet, it has the task of integrating the experience in order to give it meaning and value for building up the one who experiences the Spirit and his gifts *as a member of the Church*. Both the experience and the ensuing spirituality reflect authentic New Testament witness to the nature of the Church as a community which is a special recipient of grace and the outpouring of the Spirit of God. These gifts and this outpouring witness to the newness of the covenant relationship with God, a relationship that makes the Church the people of God and the Body of Christ. Moreover, they witness to the new birth of freedom in Christ (2 Cor. 3.17). Church leaders see the tension all too often as one between charism and institution. We have mentioned this already. My point in bringing it up again is by way of arguing that judgements about the movement ought not to be prejudiced by what René Laurentin calls 'a tormented theology'.[11] The present is never simply a repetition of the past. We must look for the newness of the present and the opportunity that comes with this newness. If we believe in the newness of the gospel, then we hope that the Church is being moved by the Spirit to get beyond where it has been and where it is. We cannot appeal to the conflicts, tensions, the record of failures in Christian history. A basic claim of the gospel is to make all things new. The promise of God cannot be set aside (Rev. 21.5), our sinful condition notwithstanding. The basis of Christian hope is the faith that we can achieve in the Spirit all that is genuinely part of the Christian proclamation and promise. If Christians are unlike other men, it is because they refuse to accept the past as *totally normative*. They simply go on trying to do what has not yet been done with a measure of success worthy of the gospel. This can be applied as a principle in each situation. Therefore, it applies to the effort to integrate the neo-Pentecostal experience and its subsequent charismatic spirituality into the institutional life of the Church. What is needed is a common recognition of the validity of the neo-Pentecostal experience and a renewed evaluation of the centrality of the charisms or spiritual gifts in the life of the Church. Such recognition and evaluation will depend in great part on a Christian spirituality that relates grace and nature. Any spirituality that fails to do so cannot help being unbalanced, out of focus, and scarcely able to perform a healthy critical function *vis-à-vis* the neo-Pentecostal movement and its attendant spirituality.

The relationship between nature and grace is acknowledged in the dialogue that has been set up between classical Pentecostals and Roman Catholics.[12] In the first meeting of the participants of the dialogue there seemed to be common agreement:

> Both sides agree that life in the Holy Spirit can be manifested in signs and be accompanied by charisms which are gratuitous manifestations of the Holy Spirit working in and through, but going beyond, the believer's natural ability for the common good of the people of God. (Mark 16.17–18)[13]

This position tries to avoid the extremes of over-supernaturalizing the charisms where every manifestation is a miracle or of reducing them to psychological states, or presenting them with a purely sociological explanation. For example, the gift of tongues presupposes the natural faculty of speech. It brings a new function to this faculty so that by the power of the Spirit one receives the power to pray and praise God at a very deep level. In this way his personal spiritual life is built up and the life of his church community. Therefore McDonnell says that 'a charism is a gift because that capacity has a new function and a new power'.[14] A charism is more than the 'exercise of a capacity which pertains to the fullness of humanity'.[15] While Christian experience has taught the Church to respect the gift of discernment of spirits (1 Thess. 5.19–22) where spiritual-paranormal phenomena are in evidence, it is important to recall that the genuine spiritual nature of such an experience cannot be judged solely by a phenomenological approach according to the isolated method of natural science. It must be judged in a Christian context and the results of scientific method must take this wider context into account (Gal. 5.22). In this way psychology, sociology, anthropology, and linguistics all become valuable tools for such discernment.

Another difficulty with the neo-Pentecostal movement stems from an impression that it prefers to keep its independence, reluctant to fit into church life, to be part of the church community. This is certainly not true of the Roman Catholic stream. I would doubt that it is true of other mainline Churches. There is no evidence at this stage of the movement sliding into schism nor of widespread contempt for the organized Church. This seems to be a much more common attitude outside the movement. There is often sadness and disappointment and even chagrin that ordinary church life and worship is so dull and spiritless, so uncreative, unimaginative, and uncaring. But this is a complaint heard as often from people not attached to the movement. So, there is no extensive evidence that the movement wants to be a Church within a Church. Nor is there evidence that neo-Pentecostals are less orthodox in the tenets of their respective churches than other church members.[16] It is fair to suppose that they do not understand how the integration into wider church life takes place, how the freshness and dynamism of the movement is to be preserved in such integration. They do not wish to be marginalized. They do not wish history to be repeated either by rejection or by a devitalizing assimilation into church life. For this reason neo-Pentecostalism will remain a movement for some time to come.

Movements of the Spirit are very subtle. They are seldom like political decisions. In this sense the integration of neo-Pentecostalism is already under way and the spiritual renewal represented by it is being shared with many who would not count themselves in the movement, particularly through shared prayer groups and days of renewal. A Roman Catholic writer says:

> The charismatic renewal just may be one of the doors the Lord is asking Christians of our day to open . . . not necessarily in the sense of joining and associating with 'charismatic groups', but in the sense of living by the Spirit and having the gifts of the Holy Spirit at work in their lives.[17]

The process of integration will stand a better chance if such openness can be created in the practising Christian community. However, if neo-Pentecostalism is going to remain a movement for some time to come, then it ought to be recognized as such. It is not a fad or passing enthusiasm. It is a movement. René Laurentin defines a movement as 'a spontaneous, collective impulse that arises from the ranks in response to needs and that creates from within its own coherent structure'.[18] Laurentin maintains that neo-Pentecostalism shows all those characteristics and consequences, namely it answers a need, it focuses on essential values, it provides a synthesis of these values. What would some of these values be? Looking especially at the neo-Pentecostal renewal in the Roman Catholic community, aware that similar needs and values are present in other Churches, with some variations perhaps, we can list the following:

(1) Dissatisfaction with social involvement alone;

(2) dissatisfaction with ecclesiastical reform, e.g., the institutional bureaucratic approach to Christian unity, liturgical reform;

(3) dissatisfaction with the lack of spiritual fruition and fulfilment, i.e., mission and adaptation without inner renewal of the Church and the person;

(4) a turning to prayer and a searching of the heart for answers to the spiritual malaise, joined to a desire not to abandon social involvement or church reform, but to renew and transform this involvement and reform.

(5) a new expectancy through reflection, reading, and contacts

with other Christians, that the Holy Spirit can transform,
renew, and empower our lives;

(6) 'baptism in the Holy Spirit' becomes a deeply personal
event that brings gifts for one's own needs and for others,
transforming, empowering, renewing;

(7) this experience creates a desire for prayer, a love of Holy
Scripture, the revival of piety and devotion in daily living;

(8) a new sense of Christian community with its appropriate
outreach;

(9) an attempt to 'order' the new experience through theological articulation, an effort to stay in touch with church authority, and a measure of internal organization.

Looking back over this relatively short period of church history,
the blessings of this experience seem so abundant and evident that
I never cease to wonder at the virulent opposition towards it, the
distrust of it. It has helped millions of Christians understand that
their effectiveness lies in their real sense of dependence on the
power and presence of the Holy Spirit in their lives and activities.
When people come close to this renewal movement, their faith
comes alive in an unprecedented way. God is giving the Church
a sense of being his people and a sense that his people must be
one in essential matters of faith and seen to be so. It gives them
a sense of vocation (1 Pet. 2.9–10). It has restored to the Christian
churches the experience of a diversified and ranging ministry that
God intends for our time. Tongues, healing, prophecy, and other
gifts of the Spirit with which we have been unfamiliar too long
are symbols of the power and relevance of the gospel to change,
to heal and make whole, to discern the many things that have
gone wrong in God's world and how God is asking us to put them
right. All this has been experienced on an unprecedented scale as
part of ordinary Christian life, to open it up and unfold it through
growth, to empower and release it as a force to renew the face of
the earth.[19] But it is a movement that must be taken into the life
of the Church, not the life of the Church as an imperturbable
massive force destined to preserve a moral and spiritual *status
quo*, characterized by its anxiety over doctrines evolved under the
Spirit in response to an historic revelation. It is meant for a Church
that is still on the way, a pilgrim Church, a Church that 'is still in
the making, that Church which is ahead of us'.[20] It would be a

mistake to talk about the integration of any movement into a closed Church, a Church convinced of its own final and fully formed entity. The Church has always had the gifts of the Spirit essential for its life and mission. Its claim to faith in the Holy Spirit as an abiding presence shows the ongoing need of this Spirit to make manifest experientially its holiness, unity, catholicity, and apostolicity. It is a Church with a present need and a future mission as well as the possessor of gifts bestowed in the past for its ongoing life. It needs new and fresh gifts for a new and fresh response to God. The faith and spirituality of one time and place may not provide the response of faith or spirituality needed for another time and place. The faith Peter needed to leave possessions and family to follow Jesus was not the same proportion of faith he needed to walk to Jesus across the water. The Church is conditioned by its history. To be faithful to God it must remain unconditionally open to its future and not condition its hope by a precipitous, unthinking determination of what its life must be in the future. This is precisely why it needs the experience and spirituality of the neo-Pentecostal movement. The Church cannot stay where it is. As Hollenweger says, 'too much has happened in the charismatic and ecumenical field'.[21] I would add that too much has happened in our world. Only a spirituality that sustains the Church in facing a particularly opaque and risky future will be good enough. Only a spirituality that builds on the ecumenical foundations being laid will be in a position to show a genuinely catholic face to the world. Again Hollenweger: 'For it seems to me, the spirituality of our ecumenism and the ecumenicity (or catholicity) of our spirituality will be the acid test for all we do in the Church.'[22] There is no expression of faith, spirituality, or ecumenicity that better synthesizes these elements than the neo-Pentecostal movement. In an interview given in 1973 by Cardinal Suenens to Ralph Martin, at that time editor of *New Covenant*, the Cardinal said that he believed very strongly that the implementation of Vatican II involved a renewal of the structures and forms of the institutional Church.[23] During the Council it is well known how hard the Cardinal worked to have the principles of collegiality and co-responsibility adopted in letter and spirit by the Council. He wanted life in the Church to be more conducive to the full participation of all members of the Church. This was the practical meaning behind the images of the Church as the people of God and the Body of Christ. In this interview he said:

> But now I see more clearly than ever the need for the development of a grassroots charismatic renewal if co-responsibility and collegiality are ever to come to life. I see a profound complementarity between the achievement of true co-responsibility and the development of an authentic charismatic renewal among *the whole people of God*. We need a renewal in the *widespread experience* of the gifts of the Spirit for co-responsibility to become a reality. . . . The Church is the Body of Christ. The structures and forms of the Body are important, but it is the Spirit that gives it life. We need to continue to work on the structures and form, but the more important thing is the renewal of the life of the Holy Spirit within the Church. I think it is very logical that my concern for co-responsibility should lead me to see an *authentic action* of God in the charismatic renewal.[24]

On the occasion of the tenth anniversary of the entrance of Roman Catholics into the neo-Pentecostal movement, a Professor of Religious Philosophy at Heythrop College in London pressed the claim for integration directly. In an article in *The Tablet* Michael Simpson said:

> It follows that it is quite wrong to speak of 'charismatic renewal' as if this were some movement alongside others in the Church to which one might or might not belong. The Christian life as such *is* the work of the Spirit forming us into the life of Christ and empowering us to communicate that life to others. It is the Christian life that by its very nature is charismatic: there can be no life in Christ other than through the free gift of God's Spirit.[25]

These are examples of how Christians of the largest Christian tradition esteem and relate this movement to the spiritual renewal of their Church. I think that the ecumenical value associated with the people-of-God image of the Church is important for this work of integrating neo-Pentecostalism into our understanding of the Church. I mean that the Church is a special locus of grace and the activity of the Holy Spirit. In his letter to the Romans Paul mentions the gifts Israel had received from God as predilection, namely sonship, God's special presence (his glory), the covenants, the law, the worship, the promises (Rom. 9.4–6). He quotes Hosea: 'Those who were not my people I will call "my people", and her who was not beloved I will call "my beloved" ' (verse 25). This vocation as the beloved community of God has brought the Church into existence. Extended and fulfilled by a new covenant with new glory (2 Cor. 4.6) and new promises, an even more intimate sonship (Rom. 8.14–16), a perfect heavenly worship (Heb. 7.23–8; 8.1–7), the law of love (John 13.34–5), the Church 'was prepared for in a remarkable way throughout the history of the people of Israel and by means of the Old Covenant'.[26] The Church, and it cannot be insisted on too much, is an institution born of the Spirit and related to the coming Kingdom of God. 'Established in the present era of time, the Church was made manifest by the outpouring of the Spirit.'[27] It is to this community that God gives special gifts as the special object of his love and favour. Since the extension of God's saving plan is to all men, God has no favourites (Acts 10.34–5). But because the Church is meant to be a sign and light among the nations, it shares in a special way the mystery of God's love for all. As a beloved community, a pledge of the coming Kingdom of God, it is the recipient of special gifts. These gifts are functional in so far as they maintain the life of the church community. These may be offices of authority, sacraments to celebrate the life of the community in life and worship, inspired Scriptures to record the activity of God among men, his relationship with them, his promises to them. But the Holy Spirit is *the* Gift, the Lord and Giver of Life. He is the 'first gift to those who believe' (RC Eucharistic Prayer IV). He is the very soul of the Body of Christ and reaches every part, every member of it. In this sense only are his gifts ordinary. But there are gifts which anticipate the life of the Kingdom and promote the good news of its arrival in Jesus Christ. These gifts are the word made flesh; they break into our temporal existence to remind us that the advent of our God is near. They are prophetic gifts. And while I am aware of differences among theologians on the most suitable adjectives to associate with spiritual gifts, i.e., *charismata*, it seems helpful to distinguish those more *functional* from those more *prophetic*, knowing full well that one can never exclude the other. Both functional and prophetic gifts build up the believing community in its life and in its mission. The Church as a prophetic community and institution is open to each and every authentic manifestation and gift of the Spirit. The prophetic and functional distinction of spiritual gifts is not a rigid one and there is no evidence in the New Testament that they are meant to be such. Thus, if we can speak of a ministry of healing, it can imply the skill of a Christian doctor or nurse, the sacrament of healing, or the spiritual gift exercised by one who has the gift. All three are an exercise in the healing ministry of Jesus. Those whose life is in Christ are involved in all three. Yet the first is closely allied with the professional cultivation of a natural talent; the second with a formal external sign of Christ's healing grace administered in the name of the Church by an ordained person; the third with a personal gift exercised in virtue of a free bestowal. All three are of the Spirit and in Christ. However, the third exercise of the healing ministry manifests the prophetic activity of Christ's ministry announcing the Kingdom in a more prophetic way. It manifests and anticipates the newness of the Kingdom.[28] One thing is certain. The spiritual gifts are in the context of faith and increase the faith Jesus demands for those who follow him and announce his Kingdom. Neo-Pentecostalism is a movement to renew Christian faith. This is about healing and salvation. It is also about receiving God's word, not simply hearing it, to proclaim among men. Along with healing neo-Pentecostals value prophecy (1 Cor. 14.1) as a very important spiritual gift. This gift ought not to be defined as a prediction of the future in any sense of crystal-ball gazing. It is a gift for understanding and articulating through teaching and preaching how the Holy Spirit is acting here and now in the life of the church community or within the human situation. What people find strange in the claim to the gift of prophecy is that the ordinary Christian dares to say 'thus saith the Lord'. Peter Hocken says of the classical Pentecostal belief that prophecy is for all generations that it 'adds little to received theologies of the word and of its ministry', but 'in practice their prophecy challenges other Christians to believe that they can receive a word from God to speak in the name and strength of Jesus Christ'.[29] Hocken sees important consequences for the theology of revelation that figures so centrally in Protestant–Catholic dialogue. He says:

So whilst classical Pentecostals have little time for the notion of tradition, their practice and beliefs concerning prophecy imply a high degree of continuity between the apostolic Church and subsequent generations, with a view of Christian co-operation in the one completed work of Jesus Christ that is closer to the Catholic than to the Pentecost tradition. A greater appreciation of the Pentecostals could then help to widen the theological debate on Scripture and tradition, by extension to the spheres of worship and preaching, of prophetic use of Scriptures and of experience in discernment. In this they have something in common with the Orthodox, who would also criticize western Catholics for limiting the theology of tradition to the context of doctrine, theology, and church government.[30]

That neo-Pentecostalism has been led to incorporate this practice and central insight into itself speaks for itself in terms of renewal and ecumenism. I am in full agreement with Hocken's analysis of the ecumenical potential and significance of both classical and neo-Pentecostalism.[31] The exodus of classical Pentecostals from the mainstream Churches at the beginning of the century with its subsequent isolation has indeed 'enabled them to pursue their genius and develop a complete corporate life in fidelity to their basic inspiration. . . .'[32] Seventy years later it penetrates other Christian churches where its identity is preserved, yet becoming part of the other. Hocken sees the ecumenical potential 'latent in this combination of identity and otherness'.[33] He is aware of the risks and divisiveness of the neo-Pentecostal movement. For myself I would think that this is part of the challenge to the mainstream Churches to integrate the spiritual dynamic of the movement into their own renewal and into their ecumenical life. 'Ecumenism means that no Church can adequately define itself by exclusion, and that each tradition needs to keep redefining itself by increasing inclusion.'[34] Moreover, the catholicity claimed by the Churches, though it may vary in terms of precise theological understanding, is more or less understood *extensively* or *intensively*. By this I mean that extensively there is the recognition that the Church is committed to mission and service throughout the world. Intensively catholicity bespeaks a capacity to absorb and integrate what is good, beautiful, and creative in itself from human culture and civilization for its own richness and fullness of life. True in the natural order of things, it ought to be even more true

in the spiritual order. The Christian Churches have claimed the
riches of the gifts of Christ (Eph. 4.4–8). This claim has divided
them into traditions and denominational loyalties in the course of
history, though there are other less worthy reasons for these
divisions. To rediscover the fullness and richness of their claim to
be Catholic, all our Churches have been forced to look at each
other in life and work, in faith and order, in dialogue and mission.
This has been pretty much the development and meaning of the
modern Ecumenical Movement since the beginning of the century.
Efforts to bring a more spiritual dimension into the movement
were not given the consideration they merited in the hustle and
bustle of theological-social-bureaucratic ecumenism. But now, in
an age of renewal, and by extension of the dialogue to include
Christian and non-Christian spiritual insights, the spiritual dimension of ecumenism is assuming the primacy proper to it as 'the
soul of the whole Ecumenical Movement'.[35] In our modern ecumenical search for visible, organic, full communion with each
other as Christians we are looking for the fullness and richness of
the Church *as Catholic* in its life and mission. Could we possibly
undertake such an enormous task and ignore the spirituality of
classical Pentecostalism and its adoption by millions within the
Churches? Is it not time to bring the word and the Spirit more
closely together in our Churches and in our ecumenical quest?
Herein lies a whole new area of hope. As Hocken says, 'without
denying what is alive in the older Churches, we can see in the
Pentecostal movement an important, though not the only, force
for the breathing of new life into the bones and sinews that we
have inherited'.[36] In a statement on the theological basis for
Roman Catholic participation in the neo-Pentecostal renewal, the
following was noted:

> Charismatics make no claim to a special spiritual endowment
> or to a special grace which distinguishes those involved in the
> renewal from others not so involved. If they differ at all they
> differ in awareness and expectations, and therefore in experi-
> ence. The purpose of the renewal is not to bring to the Church
> something she does not have, but to bring local churches and
> the Church universal to release that which they already possess,
> to deepen the commitment to Jesus Christ, and to widen the

expectations of how the Spirit manifests himself in the charisms within the life of the Church.[37]

Whatever else we may want to say about the new Pentecostal experience, it creates in the heart of the one experiencing it deep joy and peace, a hunger for God, a commitment to Christian community. There is a fullness of Christian life experienced in a way that is at the same time continuous and discontinuous 'in relation to what one has experienced before'.[38] This does not mean that neo-Pentecostal Christians do not need the ordinary ministry of their respective Churches. In the moving account of his own Pentecostal experience, John Sherrill expressed himself on this point:

> Thank God for the organized Church during this period. There it was, an institution, running along perhaps a little mechanically, but independent of the ups and downs of individual members of the congregation. We went each Sunday to church, and were aware that there was a steady consistent quality about the services that was important.[39]

On the other hand, apart from such experience and ongoing growth in a spirit of freedom, prayer, and spontaneity more Christians than ever before are openly complaining of sterile mechanical worship, more like a literary performance than an act of worship. They are left cold by the canned spiritual rhetoric they endure rather than prophetic preaching about real issues. In the neo-Pentecostal movement they have had their first real awareness of God present and active in the life of a worshipping congregation. Many would testify to having deeply and personally prayed for the first time in their lives, to having an experience of the Body of Christ through shared prayer. For many shared prayer groups serve as an introduction to the neo-Pentecostal experience and charismatic spirituality. For others these groups bring deep spiritual peace and a sense of the Christian community they do not experience in their parish church. They seem content to be associated with the prayer group with its charismatic dimension. There is no doubt that such shared prayer is leading Christians more and more to a new growth and freedom in prayer.[40] Christians need this growth and freedom for they are the Church. The Church can live the life of Christ and carry out his ministry in the world only when it appropriates the freedom of Christ and the openness to God through a willingness to appropriate the undisclosed future God holds for us. Even the strange phenomenon of tongues which frightens many away from Pentecostalism has to be seen 'as part of the whole system of Christian practice and belief'.[41] For some years now Simon Tugwell has argued for the classical Pentecostal insistence on speaking in tongues and against neo-Pentecostals whom he feels have put too much theological weight on the central experience of classical Pentecostalism referred to as 'baptism in (or of) the Spirit'.[42] He views the experience of speaking in tongues as a liberating experience, first for the praise of God and for being with God. Second, 'the word which we must utter is a word which comes from deep within us; but it is a word which we do not choose for ourselves: it is a word that is given to us. We are a word that God speaks.'[43] Third, the experience spontaneously and creatively enables us to have the mind of Christ, 'to see things God's way'.[44] Fourth, it is an eschatological anticipation of new powers in God's Kingdom.[45] Tugwell is concerned to place the experience of tongues securely within the Catholic tradition, but he perceives the ecumenical value in relating traditional sacramental liturgy with a spiritual spontaneity associated with the Pentecostal tradition. In this experience is a 'strand of unity' bringing together Christian truth and praxis.[46] For some perhaps all this is to put too much theological weight on tongues as a spiritual gift and practice, for it is not all that highly rated when compared with a gift such as prophecy (1 Cor. 14). It is not our purpose here to explore differences in approaches among neo-Pentecostals in interpreting and understanding the spiritual gifts associated with the baptism in the Holy Spirit. The point in noting this is to stress the liberating and maturing nature of neo-Pentecostal prayer. A lady told me that her first memorable spiritual experience happened when a Roman Catholic friend of hers sang in tongues in the course of a shared prayer house group. She had always thought of prayer principally as petition or intercession. At that moment she was caught up in a movement of the Spirit into the praise and thanksgiving of her friend. She knew with spiritual knowledge that this was the centre of prayer. And so the gift given by the Spirit to one member of the group, was given for another, indeed to build up the whole group. They could experience the presence of the risen Lord in their lives.

Without denying its sign-value, this gift of tongues was recognized as a gift of the Spirit for that group of Christians. Those who have received this gift and use it privately know what a blessing it is to focus attention on God, to give freedom for the spontaneity of praise and adoration, thanksgiving and petition, to free the heart from temptation and receive a cleansing in the Spirit that opens the whole person to God. Often it prepares us to receive other gifts of God and to listen to his word.

A new appreciation, a new love for the Bible has always been a characteristic mark of the neo-Pentecostal experience. It is a love for the Bible as a living word with meaning for life here and now. As such it pierces minds and hearts like the two-edged sword it is, living and active. The Bible touches our sore spots, our weak points. It is balm and it heals. We hear things we need to hear rather than those we want to hear. Like the prodding spear of the Bayeux tapestry, it 'comforteth' us. 'This is why there is no substitute for the Bible in facing us with all the dimensions of the call to wholeness.'[47] And that is one of the principal tenets of the classical and neo-Pentecostal movements. The experience of the Holy Spirit is a call to holiness and wholeness. That is why the ministry of healing has developed so much in Christian consciousness over the last several years. The biblical word of God has become once more the work book, the field book, the common possession of rank-and-file members of the Church. The Bible reminds us that everything is God's gift – this moment, this situation, this meeting. All is gift, all is grace! The language of the Bible becomes familiar language. When we come to liturgy and formal worship we listen more eagerly and expectantly, rendering both word and sacrament more fruitful in our lives.[48] Moreover, in whatever way we approach the theological question of how the Bible functions in the Christian life as normative for faith, in seeking to discover and obey God's will here and now the Christian will be led to the Bible as the unique record of how God has spoken and acted among men, a true record of the promises he has made to them through all generations (Luke 2.55). And God is faithful! The Bible is God's gift to the believing community as promise and fulfilment. It must be a significant factor in any act of Christian discernment. One of the criticisms of both classical and neo-Pentecostal Christians is their failure to evaluate and appreciate the spiritual gift of discernment (1 Cor. 12.10).[49]

Instead of trying to get a preview of the future, this gift along with prophecy is meant to be a gift of the Spirit for understanding and obeying God's will in the present moment, situation, or meeting. Since discernment 'is an attempt to evaluate religious impulses within a context of faith', it is difficult to see how this gift could be fruitful apart from some reference to the Bible.[50] This does not mean that the Bible is the sole norm of either faith or discernment in faith. Neo-Pentecostals do a great disservice to the Bible by treating it as the I-Ching. They discredit the central experience of baptism in the Spirit and charismatic spirituality with this kind of fundamentalism and naive piety. The Pentecostals are right to point to the importance of the Bible as a special record of faith and its response, a book of divine promises that will make us aware of what God has done already. In this way the Bible provides a solid spiritual foundation for our real contemporary needs, disposing us to receive what God wishes us to receive as men and women of faith received in the past. The Bible is not a record of uniform activity on the part of God. He deals with men and women in different ways in different situations at different times, with a personal 'pathos' for everyman and all men.[51] The Bible is of unique help in our waiting upon or seeking God's will for our decisions and actions and behaviour. If we are listening to God's word in silence and with no indication of what is being asked, the Bible will help us to do this in peace and without anxiety. We may feel tempted through a certain malaise in our spiritual lives to go for a big breakthrough, a fundamental option, a radical conversion, when what God is really asking us is to keep pushing on, one step at a time but with steadiness and perseverance. In other words we need to discern whether we are in a growth pattern or one of crisis. The Bible has a lot to say about what God is asking because it is about our future and the promises God makes to us. It teaches us an invaluable lesson about the spiritual quality of expectancy, of waiting on God, of the need to combine quietism and enthusiasm, bringing both elements to maturity, preparing us for God's action, preparing us to act. The neo-Pentecostal spirituality matures where discernment is appreciated, creative silence observed, and an openness to all God's spiritual gifts can be found. Through the Bible we learn how to use God's gifts. United to other criteria of moral and scientific life the Bible teaches modern man the full extent and meaning of obedience to God as the absolute condition for sharing life in his Kingdom. It is the pain and anguish born of the complexity of modern man's discernment that the reality of his fellowship and sharing in the realities of death and resurrection, faith and hope, become vision and fulfilment. It is this spiritual vision inherent in the experience of a new Pentecost that makes the neo-Pentecostal movement a sign of hope for the renewal of Christian life in our time.

## New Pentecost – new mission

The power to speak of Jesus as Lord is the decisive operation of the Holy Spirit (1 Cor. 13.3). This is the revolutionary and missionary character of the neo-Pentecostal movement. As a movement involving millions of men and women its motivation lies in the promise of the gospel to transform personal and social life in this world. It demands fundamental changes in the life of the individual and within the life of the Christian community. It has missionary dynamism and outreach as it matures. The spiritual gifts testify to the action of the Spirit by the quality of the new life that is manifested (Gal. 5.22) and by a new commitment to the Church's mission. The reception of spiritual gifts or *charismata* is for the life and mission of the whole Church. The Pentecostal experience is the beginning of mature involvement with the Church in society. Another way of saying this would be to note that the realities behind the Pentecostal and liberation movements are compatible and mutually inclusive and nourishing. A lot of present-day teaching energy in the neo-Pentecostal movement is used either to authenticate the central experience, or to get people to enter fully into this experience, or to orientate the experience and its accompanying gifts theologically. The next big challenge for the movement will be to create a new missionary mentality beyond personal enthusiasm for proselytizing on a one-to-one recruitment basis and edifying personal testimony. When I say 'beyond' I do not want to give the impression that such enthusiasm ought to be set aside, provided the proselytism is honest and sound. Such enthusiasm is essential and ongoing. It belongs to the nature of 'life in the Spirit'. It is part of the proclamation of the good news. Yet the good news of Christ is so much more, as the liberation movements have revealed and which we have discovered anew through the development of a theology of hope. We cannot speak realistically of integrating or incorporating the movement into the life of the Church unless we intend to relate it to this new sense of mission that has taken the liberating message of the gospel seriously and practically. Classical Pentecostalism flourishes in the Third World. From its inception the movement has been marked by a lack of racial and social discrimination. It has been a Church of the poor and weak (1 Cor. 1. 26–31). Moreover, it left mission Churches free to create native liturgies, retaining community ethos, even elements of native theology. Today they feel that the gifts of the Spirit need not exclude elements of pagan secular culture which can be incorporated into Christian congregational life and liturgy. In the light of Walbert Bühlmann's thesis which we mentioned in the previous chapter, i.e., the projection for the Christian population by the end of the century, there can be no doubt of the significance of the Pentecostal Churches in Africa and Latin America, South-east Asia and Oceania. In this they will witness more directly to their elder sister Churches inasmuch as they have anticipated certain elements that belong to the new sense of mission that has been developing. For example, Latin American Pentecostals are not fundamentalists in the sense of having a rigid literal biblical theology. They emphasize Christian freedom and authenticity in terms of tangible witness. They would not have difficulty accepting Barbara Ward, Helder Camara, or Mother Teresa of Calcutta as in the Spirit. Pentecostal preachers may indulge in literalistic and imaginative interpetations of Scripture, something multitudes of preachers in all Churches have done, but they do not champion a dogmatic fundamentalism. Their constant appeal to Scripture as the locus for discovering the essential Christian message finds rapport with other Christians, and this increasingly so. As for the charge that Pentecostalism is a non-starter on issues of social renewal and revolution in the Third World, this is more and more approaching dissolution as Pentecostals expand their horizon. Emilio Castro has said:

> Pentecostalism is now facing one of the most important options of its history. Well aware that it can no longer avoid political problems, it is asking itself what its specific responsibility is in this realm. Up to now the prevailing Pentecostal attitude towards politics has been one of omission. . . . But the movement has grown so tremendously that its members are a large

sector in many communities and are compelled to participate in community affairs.[52]

It seems to me that this numerical factor and an increasing interaction with both Protestant and Roman Catholic neo-Pentecostals could tip the balance for new prophetic social commitment on the part of these Pentecostal Churches. Then the liberation movement may well experience the 'third force' of Pentecostalism. The alternative is alienation and diminishing returns because of the magnitude of the social issues facing Christians. Africa will be faced with a challenge somewhat the same, somewhat different, not unlike the North American and British multi-racial issues of integration and development. I believe the first alternative will be the one chosen by a new Pentecostal force in the Third World – north and south.

Neo-Pentecostals and classical Pentecostals are experiencing a renewed conviction that the gospel must be studied, taught, and proclaimed, not simply as Scripture, but as gospel. Neither believe in silent witness. Believing that Jesus is Lord entails proclamation at any cost. This proclamation is inspired by the example of the apostles and disciples as recorded in Acts. Nor are they afraid to challenge the spiritual mediocrity of fellow Christians. They would say that there is a big difference in knowing *about* Jesus and *knowing* Jesus. Because of their recruitment on a one-to-one basis rather than through mass appeal, though this is not necessarily excluded, they are good subjects for dialogue. They are looking for some degree of expectation, readiness to change in the other partner in the dialogue, an openness to the Holy Spirit. It is this sensitivity to the person and to the Holy Spirit that makes the one-to-one mission of Pentecostal Christians so effective. Pentecostals know that in some sense you have to put your life on the line for your brothers and sisters (1 John 3.14). This is not theory. It is life. One of the best ways to live our spiritual ideals is to lend them our lives, give them a chance to live through our lives. 'Greater love has no man . . .' (John 15.13), and 'the Word became Flesh . . .' (John 1.14). The personal witness of Pentecostals presents a God who is a personal God who deals directly with the lives of his children, not an impersonal God to be kept at a safe distance. Neo-Pentecostals have much to learn in this respect. Their witness is for Christ – not themselves or their pet

167

ideas and enthusiasms. The testimonies of spiritual experience are too often in the spirit of 'Look, it happened to me!' Humble witness looks always to the action of God in us. Built upon mature reflection and prayer the witness becomes a genuine act of love for another with whom God is willing and for whom God is waiting to share his life. The witness is looking towards the same commitment that is at the heart of all Christian mission – commitment to Jesus as the Way, the Truth, the Life, and the Resurrection (John 11.25–6; 14.6). While this is a personal commitment to the person of Jesus Christ, it is likewise a commitment to what Jesus through the contemporary action of the Holy Spirit offers men and women today in the praxis and concrete situations of contemporary life and human needs. This commitment is to the liberating message of Jesus at every level of life. The Pentecostal movement wants to authenticate the person of Jesus; the liberation movement wants to authenticate his message. They belong to each other, for in Jesus they are one. The Pentecostals have put this personal dimension into Christian mission, but the Liberationists have got the practical insight of Christian mission. The Pentecostals have the fire of conviction and assurance and the Liberationists have the passion for justice on their side. Together they can bring the intensity and drive, the single-minded devotion to the Kingdom of God that is needed. Out of such stuff missionaries are made and both Pentecostals and Liberationists must become. While theological orientation and articulation are vital for understanding and direction, theology is not a substitute for faith. It may not be a relevant theology. Faith must always be relevant if it is true faith. Robert Wild says: 'No age may be able to claim the perfect theology, but each age should have its own right to relevance.'[53] The neo-Pentecostal movement has an ethos that is true to the mission mandate of the gospel (Luke 24.45–9). It needs a relevant theology to make that mandate relevant and its own faith authentic. Pentecostals know well how to want and how to abound. In Mexico and Latin America they have enabled peasants to break through traditional patterns and adopt new agricultural methods that represent economic development. They are not afraid to depart from cultural patterns of a more subtle type, such as middle-class suburban life. They live with faith and the provisional in matters of financial security. If a need is not met, the Lord must have something else in mind.

The gospel mission has for its trademark the spirit of poverty (Matt. 10). In an environment of affluence and power, this witness possesses a special value. The neo-Pentecostals are beginning to recognize the superficial character of a great deal that passes for renewal in the Churches, i.e., mere adaptation. The neo-Pente-costal Christians have experienced the Church building on sand instead of rock. The basic Christian message has yet to be appro-priated by the church community at large. There are certain cor-rect noises being made with attendant flurries of apostolic action. A lot seems to happen more democractically than heretofore. But the Pentecostals are insisting that they have discovered a deeper need and priority for personal commitment to Jesus Christ and openness to his Spirit in their own lives. The neo-Pentecostal movement really wants the Church to be a community of love and sharing. The Pentecostals are convinced that it is the extension of such a community throughout the world that constitutes the wit-ness Christians give in their mission among men. 'In this way the Church simultaneously prays and labours in order that the entire world may become the People of God, the Body of the Lord and the Temple of the Holy Spirit . . .' (*Lumen Gentium*, Abbott edn, ch. 2. n. 17). The hope neo-Pentecostalism brings the Church is a basic renewal of its spiritual life, its ecumenical vision, and its mission to the world.

I have not gone into an analysis of neo-Pentecostalism. There is a growing body of testimonial literature and theological writing on the central experience of baptism in the Spirit with its accompanying spiritual gifts. My purpose has been apologetical in part, content to indicate that if it is integrated within church life, it has a potential for renewing and uniting the Church's life and mission that is generally underestimated. It has to figure in any writing around the theme of Christian hope. However, before closing this chapter I feel it is important to look at the reality of the spiritual experience taking place in the lives of millions of Christians of all denominations and backgrounds, an experience that has to be related to the church community. At this moment of writing, several news items are on the desk before me. There is one reporting, 'Charismatics hear opposing views on relating to the Church'. This report divides RC neo-Pentecostals into those who believe that renewal strategy calls for the resistance of evil in the world and those who believe it calls for involvement in the world. One sees stars, the other mud. At this conference, sponsored by Roman Catholics but ecumenical in membership, the issue of whether Christians were salt or leaven in the world was raised for some 40,000 people. Another item on my desk is the smiling photograph of a young RC priest testifying to his own experience of inner healing at a conference of some 50,000 people at which the gifts and fruit of the Spirit were manifested. Hardly a week goes by without some such issue or testimony coming to my desk. For me it is a sign of vitality and renewal among Christians. Just now I have been re-reading a news account in which an Anglican priest described his baptism in the Holy Spirit. A stream of light flowed over him from above. He felt it all over. He saw it. The experience lasted for a long time. He had never read or talked about the neo-Pentecostal movement and did not use the in-language often associated with the movement, i.e. biblical phraseology. He intended to keep the experience private until he came upon several of his parishioners who had had their own 'baptism in the Spirit'. A few weeks later he found himself publicly speaking in tongues, something he had wished not to happen. The story has a happy ending. His parish church is a centre of spiritual growth and attracts increasing numbers. He and his congregation remain strong in their commitment as Anglicans. Perhaps the first reaction, if not perfectly justified, yet understandable, is to decry the experience as one of emotion. It could hardly be an experience without emotion. Unfortunately many Christians have been conditioned by an unhealthy psychology to suspect, distrust, and generally misunderstand the role of emotion in human life. This brings with it a deep-set bias in the realm of religious experience. The misunderstanding is a failure also to appreciate that 'it is as non-biblical to separate emotion or passion from spirit as it is to disparage emotion or passion'.[54] If emotion is a consciousness of being moved, then it is most certainly 'inseparable from being filled with the spirit'.[55] There is no real reason for neo-Pentecostals to be defensive or ashamed and no real grounds for *prima facie* judgements that such experience or enthusiasm in the wake of such experience is due to an emotional imbalance or disorder. This is not to make the experience unquestionable. There are legitimate questions. Among these is the question of how such an experience relates to Christian sacramental baptism which for most Christians is essential as a rite of initiation into Christian life and church membership. The term which is used to describe the neo-Pentecostal experience leaves many theologians uneasy. While some have tried to shake the expression 'baptism in (or of) the Holy Spirit', it persists, and suggested substitutes seem equally awkward. At any rate it may be helpful to review the issue.[56] Here I am going to lean heavily on a noted Roman Catholic theologian, Francis Sullivan, SJ, who does his theology quite comfortably in an ecumenical context. I am indebted to him for his article in *Gregorianum*.[57] Sullivan says that the expression 'baptism in the Holy Spirit' is already a theological interpretation. We cannot avoid doing theology in assessing the experience. He would define it this way: 'A religious experience which initiates a decisively new sense of the powerful presence and working of God in one's life, which working usually involves one or more charismatic gifts.'[58] To this description classical Pentecostals would insist that the gift of tongues be added as a sign of valid baptism in the Spirit. They would describe it as a kind of personal Pentecost which follows on ritual baptism. They would claim that the New Testament shows a pattern of religious experience following conversion and baptism that can be described as an 'endowment from on high'. Only after this personal Pentecost with tongues is the Christian able to claim a 'second blessing', becoming a 'spirit-filled' Christian, anointed and sealed with the Spirit. Sullivan acknowledges the biblical scholarship of James Dunn, an Evangelical biblical theologian of the Church of England, in saying that he believes the exegesis of classical Pentecostalism will not stand the test of scholarly examination.[59] Dunn does not think this is the normal pattern. He thinks the rite of baptism and the reception of the Holy Spirit belong together as two distinct moments or acts in Christian initiation according to Luke (Acts 2.38). He says that 'if a norm is desired for the gift of the Spirit we have it not in John 20.22 or Acts 2.4., but in Acts 2.38'.[60] Nor does Pauline theology support the Pentecostal thesis. 'There is no room in Paul's theology for a Christian who is still waiting to receive his "anointing" or "sealing" with the Spirit.'[61] However:

> There is plenty of evidence . . . that St Paul expected the gift of the Spirit to be a fact of experience in the lives of Christians, that these would be abundant 'manifestations of the Spirit' (1 Cor. 12.17) in their communities. But the evidence is equally

strong that he expected this manifest and experienced gift of the Spirit to mark the very *beginning* of their Christian life.[62]

Catholic sacramental theology speaks of this neo-Pentecostal experience in terms of renewing the graces of Baptism and Confirmation; in terms of an actualization of the gifts of the Spirit with a change in our dispositions, a new commitment to Christ, a new openness to the Spirit. This theology leads to language that speaks of a release of the Spirit, a manifestation of baptism. This amounts to speaking of a hidden grace that breaks through into conscious experience. Indeed the whole experience is a prayer for greater docility to the grace of sacramental confirmation and God's answer to this prayer. Or the interpretation may lie in the Catholic sacramental theology of 'reviviscence'. Thus the explanation that at the time of sacramental confirmation there has been a lack of proper dispositions preventing the sacrament from having its full proper effect; however, in the presence of the right dispositions, the sacrament as it were 'revives' and begins to take full effect. This theology doubtlessly satisfies those in the Catholic tradition, to a great extent. But it would not seem to provide an adequately broad-based explanation that would serve the ecumenical commitment of the neo-Pentecostal movement.[63] Sullivan rightly takes up his investigation of the expression 'to baptize in the Holy Spirit' in two senses of its biblical usage:

(1) The baptism of John as a purifying repentance preparing people for judgement;

(2) the early Christian reinterpretation of the Baptist's baptism in the light of the prophecy of Joel 3.1–5. This reinterpretation is no longer a warning of messianic judgement but a promise of messianic sanctification (Isa. 32.15ff.; 44.3ff.; Ezek. 36.26; 39.29). In this reinterpretation Jesus is the one who baptizes in the Spirit, e.g., Acts 1.5 and 11.16. This conclusion of Luke's theology ought to be our understanding of the expression 'baptism in (or of) the Holy Spirit'. Sullivan reaches this conclusion by showing that Luke used the term 'to baptize' metaphorically, i.e., to be immersed, dipped, drenched in the Holy Spirit, indicating a veritable litany of expressions to convey the notion behind the metaphor. Thus we find these expressions *via-à-vis* the Holy Spirit: to send (Luke 24.49), to be clothed with (Luke 24.49), to be filled with (Acts

2.4), to receive or come upon (Acts 1.8), to pour out (Acts 2.17; 2.33); the Holy Spirit falls (Acts 10.44), is poured out (Acts 10.45), and received (Acts 10.47); again he falls or is given (Acts 11.15, 17). In using this variety of terms and images Luke is describing two events which fulfilled the prophecy that Jesus would baptize with the Holy Spirit. He uses the terms sometimes actively, sometimes passively to describe the two moments of initation of which Dunn speaks with reference to ritual baptism and the reception of the Spirit (Acts 2.38). If we are to settle for this term as an adequate expression of the neo-Pentecostal experience, it must be clearly and commonly understood that 'baptism in, of, with the Holy Spirit' is a metaphor that more literally and closely describes the reality of the event. And so Sullivan concludes his investigation of this matter: The classical and neo-Pentecostal experience is both a new sending and a new reception of the Holy Spirit, giving a new experiential knowledge of God as present within, renewing us in the Spirit and manifesting the renewal by a variety of spiritual gifts or *charismata*.[64] This conclusion seems to be fair to the reality of the experience, providing a solid theological-ecumenical basis for both the retention and common intelligibility of the classical expression 'baptism in the Holy Spirit'. This conclusion supports and strengthens my own conclusion reached in a more summary fashion in the study I undertook a few years earlier:

> It would seem best to understand the non-biblical phrase 'baptism in or of the Spirit' as an encounter with God which makes a person a more effective witness of Christ. It may well be of such significance in the individual life of the Christian, or even the non-Christian, as to constitute some mode of conversion to Christ.[65]

Can we say that there is need for such an experience in the life of every Christian? Or is such an experience to be desired by everyone? These questions demand a slightly more extensive answer than a simple affirmation or negation.

I do not see how we can answer the first question affirmatively without lapsing into the need for a twofold baptism, a first- and second-class Christian church membership. Nor do I believe we can say such an experience is to be desired by every single Christian. There are different patterns in spiritual development. There

173

is the growth pattern by which I mean a progressive sense of being called into a deeper relationship with the Lord. We might say that God's grace has elicited a fairly regular and faithful response, a developed sense of vocation. Christian baptism is patterned on the death and resurrection of Jesus. This pattern manifests itself in daily self-denial, discipline, prayer, and Eucharist. The communion with God in Christ grows into intimacy and depth. Failure to grow into Christian maturity and fullness of life can induce a crisis pattern of development, the need for a breakthrough, a conversion, a new level of Christian life. To the extent that growth has been checked and openness to the transforming grace of Christ is not what it ought to be, to that extent there often arises a desire or expectation for the renewed action of the Holy Spirit in our lives. It is this quality of openness and expectation that creates the crisis pattern of spiritual development. Crisis can mean opportunity. The person becomes aware of the potential of a new personal Pentecost, a new opportunity for spiritual growth. When such a pattern can be traced significantly in a notable segment of the Christian community, it is an opportunity for renewal in the Church. Christian life is life in the Body of Christ. Practically speaking, an individual Christian in a growth pattern cannot be indifferent to what is happening in the Body of Christ. If the neo-Pentecostal movement involves millions of my brothers and sisters in Christ, it involves me and engages my interest in what God is saying to the Church as a whole. Spirituality is not a private affair. It is the very deepest life of the Church committing each of us to concern and discernment for the needs of the Church. Perhaps it is as well to be blunt and say that because you do not experience a crisis pattern in your spiritual life, this does not mean that all is well with yourself or with the Church as a whole. We have to be ruthless with our hidden fear, insecurity, self-satisfaction, for the sake of the gospel. If one looks at his life honestly and with simplicity, it may not be too difficult to discover a converting, transforming appeal of the Spirit in the depths of the truer self moving you out of yourself towards a deeper relationship with others and into genuine apostolic action. God bestows the gift of contemplation, but he expects the fruits of contemplation to be shared. Besides, at some level of life there is always crisis, in the sense of opportunity. My aim in saying all this is not to insist on the precise experience which marks the neo-Pentecostal movement. But it does seem to me that the charismatic spirituality developed by it and associated with it is part of the normal spiritual growth of Christians. This would seem to be supported by the witness of the New Testament and a theology of the Holy Spirit that accords with this witness. Quite apart from initiating spiritual renewal for millions of Christians, as a movement it is a call to the whole Church for a life of holiness, to a life of openness to the Spirit, with all the freedom, growth, transformation this implies. This is a universal call in our time, for all of us need the gifts of the Spirit to be led into all truth. As a movement neo-Pentecostalism does not seek to displace other modes of spirituality. It seeks to *inform* them as an essential element of them. The movement exists to persuade the Church anew that of its very nature it is an institution of the Spirit, charismatic in nature. It is dangerous to pit Rome against Corinth, to oppose institution and charism. There is no alternative for leading a Christian life that is not in or of the Spirit. It is the whole institution that depends on the action of the Spirit for its real life and goals. The movement aims to reintegrate charism and institution. It does not seek to restore a delicate balance between them. Despite his qualified lack of enthusiasm for charismatic movements, Professor Lampe acknowledges the place of *charismata* in the life of the Church. 'On the contrary,' he says, 'if the Church is to be more than a society for the protection of conventional morality or an auxiliary organization to the social services, it has to be a charismatic movement.'[66] On the other hand he warns of a 'docetic pneumatology'. This is the belief that 'the work of the Spirit . . . should be expected to take place outside, or in the gaps of, the rational faculty of understanding and moral judgement'. His experience of contemporary charismatic movements leaves him convinced that 'this belief still flourishes'.[67] That such an anxiety may be justified by what one hears and observes at neo-Pentecostal gatherings is still too true. But these observations must be joined with a critical self-examination. The movement is maturing. The theology of charisms and the recognition of the importance of sound teaching are being developed and encouraged within the movement. The situation will not be improved by academic posturing or intellectualizing. Sound pastoral theology and teaching are needed, with the emphasis on the *pastoral* role of the teachers. The theology and the teaching are not meant to sterilize the spiritual experience, nor to tame and manipulate the experience. These spiritual gifts of teaching and pastoral care are meant to relate the experience to the subsequent development of charismatic spirituality and this spirituality to Christian life in the Body of Christ. Catholic neo-Pentecostals are almost too anxious about this. They want and welcome for the most part clerical participation and encouragement in understanding the Pentecostal experience, in co-ordinating the spiritual gifts with their ongoing life in the Church. One of them has said: 'It seems that the greatest danger at the present time in this area stems from the clergy – the neglect of the clergy to help these people work out the relationship between their gifts and the official ministry of the Church.'[68] The clergy are not being asked to promote a movement. They are asked to renew their understanding of what it means to live by the Spirit with his gifts operative in ordinary Christian life. They are asked to be pastors for others and Christian with others. It was more than a source of edification when about 450 Catholic priests came together at Hopwood Hall in Manchester to learn about and experience in great numbers the working of the Spirit. This took place among British clergy and represented an event of the New Pentecost going on around the world. It could only be construed as a sign of hope. Basic to this teaching the clergy are asked to give, and to the comfort of Professor Lampe, is the assurance that the Holy Spirit is in the whole of life. He is not a God of the gaps and in this sense is not a go-between God. And while he works in the whole of life, he is creating a new heaven and a new earth where God will dwell with men. This Kingdom of God proleptically anticipated in a prophetic people already holds joyful surprises for those who press forward in faith. We ought to be able more and more to define the Church as a community of faith living in the Spirit. Life in the Spirit does define the Church and supports those who say that the very nature of the Church is charismatic. It exists to provide an opening for the action of the Spirit among men – in the present age and in the ages to come. In this book I have emphasized the relationship between the Church, the world, and the Kingdom of God. It is for the cause of this Kingdom that a spiritual attitude of openness and expectation is required. There can be no limit to the way the Spirit chooses to work. If you believe in the Kingdom, you cannot confine its life and laws within the bounds of worldly–eccelesiastical intelligibility (1 Cor. 2.10–

13). God's activity cannot be limited by our understanding and our unwillingness to move into the future. He breaks into our personal and communal life. He sometimes acts with a mighty hand and an outstretched arm, though there is no doubt that he is a God great enough to work through the ordinary processes and events of creation and history. It is also true that we are not to crave for wonders and seek signs, but God in fact does give signs and does work wonders. Faith and hope in the coming Kingdom of God are part of Christian life in the world and a manifestation of the final meaning of the world's history. That the Church is renewing its essential role as a sign lifted among the nations ought to be cause for joy and sunshine in so much that is bleak and drab in the life of the Church. Most certainly the renewal of its essential function as a Spirit-led, Spirit-based institution is a substantial sign of hope. The neo-Pentecostal movement is not out of the woods yet, though I personally feel confident in its future. But if something should go wrong and the spiritual energy of the movement becomes dissipated, it will be the Church which is the loser. Much will depend on how we interpret the signs and wonders by which Jesus proclaimed and taught life in the Kingdom (e.g., Mark 1.21–8; Matt. 12.22–32). It is so easy to disjoin the present and the future, to opt for one and neglect the other. Often it is because we want to avoid the tension between what seems right and justifiable for our present needs and what God summons us to undertake or sacrifice as a sign of life to come, a life yet to be fully shared. The gifts of the Spirit are sufficiently wide in range, function, and meaning to cover those situations – present and future. A corresponding spirituality to meet all the needs of the Church as an institution in the world and as a sign of the coming Kingdom of God can be fashioned from these gifts of the Spirit, if we remain open to receive them all, not picking and choosing according to the flesh. We have learned to accept and expect and respect the signs and wonders of scientific development, signs and wonders of the universe they disclose, of which we are a part, with which we are summoned to an ever deeper communion. Yet in the midst of all these signs and wonders faith too often remains infantile, folksy, immature. The proportionate act of faith we need to match these signs and wonders and to manifest the Kingdom does not seem to be forthcoming. Complex development, high technology that is often violent, bewilders and frightens us.

177

Perhaps our lack of spiritual vision and wonder is inverse to our natural wonder. As such many feel pushed to the edge of an evolving world that threatens to destroy us or leave us behind, alienated and bewildered. If we are to respond positively to what is happening in our world, if we are to get inside it and have a place at its centre, bringing with us the essential gift of faith, we will need a largeness of vision and life combined with a renewed sense of spiritual wonder that will disclose in all its length and breadth, height and depth the Kingdom of God. Christians must bring with them to the world's life the infinite richness and variety of life that builds itself around the unique personal centre that is Jesus Christ. Such a combination of faith, vision, and wonder is our gift to our fellows, their hope and ours. Charismatic spirituality is a spirituality which by logical implication grounds the faith, vision, and wonder of God's Kingdom in such a way that we are able to respond to the magnitude and power of all that the creator Spirit summons us to share right now with himself.

The charism of healing illustrates in a simple way what I have been saying. On the whole we can say that there has been an intelligent response to scientific medicine. And faith healing has all too often represented an anti-medical bias. This has led to confusion over the significance of healing in the life of faith. The proportionate faith of which I have spoken takes into account modern medical science and technique. It acknowledges that this development 'adds a new range of instrumentalities to the process whereby healing takes place'.[69] But the development does not take the place of faith. It enlarges faith. If it does not, 'the complete secularization of healing brings less power to bear on the ills of mankind, and erroneously makes health look like a gift human beings have the power to bestow on one another'.[70] Faith enables us to understand that health and life are ultimately and profoundly the gift of God. They are signs of the wholeness and life of God's Kingdom. As such they appear through scientific medicine *or* charismatic healing.[71] As John Haughey says: 'When one reflects on it, there is no theological reason for thinking that miracles should not accompany the preaching of the Church and be in evidence in the lives and communities of Christians.'[72] J. Rodman Williams reminds us of something the great Karl Barth had to say about this:

There may be too little of the pneumatic, but never too much. It is from this too little . . . that all offences and distortions and aberrations and entanglements derive in the community. The community is healthy in proportion as it gives free course to the Spirit. Its strength, and that of all Christians, is in the defencelessness in which it commits itself wholly to the Spirit and trusts exclusively in the authority and overriding power of his rule.[73]

Another great theologian, Emil Brunner, reminding us that the charismatic gifts are strange powers to us but not in the New Testament, warns us that 'the danger for us is that, unwilling or unable to recognize our inadequacy, we might make the unfortunate attempt to judge the New Testament witness from a presumably more enlightened position'.[74] Like others who stress God's power to break into the human psyche, Brunner notes 'the power of the Spirit . . . reaches deep into the unconscious, even into the organic and physical realm, and we should beware of the attempt to judge miracles of the Holy Spirit with the yardstick of our "enlightened" rationalism'.[75] Reference has been made to a negative reaction that is quite common. This is the association in neo-Pentecostalism with excessive emotion. A good number of Christians are unable to understand the liberating action of the Holy Spirit, conditioned as they are to deep suspicion about anything associated with subjective religious experience and manifestations of emotion in the worship of God. We are only beginning to learn again in the context of modern human knowledge that the Spirit is able to break through our inhibitions, drawing us out of ourselves. Like dreams and visions, tongues and prophecy arise within us and take possession of consciousness. Their source is other than physical stimulation through sensation or knowledge arising from intellectual reflection. We might say that such events bring us into another realm of the human spirit. They signify a breakthrough of spiritual reality into everyday life. Our all too common assumption is that God can get in touch with us only through sense experience and reason. This is an expression of the materialism and rationalism of modern man that has taken over so much of church life, drying up the founts of worship in spirit and truth. The Spirit groans within all of us and within our Churches, seeking to move us closer to our spiritual centre. We need to be renewed in a kind of faith that knows God can break directly into the human psyche.[76] The neo-Pentecostal experience cuts across denominationalism. We have noted this earlier and it is extended to racial, cultural, social, economic, and educational differences. It finds its identity as a movement in terms of a oneness in Christ. The greatest weakness of classical Pentecostalism is its lack of awareness of its potential for a pluralistic approach that would save it from denominationalism. To illustrate this we can note their failure to win Evangelicals to their cause. The movement, instead of breaking into Evangelical Churches, has broken into the middle-of-the-road Churches and the Roman Catholic Church. My purpose in saying this is to indicate that the real roots of the movement are spiritual and experiential rather than finding the source of unity in theological affinity. All have learned to see that we cannot hope to be effective disciples of Jesus without a renewed sensitivity to the presence and power of the Holy Spirit in Christian life and worship. Contact is being maintained with other dimensions of Christian life. Through the movement, however, Christians are experiencing a new unity that is experienced on a scale and with an intensity heretofore unrealized since the breakup of Christendom. The neo-Pentecostal movement has already given the Church a new awareness of the breadth and depth with which God is working through a diversity of signs and gifts never before experienced on such a widespread regular basis. God himself has opened the way to full renewal and visible unity by unfolding, liberating, transforming every aspect of Christian life. The promise of Jesus to his disciples is that we shall see greater things (John 1.50) and do greater things (John 14.12). This is the spiritual ethos of renewal. We are not condemned to repeat the past, nor to live chained to it. This is the renewing breath of the Spirit proclaimed in the neo-Pentecostal movement. It would deny its own authenticity were it to create divisions in the Church. It witnesses 'to what the New Testament says as a whole on the work of the Holy Spirit in man'.[77] I once asked: Can the Pentecostal movement renew the Church? John Gunstone later suggested we might put the question the other way around. How is the Christian Church to be related to and integrated with the renewal of the Pentecostal movement?[78] His question derives from his own experience that the movement is truly of God. I share his conviction and agree that the question ought to be put as he suggests. In an age of renewal in the Church, and most likely in a very new age for the world, Christians ought to expect that the promises of Christ will be fulfilled in such a way that a proportionately new act of faith can be made, a new life of faith lived. Christians ought to expect all sorts of new and wonderful things to happen. Without faith in the promise of Jesus to send another comforter, advocate, without a vision like that of Paul for the young churches of Ephesus and Corinth, it is difficult to see how the Church will be renewed or be in a position to give the prophetic witness a new generation will demand. We shall need much more than our human talent for adaptation, more than a native genius for strategy and organization, even more than a traditional fidelity to the will of God expressed in conventional norms of behaviour. I would not want to be misunderstood. We shall need all these – but we shall need much more. We stand in need of an inspired creative force to build a new age of faith, an age of new unities and the dissolution of old polarities. For this we need the Spirit of God, we need a new Pentecost. We are proceeding in a new direction with a rather inadequate map. There is only a faint outline of the future and not much of a programme for it. Our hope rests on the faith we have to leave ourselves and our Churches completely open to be led by the Spirit into the newness and fullness of life, expecting to experience anew his presence in our midst – a cloud by day, a pillar of fire in the night.

# 6

## The Community Movement

Only together can we satisfy adequately that hunger
for the values of the spirit.
*Cardinal Hume to the Church of England Synod*

The community movement provides another substantive of hope.
In a way it is a new sense and feeling for community that is
flowering in the movements of which we have spoken thus far. It
is the search for community that motivates, authenticates, and
brings power to these movements. There is a new growth in
awareness that people belong together as people and not simply
as a crowd. It would be anomalous indeed if Christians did not
share such an awareness. For them it would be a countersign.
While it is beyond my purpose to do more than mention it, there
is no doubt that the new search for community produced by the
counterculture of the last two decades represented an effort to
bring a new consciousness to western society. The counterculture
was an attempt to shift values and priorities in such a way as to
counteract what was felt to be mass dehumanization in western
society. It questioned the manifest destiny of American politics in
favour of more basic human values like peace, like social and
racial justice. Whatever we may say of its aberrations, faddishness,
and lyricism, it achieved many of its goals and raised human
awareness on the earth. It was a liberation movement initiated in
the very heart of North America. It was to reach across the
Atlantic to Europe and across the Pacific to Japan. Indeed its
reverberations were felt around the world. It represented a kind
of conscientizing-deschooling process. That it did it through protest which was at times blatant and obnoxious, erratic and strident,
even violent at times, far from obscuring its character, identified
it as a liberation movement of an early stage. Because the forms
of protest seem to have passed, it would be facile and presumptuous to claim that things are back to normal, business goes on as
usual, the universities are quiet and the students busy with achiev-
ing high grades, the wheel has turned full cycle. The countercul-

ture has left permanent values. Among these is the desire for community life that liberates from the narrowness and privatization of affluent materialistic western life.[1] The West will never again feel the security of self-satisfaction in quite the same way. The counterculture changed this permanently.

The search for community was a new secular-Christian phenomenon. The basic value and norm of the secular phase was the creation of a climate of personal freedom and interpersonal caring. While it left great scope for 'doing your own thing' and for 'being yourself', it was conditioned by the precept of not transgressing the freedom of others. Certain forms of communal existence were orientated towards political and sexual freedom. Hence they conveyed an image offensive to many, one which still provokes a bias towards experimentation in community living. Many forms of communal living are a reaction to technological culture and represent a retreat from this culture. They often represent a quest for a more simple lifestyle, a rural retreat, a renewed cult of the 'good earth' with its ecological and organic emphasis. Some have a religious quest for transcendence attached to their lifestyle. Some stress the therapeutic need for community occasioned by the rat race of modern living. Others are inspired by political-social ideologies. For Christians many of these community values and points of orientation held great appeal. They could see the validity and authenticity of so many values in expressing their own Christian commitment. Looking at this development we can say that this quest for community is an illustration of how Church and world overlap in life, action, and goals.

For the Christian, however, the heart of community consists in breaking down barriers that keep people apart or at different levels of human opportunity to achieve dignity and purpose; in helping people to go on growing, becoming more free in themselves and in their relationships (Eph. 2.14–22; Gal. 3.28), free to pursue with others those aims that prepare the human community for the coming Kingdom of God. A special thrust has been given to the Christian community movement also from the Jesus movement or revolution as it was called in the early 1970s. The neo-Pentecostals have made the greatest contribution to the Christian community movement as they have grown in numbers and maturity. Yet the secular and Christian manifestations differ. Contrasting the hippie communal living with the communes of the

Jesus Kids, as they were called, Roger Palms noted that the hippies were in search of a better world system and despaired of building society as a whole on the basis of love and understanding. Community was a withdrawal. This did not pay off, for they had to learn that the problem was not with the system, but with the people, including the ones in their communes. On the other hand (though he is a bit lyrical) Palms notes that 'the Christian communes . . . have a binding concept of community in Jesus Christ' and he adds, 'this commitment takes the leadership out of the realm of their own ideas and relates it to . . . Christ, not a concept'.[2] The neo-Pentecostal movement seems to have created an even deeper and ongoing movement for basic Christian community living. Ralph Martin says:

> From the New Testament it is clear that God's gift of his Spirit to those who embrace the saving death and resurrection of his Son, Jesus, is intended to effect an experiential reconciliation not only between God and man, but also between man and man. It is also clear that the reconciliation between men is intended not only to produce a change of heart, a bringing about of forgiveness and universal love, but also to issue forth and become visible in a new style of life – Christian community life.[3]

The neo-Pentecostals looked beyond the experience of baptism in the Holy Spirit to the nature of Christianity itself. Very early on in the movement they saw that it is 'essentially communal, and yielding to God must mean yielding to a community form of life'.[4] Quite naturally they look to the Pentecost paradigm of Acts 2.44–7. We shall return to this paradigm and to the neo-Pentecostal role for it has made a most significant contribution to the growth of the community movement.

However, it is important to keep in mind that the need for community and its manifold forms of witness and service have always been a part of church life, be it ever so institutionalized. The history of religious orders and congregations is an obvious example. When the Church initiated its renewal, new experiments in Christian community began to proliferate. In Britain this movement towards community along with its secular counterpart became so widespread and diversified that it was felt by some that it was time to undertake some sort of survey of the scene. Communities appear and disappear or change in spirit and outreach. It was felt that there ought to be some kind of 'switchboard' for information to be exchanged and comment provided about these basic communities, a kind of network to be set up. David Clark has traced recent developments of the community movement in Britain, including an account of how this network came to be set up and developed.[5]

I am writing of the Christian community scene and will not attempt comment on the overall search for community. Precisely because this new search for community is going on at so many different levels of human involvement and service and witness, there is a danger that the word 'community' will lose its sharpness of meaning. But as Paul Davidson noted, 'that does not mean that what it stands for is out of date or valueless'.[6] As a Christian psychologist he describes this overall movement as a 'desperate quest for identity'.[7] In an earlier issue of *Community* I described the search for community as a search for 'a depth of living'.[8] I am sure that both approaches complement each other and describe what is most common to this secular-religious phenomenon. Yet, when transposed into a Christian key, they tell us that this search for community lies closest to what we understand when we use another general term. I am talking about the term 'renewal'. This new quest for community is the Church's effort to reach a new maturity, a new integrity, a sharper identity as a community of love. 'Community of love' is not spiritual rhetoric. It means that the Church is a community of persons who understand their shared life through the person of Jesus. It means that we cannot reach this ideal if we use the old models of community rooted in traditions and methods rather than persons. Traditions and methods will always be with us, but they cannot be the basis of Christian community. Only the interpersonal sharing of love to promote personal growth and deeper freedom for love can serve as the terms of any contract to build a Christian community. The newness of the contemporary summons to community reflects a new awareness that is not 'thing'-oriented but 'person'-centred. The new consciousness focuses on the centrality of Christ as a person, indeed the unique personal centre of all relationships among Christians. In him our relationship with God is defined. He is God with us, taking away a sense of alienation and isolation. He relates us to one another within and through a human community. Traditions and methods must be subjected to the spiritual scrutiny of the Spirit's gift of discernment. This gift is a light to find the way forward into the undisclosed future to which God is always summoning his people. Community is lived with this provisional outlook, this openness to move into the future of God. Christian life and Christian community are future-oriented and cannot be bound to traditions or methods. The ecumenical community of Taizé affords an example of one which has carried the spiritual traditions and methods of older forms of community life without becoming slavish to them, wise men who know how to bring the best out of both old and new ways of life. At the conclusion of the Taizé Rule we may read:

> If this Rule were ever to be regarded as an end in itself and to exempt us from ever more seeking to discover God's design, the love of Christ, and the light of the Holy Spirit, we would be imposing on ourselves a useless burden; it would be better never to have written it.[9]

So, at the basis of this renewing activity in the Church, whatever its forms and methods, lies the identity of the Church as a community of persons committed to the life and teachings of Jesus Christ, totally oriented towards the undisclosed future of God. Within this unity the Spirit creates a wonderful diversity of witness and service to the Church and to the world.

Rosemary Haughton says that all kinds of communities are both example and symbol.[10] As symbol they challenge accepted ways of doing things; they challenge the presuppositions of these accepted ways. To the extent they do this they are part of the wider liberation movement. They offer hope for people trying to live by basic enduring human values. Community formation today follows two general lines of development, namely those which are *radical* in the sense that they develop new structures from their contemporary experience and needs, and those which adopt or adapt themselves to *traditional* structures from within these structures and from which they question, renew, and summon back such structures to an essential witness of basic human values. If these are Christian communities then basic Christian values are involved. But either form of community must provide a challenge and an alternative to political and religious structures that no longer serve human development and Christian witness. These communities are part of an overall process of conscientization and deschooling. In this sense both general forms of community fit the description of a *basic community*. Such communities will continue to arise, trying to express the essential nature of man in society and of Christian life in the Church. The function may be:

(*a*) Supportive – for individuals needing dialogue, discipline, encouragement;

(*b*) model – of what the Church ought to be in its relationship with the world which is called to grow into the image and likeness of God;

(*c*) servant – through prayer, education, wider community development, parish renewal, service to the needy;

(*d*) catalyst – to promote change in the Church and in the world.

Obviously these categories are not mutually exclusive and they overlap more or less in basic Christian communities. Nor is it possible to separate the role of the Christian community from its secular counterpart. The movement reflects all the tension and complementarity of Church and world. Thus community life is a manifestation of the Church as a sacrament of the life God offers man in the Kingdom. As such it is meant to be a factor in the transformation of human life and society. By definition a Christian community cannot be exclusively Christian. It links, assimilates, and grows with all true forms of building the human community. Far from diminishing Christian witness, such human developments are an essential part of authentic community. For this reason there is always a political dimension in the shared life of Christians. Bonhoeffer defined Christian discipleship as 'life together'. Paul Oestreicher would say that the 'reduction of God to an individualized saviour rather than his acceptance as the liberator of the whole cosmos is part of the tragedy of the Church's history'.[11] He would relate this to the question of Christian community by saying that the gospel does not foster religious community or fellowship as such. It is about the transformation of the secular community into the Kingdom of God. The gospel is socio-political, not by derivation, i.e., saying that there are social, economic, political implications, but *by nature* and *in essence*.[12] Extremely radical as this may sound, Oestreicher would not divorce this dimension from its interrelational and personalized dimension or from its spiritual roots. He says:

> Organic church unity, updated concepts of Christian community, family communes, groups trained to new heights of personal sensitivity, Pentecostal fervour, Jesus People enthusiasm: All of these phenomena could be pointers to the Kingdom or new forms of escape from it. To discern which is which is one of the gifts of the Spirit we badly need. Even the commitment to politics for which I am pleading can be and often is an escape into mere activism if love of persons, immersion in the mystery of God in a little child, is not at the heart of the desired revolution.[13]

What Oestreicher pleads, as does Guttierez, is that we try to live as a Church aware of the breadth of the political and social scope of the gospel.[14] The Church has to look at itself in relation to the entire social order and contemporary man's task of building a new society. In facing this problem of the vocation of the Church to be in the world while nourishing its own spiritual roots, it is necessary to relate the ecclesial models of institution and community. These can no more be separated as models of the Church's nature than can institution and charism be separated in understanding the basis of the Church's life. Whatever tension is experienced serves as a sign of the Church being less than it is called to be in virtue of the gospel. Fidelity to the gospel in relating the Church to the needs of contemporary human society is a fundamental task, one that can be carried out only to the extent that the Church becomes aware of itself as community. This awareness is not a balance between an inward concern that is described as community and an outward concern that is described as institution. The institutional Church is called to be a community of faith. Guttierez would see this as indispensable for the Church in its mission of liberation. He believes 'we are witnessing both a rediscovery of the communitarian dimension of the faith as well as new ways of living it'.[15] In Britain we speak a good deal about a caring community with reference to the Church, though Christians find liberation for service to the wider community more in terms of individual acts of kindness and Christian participation in professional social work than they do through their churches. David Sheppard says:

In the areas of Britain where the greatest concentration of homeless poor live, the churches are generally very weak in numbers. Much of their members' leisure-time energies are taken up in keeping church organizations going, because there's no one else to do it. So they dare not get involved in anything more.[16]

Here we see a situation that reduces the effectiveness of the Church *as Church* in the wider community. The tension between the inner, the intramural life of the Church omits a political-social service and witness. Such an omission ought to be subjected to an urgent process of discernment in the Spirit. It is the direct responsibility of church leaders. The authenticity of the Church as a charismatic, prophetic, caring, serving institution is in grave doubt. A much different situation is exemplified in Michael Harper's account of the growth of the Church of the Redeemer in Houston, Texas from a nearly defunct parish to a vigorous missionary community congregation. In a chapter entitled 'Free to serve', he says:

The success of Houston has largely come about because many of the members have seen clearly what these hindrances are, and have been so sure and committed to what they knew to be the prior claim on their lives, that they have been prepared to sacrifice anything and everything to be completely obedient to that vision. The vision was to see a church free to minister fully and completely to itself and to the world around it.[17]

Here the relationship of Church and world has been made whole in the vision of one church renewed for mission. Here institution and community are one and the same reality through a proper discernment of how the spiritual gifts, *charismata* and service, *diakonia* belong together. The need for basic communities is basic. This need is beginning to command some measure of acknowledgement in strategy documents such as *Evangelii Nuntiandi* and *A Time for Building* which have been mentioned already. Stephen Clark subtitles his book *Building Christian Communities* as a 'strategy for renewing the Church'.[18] Yet one has the uneasy feeling that too much 'strategy' talk about renewal brings us back to a functional methodological way of looking at community. Or it becomes introverted and inward-looking, a means to stabilize the Church at a time of notable social change, creating the right environment for Christian life. The image of Christian life as 'salt' cannot be allowed to dominate the interpretation of Christian life as 'light' and 'leaven'. There seems to me a real need to define a bit more sharply what we are to understand when we speak of basic Christian communities. I must confess to dissatisfaction with a definition such as the following: 'A basic Christian community is an environment of Christians which can provide for the basic needs of its members to live the *Christian life*.'[19] My dissatisfaction stems from the reasons just mentioned. Moreover, the terms of the definition are loaded, namely basic needs and Christian life. I feel much easier and satisfied with the definition and analysis offered by Max Delespesse: 'A community is an organic and stable fraternal association of persons accepting responsibility for one another, through sharing both what they are and what they have, in order to bring about the union of mankind.'[20] This definition interrelates the fourfold function of community mentioned a while back, i.e., the community as supportive, as model, servant, and catalyst. It is a definition that provides for both stability and growth. Its outreach is universal in scope and it is a view of community against the horizon of human unity. It can be put forward as a definition containing elements applicable to both the secular and religious community movement. For our present purpose it provides a definition that conforms to a New Testament vision of the Church as a community. Since the church community, renewed in its self-understanding, both nourishes specific forms of community life and is nourished by them, e.g., religious orders, this definition provides a working basis for my understanding of *basic Christian community*. The Christian community movement must be rooted in some shared vision of the Church. This is not a matter of putting all our eggs in one basket. It is not a question of preferring one theological image or model of the Church to all others. It is a case of seeing the authentic life of the Church expressed *as a community through community*. The Church is a basic community of communities which expresses the fullness, the richness, the extent and depth of the mystery of Christ in the world. If the community movement is the summit as a substantive of Christian hope, it will have to be seen to reflect the pristine vision of the Church. And it will have to nourish and be nourished by that vision.

Before we try to outline such a vision it is necessary to repeat that we are not thinking of the Church as a community in the sense that community is just another image or theological model to understand the nature of the Church. We are thinking of community in relation to the Church as the most fundamental way of understanding and describing the Church. It is the most basic model and image we have in terms of the Church's visible nature. It makes Christian unity an article of urgency and high priority on the agenda of the Church's business. It does so in terms of the Church's essential message of reconciliation and liberation. It is the most basic expression of the Church's constitution. If a *lex fundamentalis* were ever needed, it would amount to this: The Church must be seen to be a community. As the theologian Torrance has suggested to Roman Catholics, it is a question of how to relate the new dynamic and ecumenical reorientation of their Church to its own inherited juridical framework on the horizon of its relation to other Churches.[21] I suggest that self-awareness as a community is the answer to the renewal and ecumenical reorientation initiated by the Holy Spirit in divided Christian Churches. Other theological models and biblical images can be related to this fundamental model and image of community. Thus the Body of Christ and people of God models manifest the Church as a communion between God and man through Christ, expressed in bonds of creed, worship, and ecclesiastical fellowship. As they are metaphors with sociological and biological overtones, terms like communion, community, fellowship more directly express the reality of the Church in its interior life of communion with the Father in Christ through the Holy Spirit. Or they express its external visible witness to Christ's message of reconciliation. The Church as sacrament signifies the Church as community tending to the Kingdom of God. It is the Church as community that reveals the Church as herald of the good news and servant of God in his loving care and service of his children. The institutional model of the Church presupposes that the Church is a structured community. In saying this I am not suggesting that these other models are dispensable. Quite the contrary. They illuminate and express the basic nature of the Church as a community with unique origin (called by God, founded by Christ) and purpose (to prepare and serve the final coming of God's Kingdom). While respecting the cautions offered by Avery Dulles in his analysis and evaluation of various models of the Church, it does seem that the community model recurs more frequently under the more significant criteria he offers for their evaluation.[22] Schematized, his analysis looks like this:

| CRITERIA | MODEL |
|---|---|
| (1) Basis in Scripture | *Community*, herald |
| (2) Basis in Christian tradition | *Community*, institution (RC) |
| (3) Capacity to give members a sense of corporate identity and mission | Herald, institution |
| (4) Fostering virtues and values esteemed by Christians | Sacrament, servant |
| (5) Correspondence with the religious experience of contemporary man | *Community*, servant |
| (6) Theological fruitfulness | Sacrament |
| (7) Enabling church members to relate to other denominations, non-Christian religions, secular humanists | *Community*, servant |

The above schema shows the primacy and theological validity in thinking of the Church as community. Moreover, it illustrates its affiliation as such with the Church's role as herald and servant. If we are to use the Church as a norm for our understanding of what a basic Christian community ought to reflect, we have to respect all images and models for they all nourish the community model. This model must be as exact as possible, for the value of a given community or specific form of community derives from its actual manifestation of the whole Church renewing its life and awareness as a basic community. This does not insert us in a vicious circle. It indicates the mutual interaction of the Church as it is called to be and as it is in its particular and localized expression. Neither the Church universal nor particular is an abstraction. In both we are dealing with God's people – in this place and throughout the world. The experimental community will be more or less an approximation of the New Testament pattern of the Church. This will depend in no little part on the state of the Church as it exists at a given time. At the same time the particular community must anticipate and signify what the Church is to be according to the call of God as a community of faith responding to the divine summons. It could be put another way. The particular community is no better or worse than the Church as it actually exists. If anything, the community of faith is a barometer. It reflects the condition of the Church. Yet it exists to improve the condition of the Church. If it lives by vision and prophecy it brings the rest of the Church closer to true discipleship of Jesus. Consequently we have to look more closely at what the Church is called to be *as a community*. Our vision has to be renewed if a clear vision is to nourish God's people. Without it they perish (Prov. 29.18). A contemporary writer laments that the more we write and talk about community, the less we seem to have. He blames this on the lack of shared vision and says: 'Community happens only when men and women have a vision together and together pursue it. The more consuming the vision, the deeper the community.'[23] The Church has a vision, all too imperfectly shared among its churches and within its traditions. Christians have not pursued the vision with much passion or commitment. Yet this is the gift the world needs, a path that leads to peace and hope, a vision shared by those who are both utopic and prophetic. Its roots are deep because it is intended to be the consummation of the hope and vision of human history.

The term *koinonia* in the Greek of the New Testament expresses the communion of spiritual life among Christians. In some modern Protestant usage it has come to mean a kind of glad hand of fellowship more appropriate for formal occasions than for a sign to express the depth of sharing in Christ. I agree with Michael Harper that *fellowship* has been overdone and I welcome a growing use of the term 'community', provided we do not lose the sense of commitment and sharing attached to it.[24] *Koinonia*, then, is expressed by our English words *communion, fellowship, community*. Its origin is in the adjective *koinos*, meaning common, i.e., what is common to all and what is shared by all. Christian community is about sharing and about something else expressed by the Greek word *diakonia*, i.e., service or ministry as an intimate form of sharing. This is not an exercise in terminology. But it is important to see the need to relearn the basic meaning of

193

community. Community logically implies commitment, sharing, and service. For the Greek pagans this sharing was done on a material and religious basis. But there does not seem to have been a link between communion with the gods and the sharing of temporal goods among friends. One was a form of initiation into cultic religion; the other was based on the concept of friendship, i.e., all is common between friends. For the Jews the solidarity of Israel with God was expressed by a concept of *covenant* which made Israel the people of God and brothers and sisters among themselves. Here we find joined together in one word the meeting with God (Deut. 6.5) and fraternal existence among men (Lev. 19.18). The basis for community, for sharing, is not philanthropy primarily but the loving initiative of God (Exod. 20.1). Henceforth the true worship of God and the sharing service of the neighbour are one and the same. The teaching of Jesus was in line with this tradition (Matt. 22.29; Luke 6.36). He preached unconditional love, indicating that his life and death were for many (Matt. 26.28). There is no ambiguity in the universal love he proclaims, a *koinonia* which knows no bounds. The very early Church of Acts understood itself as this fraternal community. In Acts 2.42 this community has its source in Christ, in his word, and in his reconciling act of giving and sharing his life for his brothers and sisters. These followers of Jesus devoted themselves to the teaching of the apostles, to the community, to the Eucharist, and to the life of prayer. Its community life was characterized by its sharing and expressed significantly. 'And all who believed were together and had all things in common; and they sold their possessions and goods and distributed them to all, as any had need' (Acts 2.44–5). And 'there was not a needy person among them' (Acts 4.34ff.). This material sharing and caring made real for these Christians Christ's word spoken for them, his body broken for them, his blood poured out for them. It made their prayer life real and expressed their inner communion (Acts 4.32). It was an authentic spiritual unity (Acts 1.14; 2.44; 4.24; 5.12) at every level of life and in every situation (Acts 12.5; 12.12). This lived community is found in two early writings of Christian history. They would seem to indicate a traditional practice and catechesis. The Didache, written at the end of the first century, says: 'You shall possess everything in common with your brother. . . . If you share immortal goods with one another, how advantageous will it be to share also perishable goods.' And the Epistle of Barnabas witnesses to the same spiritual communion and community of goods: 'You shall have all things in common with your neighbour, and you shall not say they are for your own benefit, for if you share an incorruptible good, how much more those which are corruptible.'[25]

Here is a practical expression of shared vision building a sharing, serving community, spiritual communion entailing a real care for the disadvantaged of the community. Paul with his particular insight into the depth and breadth of the mystery of Christ is imbued with *koinonia* as a participation in the mission of evangelizing the whole world by sharing the good news of God in Christ (chapters 1, 5, 7 of Philippians). This *koinonia* is closely allied to *diakonia* or the servant church of God in service to the world.

All this is the briefest possible summary of the Church's self-understanding that has developed and in which the Church is asked to renew itself in the Spirit from time to time. We live in such a time. The vision of a loving, serving, sharing community has never disappeared from the visible life of the Church. Monasticism was a movement to renew the apostolic life of the primitive community, as were the mendicant movements of the Franciscans and Dominicans in the thirteenth century and subsequent developments in the formation of religious orders and congregations. All this brings us back to the contemporary communitarian renewal going on among Christians. Max Delespesse says:

Today the Church is certainly tending to become again a community of communities. In all the countries of the world we see Christians grouping together into small communities, tailored to human dimensions. This phenomenon appears on the infra-parish or para-parish level. All the associations . . . are not necessarily communities yet but they are moving in that direction. We must add to this the continually increasing number of communities in the full sense of the word which implies both a spiritual and material sharing. . . . Without doubt the parish of the future will be a community of communities. It will group together members of different communities for certain activities, but ordinary life will find its place at the level of the basic community.[26]

This is a statement of hope for the renewal of the Church. Movements are the beginning of something larger and more permanent which they already incorporate in a pre-nascent way and bring forth when the conditions of life are right. There is never pure continuity nor pure discontinuity and we can never say how any one movement will work through the factors of novelty, transiency, and permanency present in any real movement. Neither are we able to predict exactly how its integration with other movements is to take place and what the final picture will reflect. The true picture of Christian renewal is in its very early stage of development. How the movements with which this book is concerned will grow together and find a place in the life of the Church, how they will complement and nourish one another is subject to time and grace and the response of faith the Church brings to its task of renewal for the life of the world. The Church insists on the permanency of certain values and on continuity with its past because its life is in continuity with and makes present in the world the definitive act of God in Jesus Christ. Both its development and continuity as a basic community are essential for its renewal and fulfilment. The renewal itself is necessary and provides a unique opportunity for development because throughout Christian history Christians have experienced the Church more as a spiritual society to which they belong than as a sharing community of which they are a part. Our time of renewal is to indicate the continuity of the Church of today with the basic Christian community of Acts. The Church today has an opportunity to experience itself as community on a scale and in a way without precedence. This is so because of the secular phenomenon of community that is able to set up relationships with the world and the Church that manifest the best and truest in the nature of each. In this sense hope becomes substantial, for what happens in the Church is about the world; what happens in the world involves the Church. If the world is experiencing a new exploration into the meaning of human community, the Church must explore the meaning of Christian community anew. If there is a radical attempt to return to the roots of being human, there must be a radical attempt to return to the roots of being Christian. Such

196

exploration and radical attempts are described as 'basic communities'.

Building Christian community is both profoundly human and Christian. It demands all that is truly human and all that being Christian means. In choosing one we choose the other. And there is no evidence of instant success. Building community is both goal and process. But it is a goal in itself and can never be a means to an end beyond itself. Why? Because the destiny of man is to live the life of God in a communion of saints. All forms of life are an effort and an outreach in response to a summons to that ultimate form of life. Every form of Christian community is 'an anticipation here below of the eschatological reality of the Church'.[27] For this reason we cannot stop short at building community simply at the level of comfortable functional togetherness. Christian community is about exodus and liberation, a true passover of death and resurrection. The mystery of the cross is present throughout the process. Yet the goal remains and the anticipation of it is present in all our concrete acts and practical efforts to build a joyful, celebrating community. In the long run there cannot be a loving, caring, sharing, serving community apart from a wholesome sense of play and celebration. For lack of this wholeness in human dynamics our efforts at community become an impossible task, a piece of human drudgery. Because so many of our efforts at building community are experimental and risky, people are afraid of its more daring and demanding dimensions. The temptation is to go halfway with the community effort, a charade of true community. 'We are not ready for it yet in quite this way.' Those who bring spontaneity, freedom, open relationships to the community face a battery of flashing warning signs. Too many Christians prefer clinical prevention to Christ's healing, saving love that is promised to those who come together in his name. We go on ignoring the developmental possibilities in human relationships, especially between men and women, single and married. Our safeguards and separations do not serve contemplation or inner freedom. They preserve our personality disorders, our lack of responsibility, our emotional immaturity – hardly signs of the coming Kingdom of God. Millions for defence, a pittance for prophecy! As the world talks of liberation and revolution in human relationships, it needs living signs that there is real hope for and authenticity in its aspiration for such. Can Christians justify the hope and witness to what is possible and authentic? The only way forward is to build communities that are truly basic and mixed. The mix admits a spectrum of diversity. In community there is the child–parent relationship, the married–single–celibate commitment and relationship to be worked out; the religious–lay–clerical mix; that of the professional–unskilled or semi-skilled community members; and finally the discipline and lifestyle described as monastic–mobile–secular. For some this is all too much of a possible mix. They may have to try community on a more selective basis. This is understandable and perhaps dictated by a kind of prudence. But as Christians we have to be open to a fullness of community that ultimately embraces the whole range of diversity. The quest for solidarity and affection in a Christian context of responsible unselfish love is the essential Christian witness that is needed. It is the basic need of our brothers and sisters throughout the world. And yet we are put off because all is not sweetness and light, because of our pretentious claims to 'identity'. We are broken by tensions, by things which amount to 'commonplace jealousies and everyday squabbles' in ordinary life. These things prevent or destroy community experiments because we lack commitment to the Church as a community. Here as nowhere else grace is costly and fidelity must be creative. Andrew Rigby, addressing himself to the British commune scene, said that 'apart from the problems involved in maintaining a viable economic and financial basis for a commune, the major problems that appear to confront members of the British communes at least would appear to be those involving the buildup of interpersonal tension and stress rather than those concerned with matters of "grand principle" '.[28] Christians have much more than a grand principle with which to nourish their community aspirations. We have been given a vision of life together in the presence of God (Eph. 1.3–10). Our vision can become real only by a passionate, sensitive commitment to the Kingdom of God and to our brothers and sisters in a world not yet free of poverty, injustice, oppression, anxiety, despair, loneliness, and alienation. We cannot afford our petty idolatry and insecurity if we choose to follow the pattern set by the early Christians of Acts. Christian community cannot be built on anything except Christ and the ethics of the Kingdom he proclaimed (Matt. 5; 6). A commitment to build Christian community is always a work of renewal for the Church. It seems unreal to me when I listen to talk about community as a para-ecclesial structure in the sense of being an alternative to life in the mainstream of the Church. I have heard a good deal of loose pseudo-radical talk along these lines. A lot of localized ecumenical steam has been released on the subject of community as an alternative form of church life. If the Church renews its life on the radical lines of the gospel, it is uniquely an alternative society. To renew the Church is to create an alternative society. Its catholicity is made tangible through a multiplicity of communities serving God for his glory and making his love and care for people really present in the world. My hope for the Church's renewal through new forms of community is not the basis for a new wave of sectarianism. This would be the case were we to regard experimental basic communities as alternatives to life in the institutional Church. The hope attached to the community movement is the creation of new forms of prophetic living that are linked to the life and witness of the Church to be a mirror of her true image as the people of God and the Body of Christ, dwelling place of the Spirit. In practice most of the experimental communities want to be part of church life and Christian witness, not as mutually exclusive options, but as part of one reality. In Britain, the USA, or Canada I have little evidence that these basic communities want to remain marginal or para-ecclesial bodies. They want to bring fresh life and renewed vision to the Church. At the present time many of these communities function as 'peculiars' where areas of freedom can be marked out. In general they exist to:

(1) Set up the right priorities for church life;
(2) renew Christian life according to the radical demands of the gospel;
(3) do together as Christians all that we are able to do in good conscience and according to major points of church discipline to make ecumenism a real part of the life of each church; to find a way forward in ecumenical relationships while respecting the continuity and development within the historic Churches.

However, the essential object of these basic communities is to prepare the Christian people as a whole for real living relationships that look in some unified fashion towards God at work in his world. Practically they prepare the Church for mission. Such

199

relationships need to be supported from within a group of committed people living with a vision that can be translated into loving acts of kindness and justice. In this way the Church becomes a prophetic society, an alternative society that effectively reduces conditions inimical to the true human condition and translates in a positive, loving way the gospel to attract and encourage the best that lies in the heart of man. A few years ago Norman James wrote some words I have never forgotten:

> I do not know whether the Church is meant to be an alternative society, but for leaven to work it must be from within and not outside. The life of which the Church is agent must come through a healthy cell within the organism of human society . . . The new order, the new life, must also begin within ourselves, drawing the thread of life and love out of our inmost being, not to make a cocoon, but as spiders to weave a web holding the several parts together in the lightest way. The more people who can bring their threads of unpossessive but spontaneous love and integrity out of their perpetually replenished life with God, the stronger and truer will grow the society of men.[29]

These words could be richly applied to many events and movements in the Church, but applied to the community movement we can see how profoundly they challenge us – not to observe and tolerate basic communities, but to give outright recognition and support to them. Church leaders will have to discern and respect the freedom and particular gifts of each community. Recognizing the ecumenical–renewal commitment of many of these communities is positive encouragement to their sense of serving the larger family of the Church.

It is this reflection that brings me to a very practical suggestion and hope. It deals with the problem of persuading the older established communities of traditional religious lifestyle, the orders and congregations, into this new search for community. In a period of decline, much of their own future and renewal must be reintegrated with the renewal of the Church at large. This renewal and future may well depend on a new commitment by religious to find that unity of heart and soul with their Christian brothers and sisters who carry a new fire in their hearts, a burning vision in their souls. Much of the liberation of religious will be from bondage to decaying human traditions, self-satisfaction, petty idolatries arising out of a spuriously assumed tribal identity. Pious posturing will give way to worship in spirit and truth as they learn to share their material and spiritual bread with their hungry brothers and sisters of the Church. Religious life may become once more an 'apostolic life', a eucharistic life broken and poured out for others. Delespesse rightly refers to religious communities and other basic communities as complementary.[30] He wonders 'if this sharing wouldn't be better realized by integrating the religious communities into the ordinary communities of the Christian people'.[31] He argues his case persuasively and deductively, i.e., from the theology of religious life, rather than arguing the case inductively, i.e., from religious life as it is. Those who wish to be more realistic in their approach to building new forms of community with religious would do well to balance their hope with a generous amount of inductive thinking. Religious life today is far less sure of its meaning and its future than it has been for a very long time. It has begotten an introverted breed of Christians too long separated from the ordinary life of people and from their fellow Christians. They are unprepared for open, honest experimentation in new forms of basic community living. Life and service in the main have become largely functional. They continue to skate around the edge of renewal, always at the planning board, writing endless statements and spiritual documents, drawing up constitutions. They suspect something may be happening in the depths of Christian church life and would not want to be left out. But they are not sure how to get into the mainstream of renewal. The older inherited spirituality and charism wears thin and is hardly adequate for a new act of faith proportionate to a new age of faith. Thus membership is down, age is up, with extensive property resources and former commitments of the apostolate weighing heavily. They are left with the choice of disposing of property resources and shrinking commitments. Or there is the choice of using these property resources for new co-operative ventures with other Christians. If this option is taken, these religious communities will have to be ruthlessly honest with themselves. The temptation is to keep the tribal pot boiling and the flag flying often at the expense of those who sincerely join them to create new forms of basic community. There is an honest search going on for these new forms of community. If religious are to take part in the search they will have to understand the object of the exercise: to renew the identity of the Christian Church as a community of communities. Religious community life has been content to put willing satellites in orbit around itself. This is contrary to the authentic basic communities the Church needs for its present life and witness. The Holy Spirit can transform whatever we give him and there is no doubt that this includes mixed motives, a measure of ambiguity and deviousness. Despite these the Holy Spirit is able to initiate experiments that will flower finally in Christian communities born of a rediscovery of our spiritual unanimity across the lines of canonical status. Within the religious orders there are individuals sincerely seeking to renew the charism of their particular community. But the renewal is out of context because the context is the world and the brothers and sisters the Lord sends to do a new thing. There are also those who, liberated by the Spirit in their hearts and minds, are finding ways of being with others for a genuine renewal and sharing. Certain developments in household communities allow religious and priests to be incorporated into extended families of Christians as brothers and sisters in the Lord. In this way they bring their gifts and witness of a vowed or celibate life directly to the Christian community. In turn they are nourished by the charisms or spiritual gifts along with basic human values to be discovered in the daily life of the Christian family.[32]

Yet the approach that Delespesse takes is not without some merit. Religious life by intention has its roots deep in Christian community life as a life of sharing and service to others as a means of glorifying and serving God. Whatever new insights, as well as deviations, have become attached to the vowed life of poverty, chastity, and obedience, they bear witness to fundamental values proper to the whole of Christian life and have their roots in that vision witnessed and expressed by the communities of the Acts, of the Didache, of the Epistle of Barnabas. And since our concern is with hope and the future, we have to recognize the spiritual and material potential of religious communities in the renewed search for basic Christian community. The potential will have to be actuated by authentic motivation and in the right context of sharing. As Delespesse remarks, 'this requires a profound change of mentality and of the structures of "religious life" '.[33] The very gradual work of integration has begun and the beginnings are not marked with great success. But we must be content with humble beginnings. Minorities are where the action begins – in the Church and in the world. So we need not be discouraged about the future of religious life, since the Holy Spirit will renew it as he renews the Church as a basic community. The process could move ahead much more quickly if religious communities really put their resources behind the efforts of the younger basic communities. Delespesse thinks there could be a revolution, a renewed social order, and a witness to a more fraternal, human way of life.[34] He concludes:

> The 'recommunitarization' of the Church is a movement that nothing can stop. Religious should participate in this by utilizing all their possibilities and potentialities which still are very considerable. They could change the face of the Church and resolve the problem of the religious life in today's world.[35]

In the middle of 1977 a consultation was set up with the joint effort of Alan Harrison, Secretary of the Advisory Council for Anglican Religious Communities, by David Clark to whose important community study I have referred already, and by myself.[36] The invitation was selective, to assure a manageable cross-section of old and new communities, religious life, and lay communities. We ended up with fifty-seven varieties, speaking various ideological dialects, but conscious of a common life binding them together nonetheless, conscious of the need to find a new way of sharing. The religious and the members of the newer basic communities often had to resort to spelling out terms such as *commitment, authority, poverty*, and *community* for mutual clarification as much as edification. All the difficult questions were raised 'but in the end we departed convinced that something had begun, or continued, rather than had finished'.[37] At the end of that conference we were able to formulate a simple statement:

> We thank God that Christian communities are discovering each other and we know that the Spirit will show us the way to share our prayers, members, resources, and skills. We give thanks that this is beginning to happen.

I promised to return to the accelerating force of the neo-Pentecostal movement in the Christian community movement. Community building is a very fragile task. Look at it as an ideal. It seems simple and beautiful and attractive and fulfilling. Come near it. Touch it. It falls so easily. People come to it with hidden or unconscious motives and agendas. And then one remembers that 'unless the Lord builds the house, those who build it labor in vain' (Ps. 127.1). It is interesting to note that we speak of *building* community so frequently. No one, except the novice and the hopelessly romantic, could imagine otherwise. If the hope afforded by this building of community is not to end with disappointment, it is important to look at basic issues and hard questions arising early in the movement, issues and questions demanding rigorous and radical honesty – with ourselves and others. But at the end of all our considerations and plans we cannot forget that building community is a spiritual work. Each member brings his or her devious, dishonest heart into community. Entering a community is a call to conversion – not conformity. Each is asked to put himself or herself before the Lord in anticipation and openness to have the heart changed. No matter how prepared spiritually we may think we are, no matter how we appreciate and appraise the spiritual tradition from which we come, we must be prepared to be changed. We are in a new process with new people to do a new work and give new witness. We are now obliged to serve a new common goal. We have a new vocation to build up the Church in a new way. The point in saying all this is to make very clear that the only spirituality able to meet the demands of unity and diversity is a spirituality of charisms or spiritual gifts. I speak as someone who has been directly involved in a basic Christian community experiment. I have known also the joy of being led by the Lord into the neo-Pentecostal movement. Communities rise and fall in this provisional stage of church renewal. They do not rise very high or fall very low. They just sink into the slough of mediocrity and functionalism, a kind of joyless forced march with people dropping out or falling in. You may remember that I spoke of the neo-Pentecostal experience *vis-à-vis* Christian holiness and of how the spiritual gifts or *charismata* which accompany this experience create a new openness to God. I also indicated that I considered the development of a spirituality out of that experience to be the real ongoing meaning of the experience itself. My own conviction is that though one may debate both the nature and evidence of the experience, a Christian is not free to bypass charismatic spirituality, i.e., a radical openness to the gifts of the Holy Spirit. Paul Hinnebusch in referring to the spiritual gifts as charismatic graces says that they 'are essential for building up Christian community, and have always been operative wherever there has been true community in the Lord'.[38] Their very purpose is to build up the Body of Christ. By logical implication they are for those who wish to build community in order to renew the Church as the community of communities. One of the first lessons the Lord taught through the neo-Pentecostal renewal is that much of our efforts, programmes, and structural planning end in frustration and sterility because we act without discerning what God's will is, what the true values and priorities are for building up the Church, and because so much of self, human vanity, motivates us. As Ralph Martin noted, renewal demands that we experience a new Pentecost. So much of what we do is 'of the flesh and the will of man' rather than the Spirit of God.[39] In saying this we are not denying that charismatic grace is at work in some measure in Christian homes, hospitals, schools, and churches. We are saying that there is a lack of awareness among Christians that they belong to a people of God, the Body of Christ, a community of faith. We are saying that the charismatic graces meant to be communicated and used for service have become excessively institutionalized and spiritual ministry has been carefully confined to an ordained ministry. What was meant to be the ministry, witness, and spirituality of the whole Church has been reserved to and expected from ordained clerical service. Charismatic graces manifesting the Spirit and building up church life around the Lordship of Christ make us aware that God is at work in and through the lives of all of us. God is at work among all his people who are the Church. This is a lived experience. Far from underrating sacraments or ordained ministry, charismatic spirituality views sacraments as gifts of God and an ordained ministry as an instrument of God to build up the whole life of the Church through Jesus in the power of the Spirit. Hinnebusch says that the 'life in the Trinity, still hidden in our hearts, is expressed outwardly in the body of Christ, the Christian community'.[40] He continues: 'The charisms, building up the body and manifesting its life, are therefore necessary until the full revelation of the "life now hid with Christ in God" ' (Col. 3.3). A renewal through these charismatic graces provides blessed assurance that God is renewing the Church as community. Because all charisms by their nature are to be shared, they manifest that self-transcending love which is the bond they are meant to build up and strengthen for the life of the Christian community. They prepare the Church to be a community of love living at the heart of the world. Finally, charismatic graces are signs that God is acting now. Ralph Martin says:

> The question of the re-evaluation of parish structure and the present shape and training for ministry is something that will take years to work out. But God is acting now. And already we can see outlines . . . of the 'church of the future' emerging here and there, local churches, Christian communities . . . experiencing the full range of workings of the Spirit. . . .[41]

This return to reflection on the role of charismatic spirituality in building community brings us back to the real object of community living, i.e., the renewal and refinement of the Church as a community. If we wish to be more precise and real, we can say that the object is the renewal of a sense of community in our parish churches. The parish or local church is a family of families. The parish or local church is the basic unit of the Church as a community of communities. It is at this level that the ordinary meaning of Christian life will be renewed and manifested. Whether our parish churches have spires or not, they will once more become symbols of man's life with God and his solidarity with the human community. The buildings are very secondary. A lot has been said about this. The building of one visible community of faith at the heart of the human community is the indispensable value behind all parish-church work. Where there is a real community, word gets around because community is its own attraction and witness. The work is ongoing and never finished because it is about the love and care and sharing of life at every level where people are. Community is a 'third force' uniting those left and right of centre, breaking the polarity which renders the Church helpless and hopeless, a spectacle to men and angels. It is truly a place of meeting, a 'place of synthesis' where spiritual and basic human values are preserved and integrated. Delespesse has shown how Vatican Council II had a very limited notion of community. The Council used the notion in reference to religious orders and priests.[42] But, as he indicates, this only shows that the renewal sponsored by the Council is meant to be a beginning in the process of renewal and change in the Church. It was a pastoral council undertaken for the life of the whole Church. He recalls the prophetic voice of Bishop Elchinger of Strasbourg and Bishop Himmer of Tournai, both of whom pleaded for a new openness to small basic communities like those of the early Christians.[43] The community movement is a development keeping us faithful and bringing us to a renewed sense of the radical demands and praxis of the gospel. It forces us, as a people of God, to look outward and reach outward to God's world, the *oikoumene*, the family of God. Because of our knowledge and communion with Jesus Christ, we are the firstborn of a new creation (Col. 1.15) for he is the firstborn of many brothers and sisters (Rom. 8.29). The community movement is a movement towards the unity of human life with life in Christ. Along with the other areas of hope we have singled out in this book, the community movement is a landmark and blazes a prophetic trail. Unlike the other movements it is their consummation and the goal, for the basic value it seeks to bring to the world is the reality of God's love poured into our hearts by the Holy Spirit (Rom. 5.5). It seeks to show how practical this love of God is and how necessary for the life of the world.

While I am more sanguine in my hope for the institutional Church than a number of my friends and associates, my hope does not rest on attitudes I find among Christians or the performance of the Church as an institution in the conduct of its own affairs and its commentaries on the affairs of others. My hope rests on the living God who pours out his Spirit on the Church, breaking through our wrongheadedness, making us look in the right direction.[44] I agree with David Clark that the community movement has a narrow path to tread and needs the positive encouragement of the whole Church without paternalistic protection or premature idealization. As he says, the community movement 'is robust enough to stand up for itself and it openly acknowledges that it has already run into all the problems associated with that type of human endeavour which risks going out into the unknown'.[45] There is always the question of how much continuity or discontinuity the Lord is asking of the individual or the community. There is always the need to discern what the nature of the work to be done actually requires. But in the light of what has been said I do not see in the long term how effective our witness can be if we choose to live in isolation from the mainstream of church life. Cut off from the mainline church life, whatever its deficiencies, the protest of the community experiment can easily become negative and turn sour. Such communities perhaps hope to identify more closely with secular communities which propose basic personal and interpersonal values as indispensable for healthy human life. Of course one hears the retort that this is where the renewal of life begins, not excepting Christian life. Yet it can be argued that Christian life is committed to these values because where it is healthy they are presupposed, built upon, brought to perfection and fulfilment. However, Christian life is built upon the unique value of Jesus Christ and his presence, an ongoing presence, in our world. For Christians all these values must be brought together in him, though not in an exclusivist or separatist way. Somehow we must live in such a way that both sets of values, human and Christian, are respected and integrated. Pope Paul VI in the *Evangelii Nuntiandi* expresses the worth of such basic communities because 'they spring from the need to live the Church's life more intensely, or from the desire and quest for a more human dimension such as larger ecclesial communities can only offer with difficulty. . . .'[46] The pastoral strategy document *A Time for Building* also devotes a section to such communities. It is clear that the value of and urgent need for such basic apostolic communities is increasingly recognized by Roman Catholics. Thus *A Time for Building* says:

> We foresee the formation of communities, groupings small enough to enable members to know and feel involved with each other but large enough to provide and sustain the main functions of the Church. . . . We feel that the pastoral efforts of the Church should be directed chiefly towards creating this form of Christian community life. The enterprise must be started at once and on a wide scale throughout the country. . . . Clearly as yet we do not know the exact shape, organization, or method of working of these groups and communities. There can be no blueprint. The Church must respond to human needs and possibilities and obviously changes will take place gradually, and new structures will grow both from within and alongside existing ones. Such a strategy will demand deep personal renewal at all levels.[47]

Of course different theologies of the Church in differing traditions will alter attitudes towards the role and response of such basic communities. It seems to me that we can agree that these basic communities are vital for the renewal of the Church as a community of faith. Differences will remain proportionate to Christian differences in other areas of church life. But these communities will also bring us beyond these differences to a new place of life together. As Pope Paul VI notes, these communities 'will correspond to their most fundamental vocation: as hearers of the gospel . . . they will soon become proclaimers of the gospel themselves'.[48] Such pastoral comments may seem to some only a token gesture of acknowledgement. I find it hopeful, a kind of beginning. At any rate the mantle of prophecy does not rest exclusively on the shoulders of pastors and priests. We place too great a burden on church leaders. It is the whole Church that shares in the prophetic, priestly, leading role of Christ. The statements of church leaders encourage, whatever their limitations; the movement towards community is what grounds our hope. David Clark confirms this towards the end of his study of basic communities in Britain. He says:

> Yet the winds of change have been blowing for some time, given impetus by the rising tempo of mobility – spatial, social, cognitive – and through a few prophetic voices, many not Christian, the meaning of humanity and community is being radically questioned and searchingly reappraised. And who can argue that a Church which has always claimed to offer the key to the truly human and to represent the fullness of community should not be especially ready to welcome such a challenge? The basic communities of which I have written are but a very small part of a much larger 'movement of fire' running across many continents.[49]

Those who ignore the winds of change and the movements of fire ignore the Spirit of the living God. Despite its prosaic and low-key approach, what I have been talking about in this book is about the wind, the fire, the Spirit. I have said that the community movement consummates the other movements because it is about the Church and the Church is about the world. Hans Küng says:

> But 'Church', great or small, is the *whole* community of faith

209

which proclaims the gospel . . . in order to awaken faith in Jesus Christ, provoke commitment in his Spirit, make the Church present in the world in everyday Christian witness and so to carry on the cause of Jesus Christ. . . . Whenever the Church privately and publicly advocates the cause of Jesus Christ . . . in word and deed, it is at the service of man and becomes credible.[50]

This is what community is all about – the credibility of the Church. This need not and ought not to be a joyless task and witness. In Christian affairs joylessness is always a countersign. Building community puts us directly into the stream of life itself, a spontaneous, free, joyful celebration of being called to share the life of God himself. Joy is meant to be as much a part of life here and now as is suffering. Joy belongs more to life than does suffering because joy is meant to last as a fruit of living. Suffering is meant to pass and is a temporal ingredient of the mystery of love and care that God is working out among men. The cross is part of the mystery of joy (Rom. 5.11). So joy is not a superficial, sentimental feeling. It is a fruit of grace just as the cross is a sign of the costliness of grace. Perhaps this is what draws men and women to community in significant numbers. It is a place where joy and suffering meet, are celebrated in every Eucharist, in the laughter and tears of every community where suffering can be sustained, joy given depth and permanence. Community can be 'serendipity', i.e., the discovery of something new and beautiful in an unexpected place. It can be the place where we are surprised by joy if we take its demands seriously. In an early editorial in *Community* David Clark reminded us that we cannot stop short at community because *joyous community* is the goal. Far from being an escape from life's realities it sets for itself the difficult aim of living out the mystery of joy through the cross. Through the cross Christians in community are able to experience the discovery that 'joy is the exhilaration of having discovered that love is eternal'.[51] If a community is authentic, therefore, it is led into a spirit of celebration, and the particular times of celebration nourish joy as a 'pervading spirit in the community'.[52] Jean Vanier describes the effects of joyful celebration:

> The celebration is that which relaxes the person in the depths of his sensibilities, that which opens him to others and to the

universe. It softens hardness of heart and spirit. It creates unity between persons. It is the sign of the happiness of the eternal celebration.[53]

Introducing this element of joy might seem to be an overextended footnote to my other reflections on the community movement. Yet it is the secret of the perennial attraction to community. Community is not a romantic aspiration to something past and precious to folk memory. It is the anticipation of joy discovered through love and the sharing of life. Community is neither fool's gold nor a fool's world. It is the place and condition for life's synthesis. Its components are suffering, joy, celebration. It makes life real, credible, and strangely fascinating. It is meant for the world and through the mystery and community of the Church in the world. It is neither a luxury nor dispensable. Whatever forms it takes, whatever apostolates it serves, it is the supreme gift of God offered to the world through the mystery of men and women prepared to enter the depths of their humanity, sustained by the unifying gift of Christ's love.

# Epilogue

In an essay for *The Times*, 29 October 1977, Cardinal Hume spoke of the image of the Church changing from that of Solomon's Temple to Abraham's tent. The old image of the Church shrouded in clouds of majesty, perfect and unchangeable, was in fact changing. The new image of the Church was that of pilgrim. The Church has undertaken a pilgrimage of faith. It is on the move, listening obediently to the voice of God, putting its trust in his promises. The Cardinal said: 'Now the Church tends to listen as well as to teach, to be humble and searching as well as being guide and beacon. More than anything else the Church has become aware that it can learn more about the revelation of God entrusted to it: it can grow in knowledge and self-realization.'

I would like to add that this new awareness is to be conditioned more by the future tense than previously. The Church is going to be more concerned where God is calling it to move than by its past. The past is a lifeline, a vital cord not unlike the one attached to an astronaut for a spacewalk. The cord makes exploration possible. Man does not step into the vastness of space simply for the thrill of it, though he may well feel thrilled. For example, the definition of Jesus as both God and man that emerged from the doctrinal Council of Chalcedon (A.D. 451) is important in the life of the Christian Church. It provides a parameter for Christian life, work, theology. It is a factor that remains constant in the Christian equation and stubbornly resists dissolution in the name of modernity or contemporaneity. The faith expressed and worked out from Chalcedon makes possible a basic relationship with God in Christ. But this faith does not exempt Christians from that act of faith that discerns what God is asking them to be and do here and now in obedience. The future is something positive even if it is discerned faintly at times. Men search, look for, reach for the future in obedience to God. Hope sustains their obedience and discernment. This book is a very preliminary contribution to encourage the discernment of church leaders and committed Christians. Christians are called to mediate, anticipate, lead towards the future God wants for everyone. To this end a Christian is baptized into Christ and into hope. This book is about the future and even as it is being written that future is becoming present. It has not been written on the basis of a simplistic intuition or guess. It is based on more than a vague, visceral feeling that amounts to little more than a naive optimism about the future of the Church. This book has been inspired by the virtue of hope, given in baptism, communicated in a vision of faith, substantiated by an experiential awareness that God is working in an unprecedented way and on an unprecedented scale in both the Church and the world. This new consciousness is revealed in a number of significant movements which curve towards each other in a promise of convergence. Under a new creative act of God's Spirit a new pattern of Christian unity and community, of liberation and mission, is being fashioned from the chaos of history and human mismanagement. Such awareness, such unprecedented participation in these movements is itself a component of contemporary Christian hope. Cardinal Hume in his essay in *The Times* noted four points that coincide remarkably with the substantives of hope which make up this book. He referred to them as areas of thought and behaviour, areas which were becoming increasingly important to many people. He suggested we should concentrate on these because they are seeds of promise for the future. They provide a challenge for a united Christian conscience. He listed them as *prayer, a feeling for universal justice, a respect for human dignity,* and *a longing for community*. Despite a sense of urgency in matters of church renewal, in matters of Christian mission and unity it will be important to keep these movements flexible and free to mature and converge. Hopefully they will not be subjected to ecclesiastical organization that will thwart the new life they promise for the Church. Christians are called to bear witness to the resurrection through the renewal of spiritual life, Christian unity, community, liberation, and mission. We cannot be deterred by the magnitude and complexity of human problems. We were called out of darkness into light, so we cannot sympathize with the doomwatchers. We are God's people, affirming that light has come into the world and darkness cannot extinguish it. However deep the darkness of the night with its terrors and tears, joy comes with the dawn (Ps. 30). The Christian people are called to announce with one voice that God has visited his people and with tender mercy gives light to those who sit in darkness and the shadow of death, to guide our feet into the way of peace (Luke 1). We need sophisticated analysis and planning, pastoral care and strategy. These too are expressions of real hope. They are our response to God in hope. But the heart of hope is a renewed spirit, a new openness to do the right thing, to love the right way, and to walk humbly with God into his future and ours (Micah 6).

# Notes

*The place of publication is London unless otherwise stated.*

## CHAPTER 1
## BAPTIZED INTO HOPE

1 Christian life means a reshaping of man. Our very being is transformed. A special relationship to Christ is established in association with his saving death and resurrection. It is a commitment to new life, new creation, and the renunciation of whatever is judged to be incompatible with the new life in Christ.

2 *The Birth of the New Testament*, C. F. D. Moule, Black's New Testament Commentaries, ed. H. Chadwick, companion vol. 1, (A. & C. Black 1966, 2nd edn), pp. 25–6; 112–13. Commenting on Eph. 1.3 and 1 Pet. 1.3, Moule says they 'are undoubtedly liturgical in *type*'. The Jerome Biblical Commentary says that it is better to regard 1 Peter as a real letter into which a baptismal exhortation has been incorporated or materials from such an exhortation rather than the shape of an actual baptismal liturgy.

3 *The Experiment Hope.* SCM Press 1975. Trans. M. Douglas Meeks, p. 41.

4 Ibid.

5 Trans. Edward Quinn. Collins and Doubleday 1976, 1977.

6 Ibid., pp. 223–5.

7 As renewed biblical reflection develops, thinking about God as the one who acts in time and history leading us to action and fulfilment, the one who is always ahead of us becomes more familiar to Christian thought.

8 Op. cit., p. 189.

9 Ibid., p. 187. José Miranda says: 'Biblical faith understands itself as hope, but truly as hope that recognizes no limits.' Cf. his *Mark and the Bible* (SCM Press 1977), pp. 226–9.

10 Cf. Douglas Rhymes, 'Contemporary Spirituality', *The Month*, May 1976, pp. 153–6.

11 The Bible is a book of God's promises, a book of hope; cf. Moltmann, op. cit., p. 187.

12 Moltmann says: 'In fact, there is no true *theology of hope* which is not first of all a *theology of the cross*.' Op. cit., p. 72.

13 Thomas Merton's development as a monk is one such example and is reflected in his more mature writings, e.g., *Conjectures of a Guilty Bystander.*

14  Trans. William Glen-Doepel (Herder & Herder 1969), p. 102. Metz explores this question of Christian asceticism to support his understanding of biblical hope as radically oriented towards the future in the context of responsibility for the progress of the world in both the New and Old Testaments; cf. pp. 92–3.

15  Cf. Moltmann, op. cit., p. 185: 'Without the hope of faith, there is no ground for hope in action. Without hope in action, there are no results from the hope of faith . . . Without the growth and spread of the hope of faith, however, all programs for peace and campaigns for liberation fall short of their marks, become pragmatic, and quickly succumb to weariness.'

16  *Study Encounter*, vol. 12, nos. 1–2 (1976) takes up this theme of accounting for hope. I have taken this quote from a paper of the Division of Ecumenical Affairs of the British Council of Churches (DEA/4/75), pp. 23–4.

17  An example *vis-à-vis* Roman Catholics would be Hans Küng's *Infallible?*; another example that has more recently bewildered many Christians is *The Myth of God Incarnate*.

18  Cf. Hans Küng, *The Church* (Burns & Oates 1968), pp. 433–6; also pp. 179–91, 396–8.

19  Though I do not use him as a source in this book, Wolfhart Pannenberg shares with Metz and Moltmann an important place among the theologians who have stressed the significance of the *future* in theology.

20  Gustavo Guttierez, *A Theology of Liberation* (SCM Press 1974), p. 225.

21  Bloch's *Das Prinzip Hoffnung (The Hope Principle)*, which has been so influential, was written between 1938 and 1949 when he was a refugee from Nazi Germany living in America. Cf. chapter 3 of Moltmann, op. cit.

22  The two complementary works of Moltmann are *Theology of Hope*, New York, Harper & Row, 1967 and *The Crucified God*, New York, Harper & Row, 1974.

23  *Theology of Human Hope*, Washington, D.C., Corpus Books, 1969; quoted by Guttierez, op. cit., p. 217.

24  *Revolutionary Theology Comes of Age* (SPCK 1975), p. 144.

25  Guttierez, op. cit., p. 218; an example of how Moltmann has corrected himself may be cited from his work *The Experiment of Hope*, pp. 57–8: 'The cross of Christ is the sign of God's hope on earth for all those who live here in the shadow of the cross. Theology of hope is at its hard core theology of the cross. The cross of Christ is the presently given form of the Kingdom of God on earth. In the crucified Christ we view the future of God. Everything else is dreams, fantasies, and mere wish images. Hope born out of the cross of Christ distinguishes Christian faith from superstition as well as from

disbelief. The freedom generated by the cross distinguishes Christian faith from optimism as well as from terrorism.'

26  *The Experiment Hope*, p. 28.

27  Ibid., p. 27.

28  Ibid., p. 52; chapter 4 is in fact an introduction to the 'theology of hope'.

29  Ibid., p. 42.

30  *Eschatology* means essentially that there is faith that human history has an end. There has been a development of this faith in Judaeo-Christian thought and faith. It is a faith that God acts definitively in that history with its human sin and chaos to create a new heaven and earth (Gen. 1.1) where there will be no conflict between God and man, nor between man and man. *Systematic theology* is a general term to describe an approach to theology that uses a set of language, symbols, and images in a consistent way to articulate relationships between various articles of faith, analysing and distinguishing these elements of faith, emphasizing the difference between the content and language of faith. It is done with the purpose of providing a coherent understanding within the limitations of human reason of the things of God.

31  Alfredo Fierro, *The Militant Gospel* (SCM Press 1977), p. 257; cf. also pp. 257–301.

32  Ibid., p. 260.

33  Ibid., p. 270; this is a not uncommon criticism of the work of Teilhard de Chardin, namely that matters of violence, social justice, exploitation of man by man do not occupy an important place in his system of thought; cf. Guttierez, op. cit., p. 178.

34  For example, see Fierro, op. cit., pp. 257–301.

35  Ibid., p. 299.

36  Guttierez, op. cit., p. 232.

37  Fierro, op. cit., p. 274.

38  Cf. ibid., pp. 274–5.

39  Guttierez, op. cit., pp. 234–5.

40  Quoted by Fierro, op. cit., p. 279.

41  Op. cit., p. 281.

42  There are more subtle difficulties, conceptual and linguistic, but they do not serve our purpose here. They are important to the theologian with reference to political social action and liberation theology. Our terms of reference are wider and more diversified. I can only suggest more extensive reading for the curious, e.g., *The Militant Gospel* by Fierro, pp. 282–301 and Bonino's *Revolutionary Theology Comes of Age*, pp. 132–53. The future cannot be discerned solely in terms of socio-economic-political structures. I would want to question seriously Fierro's assumption that 'theology refers to the future in

mythical and symbolic terms; utopian thought refers to the future in rational terms' (p. 282). There seems to be an older rationalistic epistemology at work behind such a statement. Today the limitations and symbolic function of all language, including scientific language, are recognized; in this respect *The Structure of Scientific Revolutions* by Thomas S. Kuhn, University of Chicago Press 1970, 2nd edn enlarged, has become a standard reference.

43  Cf. *The Protestant Era* by Paul Tillich, a Phoenix Book, University of Chicago Press, abridged edn 1957, with special attention to chapter 4: 'Religion and Secular Culture'.

44  Ibid., p. 59.

45  Op. cit., p. 93.

46  Ibid., p. 94.

47  Ibid.

48  *On Being a Christian*, cited above, p. 215.

49  Ibid., p. 478.

50  'Our Hope: a Confession of Faith for this Time', *Study Encounter*, vol. 12, nos. 1–2, pp. 65–87.

51  *The Christian Commitment* (Sheed & Ward 1963), p. 60, first published as *Mission and Grace*, vol. 1.

52  One thinks of the explanatory work of Nicolai Bulgakov, Orthodox priest, theologian, philosopher, and economist. His work popularized in English under the title *The Wisdom of God* (out of print) in 1937 never found acceptance in his own Church. Perhaps the neo-Pentecostal movement will provoke more theologizing along these lines beyond the neo-Pentecostal experience itself.

53  Selected papers from a symposium sponsored by the Graymoor Ecumenical Institute in September 1969 under the general title *Conversations 69*; the institute publishes *Ecumenical Trends* and is particularly active in North American ecumenical affairs. The address is: Graymoor Ecumenical Institute, Garrison, New York 10524, USA. The institute was established in 1967.

54  Cf. the Constitution on the Church (*Lumen Gentium*) of Vatican II, ch. 2, n. 17 (Abbott edn).

55  Christians are divided in their understanding of how Scripture and Tradition function as one source of revelation and how both relate to the question of teaching authority in the Church. There are a number of questions unresolved in both Catholic and Protestant theology. Cf. Hans Küng's *Justification* (Burns & Oates 1964), pp. 106–17; *On Being a Christian*, op. cit., pp. 463–8; also his *Structures of the Church*, Burns & Oates 1965.

56  *Theology*, vol. 75, no. 627 (Sept. 1972), pp. 451–62. I am indebted to Dr McDonagh for this reflection on the moral dimension of human experience in relation to hope.

57 *Crosscurrents*, vol. 5, no. 4 (Autumn 1955), trans. Maurice S. Friedman.

58 Article cited above, in *Theology*, p. 453.

59 'The Christian attitude here clearly derives from the creation story of man as a social being; the salvation story always dealt with man-in-community so that the key Old Testament figures Abraham, Moses, and the prophets, as well as the key events such as Exodus and Sinai, were figures and events in the formation of a people in whom God's action in the world would be embodied until it reached its climax in Jesus Christ. And he was the key figure in the formation of the New People of God which is a sign and realization of the unity and fulfilment of all mankind . . . In this extension of the reconciling work of Jesus Christ which is through community and for community of all men, the reign of God is achieved together with the growth in humanization, the fuller development of all men in an increasing realization and sharing of their human potential. In such humanization the Christian discerns the thrust of God's activity in the course of human history.' (*Theology*, op. cit., pp. 457–8.) The search for further human development comes from this quest for the fullness of life in the Kingdom of God which Jesus preached. Human motivation and energy are informed by a unique energy of love (*agape*) which saves man from the dual oppression of collectivism and uniformity on the one hand and narrow individualism on the other. That this agapic energy is found only within the Christian community and not within the wider human community is open to much debate, i.e., the question of anonymous Christianity.

60 Cf. *The Month*, July 1977, 'The Church: Sign of the Kingdom in the Pluralistic Secular Society', pp. 226–30. A talk delivered at a conference on 'Christian Mission and Evangelization' sponsored by the Franciscan Friars of the Atonement.

61 Ibid.

62 *The Times*, 2 December 1972, and reprinted on 30 October 1976.

63 *The End of Our Time*, trans. Donald Atwater (New York, Sheed & Ward, 1933), p. 11.

64 Ibid., p. 33.

65 The Bodley Head (1970), p. 14.

66 Op. cit., pp. 27, 39.

67 'Nowhere and in no single matter is solid earth felt underfoot; we are on volcanic ground and any eruption is possible, material or spiritual.' (Berdyaev, op. cit., p. 12.)

68 *God's Tomorrow* (SCM Press 1977), pp. 4–10.

69 Op. cit., p. 12.

70 Cf. an excellent essay by John Mills, OP, on the true nature of apocalyptic thought, language, and literature in *New Heaven? New Earth?* (Darton, Longman & Todd 1976), pp. 71–118. He notes that

apocalyptic literature: (a) represents a break in history; (b) conveys hope rooted in the new vision of history as wholly in control of God; (c) stresses the cosmic dimension of the conflict of good and evil.

71  This is not the place to argue the case for our present time to be a time unique in the evolution of human consciousness. There are many assumptions and unprovable hypotheses. However, we are not resting our conviction on any naive optimism or enthusiasm for the so-called 'age of Aquarius'. The conviction rests on the scale and magnitude of human events and human behaviour and human knowledge.

72  *The Times*, 27 January 1975, from an article headlined 'Religion has a major role to play in leading civilization away from the brink of disaster'.

73  John Hughes, *Sociological Analysis: Methods of Discovery* (Thomas Nelson 1976), pp. 15–16.

74  Cf. Barry Till, *The Churches Search for Unity* (Penguin Books 1972), p. 15.

75  'The New Testament gives witness to the Church as the unique instrument of grace, and at the same time it acknowledges the universality of God's salvific care for his people. It would seem, therefore, that the New Testament does not commit the Christian Church to a particular understanding of her mission. It may well be that several concepts of the mission are in harmony with the teaching of the apostles and that it depends on the historical situation of the Church and on the guidance of the Spirit what particular understanding of the mission the Church acquires in a given age.' (Gregory Baum, 'The Doctrinal Basis for Jewish–Christian Dialogue', *The Ecumenist*, May–June 1968, vol. 6, no. 4.)

76 · SPCK (1976), pp. 112–13.

77  Op. cit., p. 117.


## CHAPTER 2
## THE ECUMENICAL MOVEMENT

1  From his enthronement sermon as Archbishop of Canterbury in 1942.

2  *Oikoumene*: cf. Acts 11.14 and 19.27; Matt. 24.14; Luke 2.1.

3  The Orthodox Church considers herself to be the One, Holy, Catholic and Apostolic Church though recognizing the historical actual (ontological) existence of Christian Churches and confessions. The Roman Catholic Church 'recognizes that in many ways she is linked ' with those who, being baptized, are honoured with the name of Christian. . . .' (Vatican II Constitution on the Church, Abbott edn., no. 15; cf. also no. 8). Moreover, the RC Church is convinced that '. . . as the obstacles to perfect ecclesiastical communion are over-

come, all Christians will be gathered, in a common celebration of the Eucharist, into that unity of the one and only Church which Christ bestowed on his Church from the beginning. This unity, we believe, dwells [subsists] in the Catholic Church as something she can never lose, and we hope it will continue until the end of time.' (Decree on Ecumenism of Vatican II, Abbott edn., my parentheses, no. 4.) This represents a development of self-understanding, i.e., unity subsists in the RC Church rather than a simple identification of herself as the 'one true Church'.

4   I am not writing a history of the movement and suggest as a reference Stephen Neill's *A History of the Ecumenical Movement*, 2 vols., SPCK 1967, 1970; or Barry Till's *The Churches Search for Unity*, Penguin Books 1972.

5   Charles La Fontaine, 'The Many Faces of Ecumenism Today', *The American Ecclesiastical Review*, vol. 169 (1975), p. 330.

6   While there are many confessional dialogues going on around the world, two such dialogues have provided outstanding evidence of a growing consensus in matters of faith. These are the ones carried on by the Anglican–Roman Catholic Commission established in 1966 and which has dealt with the areas of Eucharist, ministry, authority; and the Lutheran RC dialogue in the USA which with even greater theological depth has undertaken since 1964 to discuss the Nicene Creed as dogma for the Church, i.e., one baptism for the forgiveness of sins, the Eucharist as sacrifice, followed by Eucharist and ministry.

7   As quoted by Barry Till, op. cit. Till questions this thesis in ch. 1, pp. 20–31.

8   Ibid., pp. 22–3.

9   *The Church and Christian Union* (Oxford 1968), p. 75; cf. Barry Till, op. cit., pp. 33–5.

10   The RC position is that the *data* of unity have not been lost. Cf. footnote 23 of the Abbott edn of *The Documents of Vatican II* with its comment on *Lumen Gentium*; referring to the document's statement that the Church *subsists* in the RC Church, the footnote says: 'The Constitution here takes up the very delicate point of the relationship of the Catholic Church as it presently exists . . . to the Church of Christ. According to the Constitution, the Church of Christ survives in the world today in its institutional fullness in the Catholic Church, although elements of the Church are present in other Churches and ecclesial communities – a point which will be more fully developed in the Decree on Ecumenism. These "ecclesial elements" in other Churches, far from shattering the unity of the Mystical Body, are dynamic realities which tend to bring about an even greater measure of unity among all who believe in Christ and are baptized in Him.'

11   *Towards Christian Unity*, a CTS (Catholic Truth Society) publication, 438 (1971), pp. 8–9.

12   Eugene Carson Blake, *The Church in the Next Decade*. New York, Macmillan, 1966.

13   Avery Dulles, *Models of the Church* (Dublin, Gill & Macmillan 1976), pp. 138–42.

14   Ibid., ch. 2.

15   Quoted in *Time* magazine, 30 October 1964. The Catholic Truth Society (CTS) published the *Ecclesiam Suam* under the title *The Church in the Modern World*, 1964. This is not to be confused with the document of Vatican II sometimes translated by the same title. The official designation for the latter document (1965) as a pastoral constitution is *Gaudium et Spes*.

16   David Tracy, *A Blessed Rage for Order: The New Pluralism in Theology*. New York, Seabury Press, 1975.

17   *A Human Apostolate* by Kevin O'Shea and Noel Meehan (Melbourne, Spectrum Books, 1971), pp. 103–4.

18   In Britain there have been some very well-intentioned efforts at joint mission, especially at the regional level. One thinks of the 'call to the north', the SWEC meeting which was national but grew out of fruitful joint ecumenical ventures in the Bristol area. But on the whole such efforts have achieved very little beyond some measure and manifestation of good will among some Christians. It is here that Catholic versus Evangelical approaches to joint mission meet head on. Where the mission has been limited to the distribution of the Bible, there has been success.

19   An example of such a fellowship would be the International Ecumenical Fellowship (IEF); it has seven regions to date, namely Belgium, France, Germany, Holland, Spain, UK, USA. The fellowship tries to organize an international conference annually as well as regional conferences. The present headquarters are in London: 42 Crutched Friars, London EC3N 2AL.

20   Cf. Barry Till, op. cit., pp. 199–202. The opening sermon spoke of setting up the Kingdom of God and was counterblasted by a German bishop who did not think it the business of mortal men, even Christians, to build up the Kingdom of God in this world. Obviously you need theology for that kind of debate. By 1937 the saying 'doctrine divides, service unites' was dropped in favour of 'let the Church be the Church' which is a faith and order statement. It reopened the question: What is the nature of the Church? The impotency of the Church during the First World War was replaced by the failure of optimism in building the Kingdom of God as the Second World War enveloped the Church.

21   Op. cit., p. 289.

22   *Local Councils of Churches Today*. Publications Department of the British Council of Churches, 2 Eaton Gate, London SW1W 9BL, 1971.

23  Cf. *Uppsala Report* by Kenneth Slack (SCM Press 1968), p. 53.

24  Ibid., p. 52. A full report has been edited by Norman Goodall entitled *The Uppsala Report 1968*. Geneva, WCC, 1968.

25  *Breaking Barriers: Nairobi 1975*, ed. David Paton, SPCK 1976, reporting remarks made by a Roman Catholic observer at the request of the Moderator, p. 207. Paton offers his tentative evaluation of Nairobi as a determination on the part of the Churches to suffer and struggle together in love for truth and justice, pp. 35–6.

26  Ibid., p. 208.

27  Paton, op. cit., reference in footnote 25.

28  Op. cit., p. 68.

29  Quoted by Jeffery, op. cit., p. 69.

30  Cf. *Breaking Barriers*, cited above, p. 258.

31  Cf. *The Third World Conference on Faith and Order*, ed. Oliver Tomkins, (Geneva, WCC, 1953), p. 34.

32  This is not the place to discuss the presuppositions behind a commitment to evolution. My assumption rests on a commitment to the analysis of the structures inherent in theological, scientific, and psychological thinking as revealing the essential structures and processes of man and his world in relation to God. Confirmation of such an assumption is to be found in a sampling of recent works: *Myths, Models and Paradigms* by Ian Barbour, SCM Press 1974; *Introduction to Theology* by Theodore W. Jennings, Jr., SPCK 1977; *In the Human Grain* by Walter Ong, SJ, New York, Macmillan, 1967, esp. chs. 5–7; *Theology in Reconciliation* by T. F. Torrance, Geoffrey Chapman 1975, esp. ch. 1; *Has Dogma A Future?* by Gerald O'Collins, Darton, Longman & Todd 1975.

33  Cf. 'The Church in the Modern World' by Emmanuel Sullivan, *Epworth Review*, vol. 2, no. 1 (January 1975).

34  *The Bible in the Modern World* by James Barr (SCM Press 1973), p. 143.

35  Heribert Mühlen, quoted by Avery Dulles, op. cit., p. 149.

36  *In the Human Grain*, cited above, p. 61.

37  Ibid., p. 124. He amplifies and specifies the unprecedented conjunction of nature with history, pp. 70–81.

38  An interesting comparison of this astrovision could be made on the account of the vision of the Blessed Julian of Norwich found in her Revelations of Divine Love, ch. 5.

39  *Theology in Reconciliation* (Geoffrey Chapman 1975), p. 70. Cf. also in this context *The Second Vatican Council and the New Catholicism* by G. C. Berkouwer, trans. from the Dutch (Grand Rapids, Michigan, Eerdmans Press 1965), pp. 251 ff., on the problem of continuity as a shared problem for Christians.

40  *Future Shock*, cited above, p. 348.

41  Ibid., pp. 348–9.

42  Torrance, op. cit., pp. 70–71.

43  Cf. *The Coming of the Third Church* by Walbert Bühlmann, Slough, St Paul Publications, 1976.

44  Torrance, op. cit., p. 81.

45  Ibid., p. 83.

46  Ibid.

47  'Liturgical Convergence' by Thomas J. Talley, pp. 69–70, *Episcopalians and Roman Catholics – Can They Ever Get Together?*, eds. H. Ryan and J. Robert Wright.

48  Ibid.

49  Report of the Joint Working Party on Pastoral Strategy, published by the Catholic Information Services of the Bishops' Conference of England and Wales, 74 Gallows Hill Lane, Abbots Langley, Herts WD5 0BZ. Cf. pp. 25–6 for the section on ecumenism, with special reference to nos. 64, 65.

50  Cf. Guttierez, op. cit., pp. 277–9. Here I am using the term 'myth' in a pejorative way.

51  Ibid., p. 278.

52  Peter Berger, *A Rumour of Angels* (Penguin Books 1969), p. 102.

53  Cf. B. M. C. Jeffery, op. cit., pp. 9–20. Kenneth Slack in *The British Churches Today* notes that in 1960 there were 260 local councils, and about 700 in 1970, in his second fully revised edition, SCM Press 1970. According to Jeffery, by 1971 there were 650 councils in England, Wales, Scotland, and Ireland in association with the British Council of Churches, 550 of these in England. The BCC itself was formed in 1942.

54  K. Slack, op. cit., p. 134.

55  SCM Press 1973.

56  Cf. *The Implications of Roman Catholic Membership of the BCC*, BCC Publications, 2 Eaton Gate, London SW1W 9BL, 1972. My own opinion is that prior to all objections made by the RC position is the failure on the part of the decision-makers to understand the ordinary procedures of conciliarity, an exercise Roman Catholics are beginning to take into their system. For this reason I should like it to be clear what I mean by 'conciliarity' and for that purpose borrow my definition from *Ecumenical Review*, vol. 24, no. 1, January 1972, from the text of a statement of the Commission on Faith and Order, Louvain 1941: 'Conciliarity has been, in some form or degree, characteristic of the life of the Christian Church in all ages and at various levels. By conciliarity we mean the coming together of Christians . . . for common prayer, counsel, and decision, in the belief that the Holy Spirit can use such meetings for his own purpose of reconciling, renewing and reforming the Church by guiding it towards the fullness

of truth and love. . . . The central fact in true conciliarity is the active presence and work of the Holy Spirit.'

57 At the end of 1976 this Church had 174,611 members; 87,359 children; 1795 ministers; 2063 places of worship.

58 *The Manual of the United Reformed Church in England and Wales*, ed. Percy Bush (86 Tavistock Place, London, 1973), no. 8.

59 The ten propositions with commentary may be obtained by writing to the Churches' Unity Commission, Church House, Dean's Yard, Westminster, London SW1P 3NZ. The context of these propositions has been set out by Dr John Huxtable in a book entitled *A New Hope for Christian Unity*, Collins Fontana 1977. A simple statement of the ten propositions is as follows:

(1) We affirm our belief that the visible unity in life and mission of all Christ's people is the will of God.

(2) We therefore declare our willingness to join in a covenant actively to seek that visible unity.

(3) We believe that this search requires action both locally and nationally.

(4) We agree to recognize, as from an accepted date, the communicant members in good standing of the other covenanting Churches as true members of the Body of Christ and welcome them to Holy Communion without condition.

(5) We agree that, as from an accepted date, initiation in the covenanting Churches shall be by mutually acceptable rites.

(6) We agree to recognize, as from an accepted date, the ordained ministries of the other covenanting Churches, as true ministries of word and sacraments in the Holy Catholic Church, and we agree that all subsequent ordinations to the ministries of the covenanting Churches shall be according to a Common Ordinal which will properly incorporate the episcopal, presbyteral, and lay roles in ordination.

(7) We agree within the fellowship of the covenanting Churches to respect the rights of conscience, and to continue to accord to all our members, such freedom of thought and action as is consistent with the visible unity of the Church.

(8) We agree to continue to give every possible encouragement to local ecumenical projects and to develop methods of decision-making in common.

(9) We agree to explore such further steps as will be necessary to make more clearly visible the unity of all Christ's people.

(10) We agree to remain in close fellowship and consultation with all the Churches represented on the Churches' Unity Commission.

60 Berkouwer, op. cit., p. 250.

61 *Crises Facing the Church* (Darton, Longman & Todd 1975), p. 108.

62 Op. cit., p. 250.

63  Cf. David Edwards, op. cit., appendix, p. 61.

64  Cf. *The New Sower*, vol. 2, no. 2 (Winter 1976), pp. 17–20, for my article entitled 'Growth in Ecumenical Prayer'. This quarterly is published by Mayhew-McCrimmon, Great Wakering, Essex.

## CHAPTER 3
## THE CATHOLIC–EVANGELICAL CONVERGENCE

1  *Open Letter* from Latimer House in conjunction with the Church of England Evangelical Council (131 Banbury Road, Oxford), n. 2.

2  Ibid.

3  Ibid., n. 5, iii.

4  Ibid. iv.

5  *The Prophets* (Harper Torchbooks: Harper & Row 1969), vol. 1, p. 102.

6  *Biblical Reflections on Crises Facing the Church* (Darton, Longman & Todd 1975), p. 15.

7  Cf. *The Myth of God Incarnate*, ed. John Hick, SCM Press 1977; *The Truth of God Incarnate*, ed. Michael Green, Hodder & Stoughton 1977. While the liberal quest for the historical Jesus goes back to Herman Reimarus, who died in 1768, and ends with Schweitzer in its first phase, phase two begins with Bultmann at the time of the First World War and develops a 'new quest' in the 1950s. It is difficult to say whether the present 'myth' debate means that the quest is frustratingly ended or will be fulfilled in the emerging consensus of a common approach to Holy Scripture through historical research. For clear and easy reading may I suggest a work by Dermot A. Lane entitled *The Reality of Jesus*, Dublin, Veritas Publications, 1975; also R. P. C. Hanson's *Mystery and Imagination*, SPCK 1977, cited above, pp. 80–100.

8  *The Nottingham Statement* (Falcon Booklets, Church Pastoral Aid Society 1977), n. 2, p. 76.

9  'Finding A Leg to Stand On', published by and available from One for Christian Renewal; 169 Forest Road, Loughborough, Leics.

10  Cf. 'Evangelicals at Chicago', an article by John Yoder in *Christianity and Crisis*, 18 February 1974. It contains the declaration made by the participants of an evangelical consultation in Chicago in November 1973.

11  E.g., *The Truth of God Incarnate*, cited above.

12  Quoted in *Evangelicals Tomorrow* by John Capon (Collins Fontana 1977), p. 90. This very readable and informative account of Nottingham 1977 is subtitled a 'popular report'. Cf. also *The Evangelical Renaissance* by Donald G. Bloesch, Hodder & Stoughton 1974.

13  *Fundamentalism* (SCM Press 1977), esp. pp. 1–39.

14 *What is an Evangelical?*, a Falcon Booklet, based on a talk given at the end of the Nottingham Conference; p. 10.

15 Quoted by James Barr, *The Bible in the Modern World* (SCM Press 1973), p. 20. Barr's work is a valuable source for its survey of arguments affecting various positions on various questions surrounding biblical interpretation and authority.

16 Cf. article with this title in the *Journal of Ecumenical Studies* (Summer 1972), vol. 9, no. 3, pp. 544–55.

17 Ibid., p. 545.

18 Ibid., p. 547.

19 Ibid., p. 545.

20 Ibid., p. 547.

21 Cf. Uppsala Report cited in chapter 2.

22 The quote is from the *Catecheses* of Cyril, xviii, 23, cited by Trevor Ling in his book *Prophetic Religion* to which I am indebted for its exploration of the meaning of catholicity related to the prophetic dimension of Christianity. New York, Macmillan, St Martin's Press, 1966.

23 This 'unity in diversity', the 'united but not absorbed' principle will exercise ecumenists for some time to come. Various models of church unity will be constructed along these lines. The biblical image of the people of God under a new covenant in Jesus Christ combined with the notion of the Church as a 'communion of communions' with a plurality of 'types' within that communion seems to point a way forward. Cf. Cardinal Willebrand's Great St Mary's sermon, quoted by Barry Till, op. cit., pp. 437–8; also the results of the Presbyterian–Reformed–Roman Catholic Consultation in the USA, *Ecumenical Trends*, vol. 6, no. 10, November 1977, published eleven times a year by the Graymoor Ecumenical Institute in co-operation with the National Council of Churches (USA).

24 *Dogmatic Construction on the Church* (*Lumen Gentium*) of Vatican II, ch. 2, no. 9, Abbott translation. Cf. also *Obeying Christ in a Changing World*, a three-volume work under the general editorship of John Stott, introducing the theme of the Nottingham Conference of 1977; *The People of God*, vol. 2, ed. Ian Cundy, Collins Fontana 1977, 'The Church as Community' by Ian Cundy, pp. 17–41.

25 John Stott, *What is an Evangelical?*, cited above, p. 11.

26 The letter of Barth to Küng can be found following the foreword of the English edn, Thomas Nelson 1964. First published in German in 1957.

27 *Conjectures of a Guilty Bystander*, 2nd edn, Sheldon Press 1977. First published in 1965, pp. 165–8.

28 *Fundamentalism*, cited above, p. 12.

29 Op. cit., p. 167.

30 Cf. James Barr, *The Bible in the Modern World*, cited above, ch. 3.

31 Ibid., ch. 2. My experience within the neo-Pentecostal movement causes me to question this assertion.

32 By way of example I have the feeling that Tony Thiselton does this in his paper prepared for Nottingham 1977; cf. *Obeying Christ in a Changing World*, op. cit., vol. 1, *The Lord Christ*, 'Understanding God's Word Today', pp. 90–122. Scriptural exegesis and its modern methodology is more than a sophisticated reinterpretation of the Bible. The biblical theologian, or one working with conciliar documents, ought to help us understand more accurately the context of statements of Christian truth. Like systematic theologians their conclusions are to be checked by the faith of the Church of which we believe the New Testament is an inerrant record.

33 *What is an Evangelical?*, p. 11.

34 Darton, Longman & Todd, trans. W. J. Kerrigan from the French, 1964.

35 *The Times*, 22 September 1975.

36 Op. cit., vol. 3, *The Changing World*.

37 *Let the Earth Hear His Voice*. International Congress on World Evangelization, Lausanne, Switzerland 1974. Official Reference Volume: Papers and Responses, Minneapolis, Minn., 1975, no. 6.

38 *Evangelicals, Obedience and Change* (Bramcote, Notts., Grove Books, 1977), p. 15. The context of this remark was a comment on an answer to a question put to Tony Thiselton in an interview at the Nottingham Conference regarding biblical understanding.

39 *Evangelism Today* (Belfast, Christian Journals, 1976), p. 9.

40 Ibid., ch. 3, p. 75.

41 Ibid., p. 93.

42 Ibid., p. 94.

43 Ibid., p. 97.

44 Cf. footnote 49, ch. 2, n. 43 of the document itself; also *With One Voice*, Catholics and Joint Evangelization, a pastoral aid from the RC Ecumenical Commission of England and Wales. This document was written to clarify certain basic principles underlying RC co-operation in joint evangelization, to help pastors and people determine their involvement in certain joint missions, and prepare the ground for further discussions of the issues; n. 44: Each generation must look at its own situation, at the present needs of the people in the world, and must judge what its Christian response should be to these needs; n. 45: The response of Christians to the needs of the world takes many different forms; each member of the Church must be at the service of the world, and each has something unique to offer, according to the gifts of the Spirit and the needs of the times.

45 Cited in note 23 of this chapter.

46 Published by the Catholic Truth Society.
47 *The Ecumenist*, vol. 6, no. 4 (May–June 1968), esp. pp. 149–50.
48 *God of the Oppressed* (SPCK 1977), p. 98.
49 *Nottingham Statement*, op. cit., section D1.
50 Op. cit., esp. essays by Christopher Butler, OSB and Professor John MacQuarrie.
51 Cf. *The Semitic Background of the Term 'Mystery' in the New Testament* by Raymond Brown, Facet Books, Biblical Series, 21, ed. John Reumann; Philadelphia, Fortress Press, 1968. Hugo Rahner in an important essay says that 'the hypothesis of a strictly genetic, historical dependence of essential Christian positions on the Hellenistic mysteries is simply untenable'; 'Greek Myth and the Gospels', *Faith, Reason, and the Gospels*, ed. John Heaney, SJ, Westminster, Maryland, USA, The Newman Press, 1963), ch. 6, p. 115.
52 Ibid., p. 69.
53 This in fact is the subtitle of an important theological work by Theodore Jennings, Jr. entitled *Introduction to Theology*, SPCK 1977. I am indebted to this work for my own reflections on 'myth'. In the light of the confusion and lack of clarity in the contemporary 'myth of God Incarnate' debate, this work is timely and very helpful. Cf. also again Ian Barbour's *Myths, Models, and Paradigms*, SCM Press 1974, which is another helpful work in terms of clarifying basic notions of myth in the areas of scientific and religious knowledge.
54 Jennings, cited above, p. 42.
55 Ibid., pp. 45–6.
56 Cf. his *The Symbolism of Evil*, Boston, Beacon Press, 1969.
57 Jennings, op. cit., p. 57.
58 Ibid., p. 61. He says: 'Cosmological and theological assertions of a mythos may and must be interpreted anthropologically. . . . The function of a mythos is particularly stressed by the kerigmatic nature of the material. It presents the hearer with a summons to a decision' (p. 65).
59 Ibid., p. 66.
60 Ibid., p. 69.
61 Ibid., p. 77.
62 Ibid., p. 93.
63 Cf. Jennings on the development of Christology and the formulations of Nicea and Chalcedon. With reference to Chalcedon he says that 'the task of theological reflection' is 'not to compromise such a claim but to elaborate its meaning for contemporary human existence', pp. 154–5.
64 Facet Books, Biblical Series, 5, ed. John Reumann (Philadelphia, Fortress Press, 1970), p. 54.
65 Op. cit., section 11.

## CHAPTER 4
## THE CHRISTIAN LIBERATION MOVEMENT

1  Cf. *The Times*, 22 September 1975.

2  This is the language of the Evangelical declaration called 'The Berlin Declaration' of 1974, under the theme of 'Freedom and Fellowship in Christ'. It is an extreme statement characterized by its bias towards the Ecumenical Movement, the WCC, and liberation theology, e.g., 'In the "Theology of Liberation", which is also promoted by Geneva, the classless society is even made to be equal to the Kingdom of God on earth.'

3  'Education, Liberation, and the Church', an article published in *Study Encounter*, 38, vol. 9, no. 1, 1973. WCC, Geneva.

4  Cf. Gregory Baum's report on the meeting at Detroit, Michigan in August 1975 between Latin American theologians and North American theologians to illustrate and expand my general remarks. The Latin Americans asked the North Americans not to use this theology as a new toy to make their classes more interesting: 'The Christian Left at Detroit', *The Ecumenist*, September–October 1975, vol. 13, no. 6; cf. also an article in the newspaper *Caribbean Contact*, January 1977, vol. 4, no. 10, a monthly of the Caribbean area, entitled 'What is Black Liberation Theology?'

5  *Study Encounter*, cited above.

6  Freire was Professor of History and Philosophy of Education at the University of Recife around 1960 and experimented with new methods of teaching adults how to read and write. He was exiled by the Brazilian military leaders in 1964. He was imprisoned for a short while and then spent five years in Chile at the Institute for Agrarian Reform; he went to Harvard University to the Center for the Study of Development and Social Change, then from there to Geneva in 1970 to work in the WCC Office of Education. In his book *A Theology of Liberation* Gustavo Guttierez refers to Freire's pedagogy of the oppressed as 'one of the most creative and fruitful efforts' of liberation in Latin America, op. cit., pp. 91–2. Illich, a former Catholic priest and Rector of the Catholic University of Puerto Rico is a co-founder and director of the Centre for Intercultural Documentation (CIDOC). For an introductory study of the thought of these two men see a study by John Elias, *Conscientization and Deschooling*, Philadelphia, The Westminster Press, 1976.

7  Freire says that 'we work out our salvation in communion'. He does not mean 'that God hasn't saved us by his presence in history. . . .' He is talking on the human level. Cf. 'What is Conscientization?' in *The Outlook*, Autumn 1975, vol. 14, no. 7, an RC missionary quartrerly review: 23 Eccleston Square, London SW1V 1NU.

8  'Ideas that proved too big for a Brazilian jail', a newspaper article: *Caribbean Contact*, November 1975.

9  *The Outlook*, cited above.

10  Published by Calders & Boyars (1971), pp. 108–9.

11  Ibid., p. 123.

12  *One World*, official WCC publication, July–August 1975.

13  Cf. Alfredo Fierro's *The Militant Gospel*, cited in ch. 1, pp. 208–12.

14  *A Theology of Liberation*, op. cit., pp. 66–72.

15  Ibid., pp. 203–12.

16  Ibid., p. 203.

17  Ibid., p. 204.

18  Ibid., p. 207.

19  Ibid., p. 208.

20  Dublin, Gill & Macmillan, 1977 (first published in Spanish in 1975), trans. John Drury, p. 3.

21  Ibid., p. 5.

22  Ibid., p. 8.

23  James Cone is a professor at Union Theological Seminary, New York City. He is author of *A Black Theology of Liberation*, Philadelphia, Lippincott, 1970 and *God of the Oppressed*, New York, The Seabury Press, 1975 and SPCK 1977. For a critique of Cone's theology see Rosemary Reuther's *Liberation Theology* (New York, Paulist Press, 1972), pp. 127–44.

24  Segundo, op. cit., cf. ch. 1: 'The Hermeneutic Circle', p. 39 for another statement of this basis for biblical interpretation.

25  Ibid., p. 33.

26  Ibid., pp. 41, 44.

27  Segundo cites the Falange or Christian Democratic movement, as it came to be known in Chile, as an example of interpreting the gospel message by way of a social doctrine of the Church. This social doctrine was written with a European situation in view. Its norms were *deduced* from divine revelation or based on a natural right *deduced* from an immutable natural law. In this context socialism was condemned as an abstract ideal opposed to a natural right to private property. It evolved to a halfway position, but when the crunch came, under the Allende régime in Chile, the Christian Democrats handed over the government to the military junta. Segundo says: 'It is hard to find . . . a more convincing confirmation of Assman's basic hypothesis: i.e., that "evangelical" conditions imposed on the revolutionary process in *a priori* terms eventually turn into third-way stands; and that they also turn into counter-revolutionary forces when and if the revolution becomes feasible' (*The Liberation of Theology*, op. cit., pp. 91–4).

28  Ibid., p. 97.

29  Ibid., p. 120.

30 *Christians, Politics, and Violent Revolution* (SCM Press 1976), p. 164.

31 Ibid.

32 Ibid., p. 174.

33 Ibid., cf. the entire section, pp. 172–7; also *The Militant Gospel*, op. cit., pp. 201–7.

34 'The Ethics of Liberation', *One World*, September 1975.

35 Cf. Hans Küng, *On Being a Christian Today*, op. cit., pp. 171–91; also Alan Richardson's *The Political Christ* (SCM Press 1973), esp. pp. 44–8.

36 J. G. Davies, op. cit., ch. 6; the word can mean a number of things to describe a situation.

37 Op. cit., p. 69.

38 *One World*, cited above.

39 'The Prophetic Principle' by Bernard Murchland, *Commonweal*, 29 April 1966, pp. 171–5.

40 Segundo, op. cit., p. 41.

41 For further light on his significance and spirit in the liberation movement of Latin America see *The Rebel Church in Latin America* by Alain Gheerbrant, trans. from the French by Rosemary Sheed, Penguin Books 1974.

42 *Revolutionary Theology Comes of Age*, cited above, pp. 165–73. For many ecumenists this approach would relativize the whole question of visible Christian unity in terms of a content of shared faith. It would render doctrinal dialogue obsolete. However, most ecumenists would agree that the dynamic way forward in the search for visible unity is shared mission. The whole ecumenical enterprise is for mission. Thus it seems to me that orthopraxy in mission is in mutual interaction with the search for orthodoxy in Christian doctrine.

43 Ibid., p. 171. He clarifies this statement under three points:
(1) putting the decision in the perspective of history;
(2) rejecting all fanaticism in favour of a theological and ethical reflection;
(3) requiring a certain latitude in the options and decisions so that the Church is made up of 'families of options'.

44 Ibid., p. 170. He claims it would be fatal to eliminate the tension between the Churches' concrete historical option and in terms of fidelity to Christ. It can be made a fruitful tension by recognizing 'that Christians live their identity as such in different levels which go from their personal historical commitment to their corporate confession of Christ'.

45 *The Prophets*, cited above, cf. pp. 195–220.

46 Ibid., p. 198.

47 Cf. *Revolutionary Priest: The Complete Writings and Message of Camilo Torres*, John Gerassi, New York, Random House 1971. Four

months after he made the decision to join the guerrillas he was killed in the mountains of Bucaramanga, 15 February 1966.

48  Best known for his *Anathema to Dialogue*, New York, Herder & Herder, 1966. Gradually he isolated himself within the French Communist Party and was expelled in 1970. In 1975 he announced his conversion to a brand of Christianity which affirms that man is always more than man. Man's life is open to thought, love, prayer, creativity, because his life is open to repentance or reconversion. Man need never feel hopelessly defeated.

49  While not sharing all his reservations or conclusions about the future of the Christian–Marxist relationship, I am indebted to him for his clear, concise, and contemporary statement of this relationship in an article in *The Month*, November 1975, entitled 'Christians and Instrumental Marxism'; especially for his more recent book *The Christian–Marxist Dialogue and Beyond*, Darton, Longman & Todd 1977.

50  Cf, above; also José Miranda's *Marx and the Bible*, SCM Press 1977, first published in Spanish in 1971. The approach of CFS would seem to justify those who think of 'liberation theology' as a profound spirituality and it validates the position of Guttierez mentioned earlier in the chapter, namely that theological categories are not enough.

51  *The Month*, cited above; also his book cited above, ch. 7.

52  *Christians and Marxists: The Mutual Challenge to Revolution*, Hodder & Stoughton 1976, first delivered as the 1974 London Lecture in Contemporary Christianity at the invitation of the Langham Trust. Chapter 8 deals with the 'promise and limits of the alliance'.

53  Op. cit., ch. 8.

54  Ibid., p. 366.

55  Segundo, op. cit., pp. 84–5.

56  *Christians and Marxists*, cited above, p. 130. Marxism becomes *in this time* the context of faith; cf. Segundo as just cited and Denys Turner, 'Can a Christian be a Marxist?', *New Blackfriars*, June 1975.

57  Cf. Paul Lehmann's *The Transfiguration of Politics*, SCM Press 1975; also Hugo Assman's *Practical Theology of Liberation*, Search Press 1975; also Freire's article in *Study Encounter*, cited above. Freire sees most of Latin America modernizing rather than developing. If development is true liberation, it must mean liberation at two levels, i.e., liberation of society from imperialism *and* liberation of oppressed social classes from an oppressive bourgeois élite.

58  *A Theology of Liberation*, pp. 22–37.

59  Ibid., pp. 34–5.

60  Ibid., p. 35; cf. *The Rebel Church in Latin America*, cited above, chs. 2 and 3; also Guttierez, op. cit., ch. 7.

61  *Christians and Marxists*, cited above, ch. 2 and *Marx and the Bible*, cited above.

62  Bob Goudzwaard, *Aid for the Overdeveloped West*, Toronto, Wedge Publishing Foundation, 1975.

63  Ibid., p. 21.

64  'Toward a Self-Renewing Society', a *Time* magazine essay, 11 April 1969, pp. 30–31. John Gardiner is a former American Secretary of Health, Education, and Welfare. The essay was excerpted from his Godkin Lectures at Harvard University. The essay would be censured by liberationists because of its failure to criticize assumed values, e.g., 'Our problem is not to find better values, but rather to be faithful to those we profess – and to make those values live in our institutions. . . .'

65  This incident is reported in his address to the Moral Rearmament Industrial Conference in Caux, Switzerland in the summer of 1977, the last public expression of his philosophy. It may be found in the MRA weekly *New World News*, vol. 25, no. 45, September 1977, published at The Good Road Ltd., PO Box 9, Tonbridge, Kent TN9 2UH.

66  Appropriate or intermediate technology (over against 'high' technology) takes into account the actual needs of real people in rural India or Latin America or third-generation Americans on welfare or in a city slum. Schumacher would say that it is a case of 'making boots that fit their feet' and not a matter of producing 500 million pairs of the same size.

67  Cited above, in ch. 2; cf. a review of Bühlmann in *The Outlook*, vol. 15, no. 3, Autumn 1976, by Arthur McCormick.

68  *International Review of Mission*, April 1975.

69  Ibid.

70  The Church Missionary Society *Newsletter* is obtainable through the SPCK Bookshop, Holy Trinity Church, Marylebone Road, London NW1 4DU. John Taylor, former General Secretary of the CMS, is now Bishop of Winchester.

71  Kosuke Koyama, SCM Press 1974 wrote *Waterbuffalo Theology*; H. S. Boyd, Cambridge University Press 1974, subtitled his work *The Cultural Context of the Church*. Black theology has been written in the context of liberation theology more than in a cultural context, e.g., James Cone's *Black Theology and Black Power; God of the Oppressed*. Cf. also *Mission and Ecumenism in Brazil* by Cary MacEoin and Ralph Thomas, published in 1973 by the Graymoor Ecumenical Institute: Graymoor, Garrison, New York 10524.

72  John Taylor, cited above.

73  Cited above, ch. 3.

74  David Brown, op. cit., pp. 82–4.

75  Cf. T. S. Eliot's *Little Gidding* and the conclusion of *The Phenomenon of Man* by Teilhard de Chardin.

CHAPTER 5
THE NEO-PENTECOSTAL MOVEMENT

1 If these terms are used with reference to spiritual gifts, the *charismata*, it is important to remember that they are descriptive or phenomenological terms, i.e., they are used in relation to their effects on us, their frequency, our practical experience of them, our expectations. The terms do not apply to the action of God.

2 I am not writing an historical account and so there is no intention of ignoring the revivalist movements of the seventeenth and eighteenth centuries in Germany, England, and the USA. Nor have I forgotten the significance of the Irvingites and the Welsh Revival of the nineteenth and twentieth centuries respectively, nor Charles Finney in nineteenth-century USA. Cf. *The Pentecostals* by Walter Hollenweger, SCM Press 1972; *The Pentecostal Theology of Edward Irving* by Gordon Strachan, Darton, Longman & Todd 1973; *The Holiness-Pentecostal Movement in the United States* by Vinson Synan, Grand Rapids, Michigan, Eerdmans Press, 1971.

3 Michael Ramsey, *Holy Spirit* (SPCK 1977), p. 87.

4 *Charismatic Renewal and the Churches* by Kilian McDonnell (New York, The Seabury Press, 1976), p. 67; a comment on the Church of Scotland Report of the Panel of Doctrine, commissioned by the General Assembly of 1972 and completed in 1974. Father McDonnell's work is extremely valuable not only as an analysis of sociological and psychological research on neo-Pentecostalism focused in the phenomenon of speaking in tongues, but also as an updated indicator of the expansion and development of the movement. It is a work with a solid ecumenical basis.

5 My feeling is that this would be counterproductive. Cf. my booklet *Can the Pentecostal Movement Renew the Churches?* obtainable from the British Council of Churches, Publications Dept., 2 Eaton Gate, London SW1W 9BL.

6 For an evaluation of the ten years of RC participation in the movement see *Catholic Pentecostals Now*, ed. J. Kerkhofs, Canfield, Ohio, Alba Books, 1977. The material of the book is reproduced with permission of the *Pro Mundi Vita* Bulletin, no. 60, May 1976.

7 Op. cit., p. 111.

8 Ibid., pp. 17–40.

9 Ibid., p. 122.

10 Ibid., p. 144; 'There is general agreement among all branches of the movement that to lead a psychologically disturbed person into the experience of tongues and what is called the baptism in the Holy Spirit is at very least imprudent' (p. 146).

11 *Catholic Pentecostalism* (Darton, Longman & Todd 1977), pp. 135–46. This is a very clear and thorough account of the movement for

those looking for an introduction to an understanding of principles and issues.

12  The proceedings and results of this five-year dialogue have been recorded in *One in Christ*, issues no. 2, 1974; no. 4, 1974; no. 4, 1975; no. 3, 1976. The dialogue was between the RC Secretariat for Promoting Christian Unity and leaders of *some* Pentecostal Churches with some leaders in neo-Pentecostalism from Protestant, Anglican, and Orthodox Churches.

13  Ibid., no. 2, 1974, p. 114.

14  Op. cit., p. 8.

15  Ibid.

16  J. Kerkhofs, op. cit. for evaluation hypotheses, pp. 112–14; 117–18. While I disagree with a number of statements in the revelation of each hypothesis, they do present a range of possibilities that have to be faced. However, the study does not take into account the significance of Catholic Pentecostalism in relation to the Ecumenical Movement and other movements of the Spirit. Cf. Laurentin, op. cit., pp. 169–71 on the charge of fundamentalism and literalism brought against neo-Pentecostalism; also *The Malines Document* (available from The Communication Center, PO Drawer A: Notre Dame, Indiana 46556, USA), pp. 40–41.

17  Robert Wild, *Enthusiasm in the Spirit* (Notre Dame, Indiana, Ave Maria Press, 1975), p. 29.

18  Op. cit., p. 178.

19  It is difficult to put forth reliable statistics on the actual numbers of neo-Pentecostals around the world. I have seen it put at three million and today those in the movement speak of millions. This of course is not the determinative of its force in the Church. Cf. *New Covenant* on a ten-year review of RC participation in the movement, February 1977: 'What Has Catholic Charismatic Renewal Accomplished?'. Cf. also *New Heaven? New Earth?* co-authored by four RC theologians, with a preface by Walter Hollenweger (Darton, Longman & Todd 1976), pp. 17–54, on the significance and potential of Pentecostalism.

20  *New Heaven? New Earth?* cited above, preface.

21  Ibid.

22  Ibid.

23  *New Covenant*, June 1973.

24  Ibid., italics mine. The Cardinal elaborates the relationship between the neo-Pentecostal movement and the development of collegiality and co-responsibility. Interesting also is the Cardinal's wish to write a book on the 'Holy Spirit, the Renewer' in the early 1970s and how he deferred this project in order to 'experience more fully the Spirit at work today' after his contact with charismatic renewal. His book was published in 1974 under the title *A New Pentecost?*, Collins Fontana.

25  *The Tablet*, 28 May 1977.

26  'Constitution on the Church' of Vatican II, under the Latin title *Lumen Gentium*, ch. 1, n. 2 (Abbott trans.).

27  Ibid.

28  Cf. J. Rodman Williams's account of earlier modern theological anticipations of neo-Pentecostal renewal in his *The Era of the Spirit*, Plainfield, New Jersey, Logos International, with special reference to Barth. Also Edward O'Connor's *The Pentecostal Movement in the Catholic Church*, Notre Dame, Indiana, Ave Maria Press, 1971, and his article in the *American Ecclesiastical Review*, 'The New Theology of Charisms in the Church', vol. 161, pp. 145–59; Donald Gelpi, *Charism and Sacrament*, SPCK 1977; Peter Hocken, *New Heaven? New Earth?* cited above, pp. 20–24.

29  *New Heaven? New Earth?*, p. 25.

30  Ibid., p. 26. Hocken is thoroughly theologically ecumenical in his treatment of Pentecostalists, careful to bring out their practical insights into body–spirit, healing–salvation correlationships; their approach to creative liturgy; and their insistence on outward signs and inner grace, not unrelated to Catholic sacramental theology.

31  Ibid., pp. 48–53.

32  Ibid.

33  Ibid.

34  Ibid.

35  Decree on Ecumenism of Vatican II, no. 8.

36  Op. cit., p. 53; Pentecostalism, though it is much more complex and varied than one imagines, has been described uniformly as a 'third force' alongside Protestantism and Catholicism.

37  *One in Christ*, vol. 10 (1974), pp. 206–15; the quote is from p. 207.

38  Ibid., no. 2, 1974, 'Pentecostal Spirituality' by J. Rodman Williams, pp. 180–92.

39  *They Speak With Other Tongues* (Hodder & Stoughton 1976 edn), p. 148.

40  I have written a short article in *Renewal*, August–September 1977, no. 70, 'Growth and Freedom in Prayer', pp. 19–21. *Renewal* is the official magazine of Fountain Trust which exists to promote neo-Pentecostal renewal, especially in Britain. There is an excellent theological supplement to *Renewal* for the more theologically oriented.

41  *New Heaven? New Earth?* cited above; cf. the essay by Simon Tugwell, 'The Speech-Giving Spirit', pp. 121–59.

42  Cf. 'Catholics and Pentecostals', *New Blackfriars* (May 1971), p. 214.

43  *New Heaven? New Earth?* p. 141.

44  Ibid., p. 144.

45  Ibid., p. 148.

46   Ibid., p. 133. Cf. also Donald Gelpi's *Charism and Sacrament*, cited above. Gelpi takes a very critical theological ecumenical approach to relationships between charismatic and sacramental worship.

47   Peter Hocken, *You He Made Alive* (Darton, Longman & Todd 1974), p. 32.

48   It is important to avoid making too great a cleavage between liturgical and non-liturgical prayer and worship; cf. Peter Hocken, *You He Made Alive*, pp. 45–7; also Robert Wild, op. cit., pp. 131–47 where he shows briefly how the concept of liturgy has moved from 'shared prayer' to 'deputed prayer'.

49   Cf. James Dunn, 'According to the Spirit', in *Theological Renewal*, February–March 1977, no. 5. This is the supplement mentioned above in note 40.

50   Donald Gelpi, *Charism and Sacrament*, cited above, pp. 91–2.

51   Cf. Abraham Heschel, *The Prophets*, vol. 2.

52   'Pentecostalism and Ecumenism in Latin America', *The Christian Century*, 27 September 1972. Cf. Walter Hollenweger's 'Charisma and Oikoumene', *One in Christ*, no. 4. 1971; 'Pentecostalism and Brazilian Religion' by Abdalaziz De Moura, *Theology Digest*, vol. 20 (Spring 1972), pp. 44–8; a summary of a sociological survey by Joseph Fichter has been presented by Kilian McDonnell under the title 'A Sociologist Looks at the Catholic Charismatic Renewal', *Worship*, vol. 49, no. 7 (Aug.–Sept. 1975), pp. 378–92; special reference must be made to the *International Review of Mission*, vol. 66, no. 261, January 1977, under the theme of 'ministry with the poor', bringing together reflections on relationships of liberation theology, the Pentecostal movement, dependence and poverty issues.

53   Op. cit., p. 52.

54   Heschel, op. cit., vol. 2, p. 96.

55   Ibid.

56   Cf. my BCC study pamphlet, cited above, p. 6.

57   'Baptism in the Holy Spirit', Francis A. Sullivan, SJ, *Gregorianum* (a quarterly periodical of the Gregorian University in Rome), 55/1, 1974, pp. 49–66; cf. also *The Baptism in the Holy Spirit as an Ecumenical Problem* by Kilian McDonnell and Arnold Bittlinger, Notre Dame, Indiana, Charismatic Renewal Services, 1972.

58   Ibid., p. 49.

59   *Baptism in the Holy Spirit*, Studies in Biblical Theology, 2nd series, 15, SCM Press 1970.

60   Ibid., p. 182; also pp. 205, 219 with the reference to 1 Peter 3.21.

61   Sullivan, op. cit., p. 51.

62   Ibid., p. 52.

63   For examples of different theological approaches see Larry Christenson's 'Baptism With the Holy Spirit: A Lutheran Perspective',

*Theological Renewal*, no. 4 (Oct.–Nov. 1976), pp. 21–4; also the joint statement of Fountain Trust and the Church of England Evangelical Council entitled *Gospel and Spirit*, April 1977 (available from Fountain Trust, 3a High Street, Esher, Surrey KT10 9RP), esp. pp. 4–5.

64  It is beyond our purpose here to do more than indicate Sullivan's analysis of the theology of Aquinas to justify further his conclusion.

65  *Can the Pentecostal Movement Renew the Churches?*, cited above, p. 6. There is no uniform blueprint for the way people are led into the experience. Thus 'Life in the Spirit' seminars among Catholic neo-Pentecostals is an exercise described by McDonnell as 'an acceptable induction mechanism' that is safe, gradual, and orderly, more a drift than a shift: *Charismatic Renewal and the Churches*, cited above, pp. 140–42.

66  *God the Spirit*, The Bampton Lectures, 1966 (Oxford, The Clarendon Press, 1977), p. 201; cf. also pp. 89–91, 198–205. This book requires critical assessment, e.g., the review by John Coventry, SJ, in *The Tablet*, 21 January 1978: 'The Basic Truths'.

67  Ibid., p. 58.

68  Robert Wild, op. cit., p. 76. The whole of ch. 4 deals with the question of discernment of the present neo-Pentecostal renewal (1 John 4.1). He notes that such renewals are not new to the Church, though whether the present one is greater in both magnitude and quality or significance, only time will tell. I am of the opinion that it presents a unique opportunity for building up a united life and mission in the Church.

69  John C. Haughey, 'Healed and Healing Priests', an article in *Charisindia*, a charismatic journal for Indian Christians, vol. 2, no. 3, November–December 1976.

70  Ibid.

71  Cf. Lampe, op. cit., p. 202; also my comments earlier in the chapter on the need to avoid ultrasupernaturalizing of the charisms. I also wish to acknowledge the fact that medical science may be a nemesis if its presuppositions are not challenged from time to time, as Ivan Illich has done in his book *Medical Nemesis*.

72  Op. cit.

73  *The Era of the Spirit*, cited above, p. 76. While I would not agree with Barth's remark in some of its presuppositions, I most certainly agree with it as a statement of theological principle.

74  Ibid., p. 79. Again I would not accept Brunner's radical position that the Church today is not the *ecclesia* of the New Testament.

75  Ibid.

76  Cf. Morton Kelsey's *Tongue Speaking: An Experiment in Spiritual Experience*, Hodder & Stoughton 1973. This book is very readable, yet presents an excellent overview of both the history of the tongue-

speaking spiritual phenomenon and a review of various psychological and theological conclusions that underwrite its authenticity with qualified criticism. The author is a disciple of Jung. The book was first published by Doubleday in 1964. Cf. also *Understanding Speaking in Tongues* by Watson Mills, Grand Rapids, Michigan, Eerdmans Press, 1972 and *The Pentecostal Reality* by J. Rodman Williams, Plainfield, New Jersey, Logos International, 1972.

77 John Gunstone, *Greater Things Than These* (Faith Press 1974), p. 30.

78 Ibid., p. 105. This will exercise the Church for a long time and will involve a lengthy process of integration with other movements taken as substantives of hope in this book. For example, one can already see the need for an authentic spirituality in the Christian liberation movement and an equal need for authentic outreach and social consciousness and mission among neo-Pentecostals. Community arises from the movement; ecumenism and the Catholic–Evangelical convergence develop in relation to it because of its nature as a unitive experience.

## CHAPTER 6
## THE COMMUNITY MOVEMENT

1 By way of example see *The Greening of America* by Charles Reich, Penguin 1971; also *The Making of a Counterculture* by Theodore Rojak, New York, Doubleday, 1969, subtitled 'Reflections on the technocratic society and its youthful opposition'. Alvin Toffler's *Future Shock*, op. cit., would take a different interpretation from Reich, by ascribing the communal movement to the search for security and permanence before the waves of novelty, transience, and alienation in technocratic society. His interpretation looks at the community movement more as a sign of despair than of hope. He would feel that much of the utopianism is backward-looking rather than forward-looking, pp. 413–16. Cf. also *Youthquake* by Kenneth Leech, Sheldon Press 1973.

2 *The Jesus Kids* (SCM Press 1972), p. 47; also see G. Corry, *Jesus Bubble or Jesus Revolution?* published in 1973 by the British Council of Churches, 2 Eaton Gate, London SW1.

3 *As the Spirit Leads Us*, eds. Kevin and Dorothy Ranaghan, New York, Paulist Press, 1971: 'Life in Community' by Ralph Martin, p. 145.

4 Ibid., p. 146. Following this essay is an earlier account of community formation by another neo-Pentecostal leader, Bertil W. Ghezzi, entitled 'Three Charismatic Communities'. The story of the proliferation of these charismatic communities is yet to be fully accounted.

5 *Basic Communities* by David Clark (SPCK 1977), pp. 256–7, 281. This is an important book based on thorough research and wide experience in the UK. This sort of work needs to be done in other

countries. At present there is an appeal being made to help consolidate the work of the newly established Community Resources Centre in Birmingham in order to extend the function of the 'switchboard' concept. Cf. the *Pro Mundi Vita Bulletin*, 62, September 1976, a survey of *Basic Communities in the Church*.

6 Cf. *Community*, no. 9 (Summer 1974), pp. 9–10 in an article 'If I hear that word again . . .' *Community* is a periodical started in Britain as part of the 'switchboard' concept already referred to.

7 Ibid.

8 Ibid., no. 4 (Autumn 1972), pp. 1–4.

9 *The Rule of Taizé* in French and English, Les Presses de Taizé, 71 Taizé-Communauté, France; cf. also the *Rule for a New Brother*, Darton, Longman & Todd 1973.

10 Cf. *Community*, no. 14 (Spring 1976), pp. 1–3.

11 Ibid., no. 5 (Spring 1973), pp. 1–4; Vatican II echoes this in *Lumen Gentium*, ch. 2, n. 9.

12 Ibid.

13 Ibid.

14 Op. cit., pp. 251–3.

15 Ibid.

16 *Built as a City* (Hodder & Stoughton 1974), p. 417.

17 *A New Way of Living* (Hodder & Stoughton 1973), 1974 edn, p. 78.

18 Notre Dame, Indiana, Ave Maria Press, 1972.

19 Ibid., p. 70, (italics mine).

20 Max Delespesse, *The Church Community – Leaven and Lifestyle*, trans. from the French. The Catholic Centre of St Paul University, 1 Stewart Street, Ottawa, Canada (1969), p. 4.

21 Op. cit., p. 69.

22 *Models of the Church*, cited above, pp. 179–92.

23 Thomas Dubay, *Caring* (Denville, New Jersey, Dimension Books, 1973), p. 30.

24 *Let My People Grow* (Hodder & Stoughton 1977), pp. 147–59.

25 Writings such as these are outside the New Testament canon, though these two quoted sources along with 1–2 Clement and Hermas were considered scriptural even into the fourth and fifth centuries. They are called sub-apostolic writings and their writers designated as 'apostolic Fathers'. They bear a special witness and have a special value. Works like the Didache and 1 Clement may well be earlier than a New Testament letter like 2 Peter. For a simple account of these writings see Conzelmann, *History of Primitive Christianity* (Darton, Longman & Todd 1973), pp. 24–9. The Jerome Biblical Commentary notes that 'the real difficulty is not why such works were thought of as canonical, but why the Church did not finally accept them as canonical'.

26  Op. cit., pp. 20–21.

27  Ibid., p. 12.

28  *Community*, no. 3 (Summer 1972), pp. 2–4, 'The Commune Scene in Britain'.

29  *The Benifold Newsletter*, no. 7, September 1974. Norman James is a retired minister of the United Reformed Church. He established an ecumenical house of prayer under the name of 'Benifold' in Hampshire in the early 1960s, experimenting with the formation of a basic community. He has been an active figure on the British scene for ecumenism and renewal. The spirit of Benifold lives on and develops in the larger ecumenical–renewal context, though Benifold ceased in 1969. Cf. also Michael Harper's *Let My People Grow*, cited above, pp. 139–59.

30  Op. cit., pp. 74ff.

31  Ibid., p. 75.

32  In making these generalizations I am not trying to undermine religious life. I am reflecting on an actual state of affairs. Nor have I forgotten the efforts of religious to establish 'houses of prayer' which are made up of a small community of people living a full-time life of prayer, but without the usual restrictions associated with monasteries and convents. These houses offer hospitality to people who wish to share the way of life of religious for a period from one week to several months. There are 102 houses in 28 states of the USA, 9 Canadian provinces, Chile, Israel, Kenya, Mexico according to the 1977–8 Directory of Prayer Houses, Clarity Publishing, 75 Champlain Street, Albany, New York 12204. Nor do I wish to discount those religious orders which keep the contemplative life of the Church vigorous and renewed. In this regard cf. Delespesse, op. cit., p. 80 and Paul Hinnebusch, *Community in the Lord* (Notre Dame, Indiana, Ave Maria Press, 1975), esp. pp. 21, 23; also M. A. Santaner, *Nearing Assisi*, trans. from the French, Slough, St Paul Publications, 1977.

33  Op. cit., p. 78.

34  Ibid.

35  Ibid., p. 81.

36  An account of this meeting at Hengrave Hall can be found in *Community*, no. 18, Summer 1977.

37  Ibid.

38  *Community in the Lord* (cited in note 32), p. 168. Hinnebusch makes the common distinction of Catholic theology between *sanctifying graces* given to the individual for his personal sanctification accompanied by the gifts of the Spirit (Isa. 11. 2–3) and *charismatic graces* which are given to individuals in diverse ways as 'manifestations of the Spirit for the common good' (1 Cor. 12.7).

39  *Unless the Lord Builds the House* . . . (Notre Dame, Indiana, Ave Maria Press, 1971), p. 62.

40  Op. cit., p. 195; cf. also Donald Gelpi, *Charism and Sacrament*, cited above, esp. ch. 7 on apostolic ministry in relation to what we have said about the sacraments and ordained ministry.

41  Op. cit., p. 62.

42  Op. cit., see pp. 28–30.

43  Ibid., pp. 54–7.

44  Cf. David Clark, op. cit., pp. 275–83.

45  Ibid., p. 283.

46  Cited in ch. 3, n. 58.

47  Cited above in chs. 2, 3, nn. 73–7.

48  Op. cit., n. 58.

49  Op. cit., p. 279.

50  *On Being a Christian*, cited above, pp. 481–4, 524–5.

51  'Something to Celebrate?', *Community*, no. 3, Summer 1972.

52  Cf. *Enough Room for Joy* by Bill Clarke, sj, an account of the foundation and spirit of L'Arche, a community founded by Jean Vanier for the love and care of mentally handicapped adults, Darton, Longman & Todd 1974, with special reference to ch. 7.

53  Ibid., p. 113.

# Index of Subjects